David Auburn

David Auburn

Collected Plays

Proof
The Columnist
Lost Lake
The New York Idea
Summer, 1976

With an introduction by Robert M. Dowling

methuen | drama
LONDON · NEW YORK · OXFORD · NEW DELHI · SYDNEY

METHUEN DRAMA
Bloomsbury Publishing Plc, 50 Bedford Square, London, WC1B 3DP, UK
Bloomsbury Publishing Inc, 1359 Broadway, New York, NY 10018, USA
Bloomsbury Publishing Ireland, 29 Earlsfort Terrace, Dublin 2, D02 AY28, Ireland

BLOOMSBURY, METHUEN DRAMA and the Methuen Drama logo are trademarks of Bloomsbury
Publishing Plc

First published in this collected volume in Great Britain 2026
Published by arrangement with Farrar, Straus and Giroux. All rights reserved.

Cover image: J. Theodore Johnson, Chicago Interior, 1933–1934, oil on canvas, 28 x 34 in. (71.2 x 86.4 cm.),
Foto Smithsonian American Art Museum/Art Resource/Scala, Florence. 2026 © Photo Scala, Florence

A catalogue record for this book is available from the British Library.
A catalog record for this book is available from the Library of Congress.

ISBN: HB: 978-1-3504-3906-1
        PB: 978-1-3504-3905-4
        ePDF: 978-1-3504-3908-5
        eBook: 978-1-3504-3907-8

Series: Methuen Drama Play Collection

Typeset by RefineCatch Limited, Bungay, Suffolk
Printed and bound in The United States

For product safety related questions contact productsafety@bloomsbury.com.

To find out more about our authors and books visit www.bloomsbury.com and sign up for our newsletters.

Contents

David Auburn was born in Chicago and raised in Ohio and Arkansas. He is a Pulitzer Prize and Tony Award-winning playwright, screenwriter and director. He lives in New York City.

The Absence of Pain:
A Reflection on the Plays of David Auburn

By Robert M. Dowling

Over twenty years ago, I conducted an interview with the novelist Annie Proulx. I was eager to ask whether Proulx believed she had won the Pulitzer Prize for her 1993 novel *Shipping News* because critics had read it as a departure away from her usual affinity for human darkness: Proulx, in short, appeared to have given her hapless protagonist, Quoyle, a happy ending. This was an illusion, she responded. Her acclaimed novel's finale was in fact produced in a spirit of defiance against such endings. "Quoyle's 'happiness' at the end," Proulx said, "is nothing more than the absence of pain. . . . Of course later I thought maybe that's all happiness is anyway."[1]

The novelist's acerbic response returned to me while I was struggling over the challenge of composing this short piece on the dramatic work of another Pulitzer recipient, for his play *Proof*, the playwright David Auburn. What was it, I asked myself, about these utterly distinctive dramas that make them cohere? I registered an unmistakable sensation while experiencing an Auburn play; it was a deeply felt emotion, yet still difficult to pin down in words or even thoughts. Then, in Auburn's heartrending portrait of a brief but impactful friendship, *Summer, 1976*, the playwright's most recent script, I discovered my answer, and it was Proulx's answer.

Summer, 1976's plot revolves around an unlikely friendship between a jaded single mother named Diana, a college visual arts instructor, and a disarmingly youthful and earnest faculty wife named Alice. Early in their friendship, Diana relates to Alice the torturous pain regularly visited upon her by migraine headaches: "It's as if someone were trying very hard but failing," she explains, "to extract your eyeballs through a hole drilled in the back of your skull." This is an apt rendering, from what I've heard, but more revealingly, Diana goes on to describe the peculiar aftermath of migraines in a passage that might well be applied to the emotional impact of each of the exquisitely humane stories collected in this book: "It's not simple joy at the release from pain—the joy you'd expect," Diana says. "It's a different feeling. . . . An awareness of how much pleasure there is to be taken in the world. That you only possess in such intensity *because* you've endured the hateful thing. And somehow, *gratitude* to the hateful thing for making the awareness possible." Life is a migraine headache, Auburn seems to tell us here, but an "awareness" of life's pleasures will gratefully arrive after the pain inevitably subsides.

This might well be Auburn's greatest gift to theatergoers—his message is one of acute relief that despite it all, we are each of us alive and not yet dead. His plays close with something far more uplifting, or at least liberating, than a happy ending: a reconciliation with life.

---

[1] Qtd. in Dowling, Robert M. "Annie Proulx," *The Oxford Encyclopedia of American Literature*, edited by Jay Parini (New York: Oxford University Press, 2004), vol. 3, 430–433: 432.

By no stretch are Auburn's plays "hateful" things, of course—far from it. They are irresistible from their opening lines. (To wit, the opening of *Summer, 1976*: "We became friends, as you often do, through our children. . . . I didn't like her child, actually.") There's an enormous warmth to Auburn's characters; you can't wholly dislike any of them. But they betray a multitude of hateful things, like migraines and sickly kids and thankless jobs and sexless marriages, that harangue each character's embattled soul, as the tensions build in their skulls over a night, a summer, a life. By the final curtain, however, Auburn compassionately reassures us that although few things in our lives are pain-free, those that matter will sustain us once we arrive at that state of relief. Only then can we open ourselves up to those of life's marvels that are not hateful—soulful friendships, healthy children, unexpected sexual encounters, rustic lakeside cabins, "hip" mathematical proofs—savory delicacies served alongside life's heaping bowlfuls of gruel.

While Auburn's dramas pull no emotional punches, they are "comedies" in a broad sense; terms such as "high comedies," "intellectual comedies" or "comedies of ideas" come to mind. These are more intellectually and psychologically rigorous than a farce or romantic comedy, more deliberate of plot and serious of purpose, less reliant on belly laughs but tremendously witty, in the mode of Irish dramatist George Bernard Shaw, Auburn's precursor Wendy Wasserstein, or even the British novelist Jane Austen. (Auburn's screenplay *The Lake House* namechecks Austen, while it reimagines the themes and plot of her novel *Persuasion*.) His dialogue is exceedingly witty and contains a masterly use of callbacks, but it's no fluke that humor is so central to Auburn's dramatic vision, as while attending the University of Chicago, he'd fine-tuned his comedic rhythms with the improvisational comedy troupe Off-Off-Campus (the Second Generation, cast in 1987). And yet a deep pathos still engulfs the plays. His endings are "happy," but in Proulx's way, without fanfare or promises of an ecstatic future. Outside of his hilarious rewrite of the 1906 "comedy of manners" *The New York Idea* (Auburn is nothing if not ambidextrous with theatrical genres, as this collection makes clear), there are no wedding bells to hear at the close Auburn's plays, just mutual understandings. It is in no way clear, for instance, that his masterwork *Proof*'s protagonist Catherine will live happily-ever-after, but she opens herself up to a love interest in the final scene, a powerful gesture of relief, and hope too.

Auburn's scripts are so rife with shocking plot twists and highwire reversals and reveals that even passing analyses would be correspondingly rife with spoilers. For my conclusion, then, I'll end with Auburn himself speaking in a passage that movingly expands the powerful relief-sensation in his plays to the theater world writ large. In 2013, Auburn presented his Harmsworth Lecture in American Arts and Letters at Oxford University with the ominous title "Theater in the Age of Twitter." In it, he contrasted the singular appeal of his chosen artform with that of the digital world's callow amusements. He admitted to succumbing to "wishful thinking" about the theater's perennially uncertain future, but was reassured by the way his drama students reacted to live theater as a communally experienced balm for their oppressively digitized young minds:

> [My students] like being taken to plays because it's a relief. It's a relief to have no competing media. It's a relief to be unconnected. It's a relief to have one's attention focused by the awareness of other people concentrating in the room

around you, and by the presence of the actors working on the stage. . . . the total absorption, the transcendence that sustained narratives can provide. . . . the more my own attention is battered by modern information technology, the more I experience the theater as a relief. And certain kinds of theater are a particularly rehabilitating escape, a place where my fractured attention, my crippled concentration, my punch-drunk, hyperlinked, multi-task consciousness can be at least partially restored, and I am betting my livelihood on the belief that I'm not the only one who will increasingly look to the theater for that restoration.[2]

Robert M. Dowling is professor of English at Central Connecticut State University and the author of the biographies *Eugene O'Neill: A Life in Four Acts* (Yale University Press, 2014) and *Coyote: The Dramatic Lives of Sam Shepard* (Scribner Publishers, 2025).

---

[2]   David Auburn, "Theater in the Age of Twitter," the Esmond Harmsworth Lecture in American Arts and Letters, Rothermere American Institute, Oxford University, May 2013: Online.

Proof

Proof was originally produced by the Manhattan Theatre Club where it opened on May 23, 2000, before transferring to Broadway's Walter Kerr Theatre on 24 October, 2000, with the following cast and director:

Director: Daniel Sullivan
Catherine: Mary-Louise Parker
Claire: Johanna Day
Robert: Larry Bryggman
Hal: Ben Shenkman

It closed on Broadway on January 5, 2003, after 917 performances and won the 2001 Pulitzer Prize for Drama and the Tony Award for Best Play.

Proof premiered in London at the Donmar Warehouse in May 2002 with the following cast and director:

Director: John Madden
Catherine: Gwyneth Paltrow
Robert: Ronald Pickup
Claire: Sara Stewart
Hal: Richard Coyle

Proof had its first Broadway revival at the Booth Theatre in April 2026 with the following cast and director:

Director: Thomas Kail
Catherine: Ayo Edebiri
Robert: Don Cheadle
Claire: Samira Wiley
Hal: Jin Ha

Characters:

Robert, 50s
Catherine, 25
Claire, 29
Hal, 28

Setting:

The back porch of a house in Chicago.

Act One

Scene One

Night.

Catherine *sits in a chair. She is exhausted, haphazardly dressed. Eyes closed.*

Robert *is standing behind her.* **Catherine** *does not know he is there. After a moment:*

Robert   Can't sleep?

Catherine   Jesus, you scared me.

Robert   Sorry.

Catherine   What are you doing here?

Robert   I thought I'd check up on you. Why aren't you in bed?

Catherine   Your student is still here. He's up in your study.

Robert   He can let himself out.

Catherine   I might as well wait up till he's done.

Robert   He's not my student anymore. He's teaching now. Bright kid.

Beat.

Catherine   What time is it?

Robert   It's almost one.

Catherine   Huh.

Robert   After midnight . . .

Catherine   So?

Robert   So:

He indicates something on the table behind him: a bottle of champagne.

Happy birthday.

Catherine   Dad.

Robert   Do I ever forget?

Catherine   Thank you.

Robert   Twenty five. I can't believe it.

Catherine   Neither can I. Should we have it now?

Robert   It's up to you.

Catherine   Yes.

Robert   You want me to open it?

Catherine   Let me. Last time you opened a bottle of champagne out here you broke a window.

Robert   That was a long time ago. I resent your bringing it up.

Catherine   You're lucky you didn't lose an eye.

Pop. The bottle foams.

Robert   Twenty five!

Catherine   I feel old.

Robert   You're a kid.

Catherine   Glasses?

Robert   Goddamn it I forgot the glasses. Do you want me to –

Catherine   Nah.

She drinks from the bottle. A long pull. **Robert** *watches her.*

Robert   I hope you like it. I wasn't sure what to get you.

Catherine   This is the worst champagne I have ever tasted.

Robert   I am proud to say I don't know anything about wines. I hate those kind of people who are always talking about "vintages."

Catherine   It's not even champagne.

Robert   The bottle was the right shape.

Catherine   "Great Lakes Vineyards." I didn't know they made wine in Wisconsin.

Robert   A girl who's drinking from the bottle shouldn't complain. Don't guzzle it. It's an elegant beverage. Sip.

Catherine (*offering the bottle*)   Do you –

Robert   No, go ahead.

Catherine   You sure?

Robert   Yeah. It's your birthday.

Catherine   Happy birthday to me.

Robert   What are you going to do on your birthday?

Catherine   Drink this. Have some.

Robert   No. I hope you're not spending your birthday alone.

Catherine   I'm not alone.

Robert   I don't count.

Catherine   Why not?

Robert   I'm your old man. Go out with some friends.

Catherine   Right.

Robert   Your friends aren't taking you out?

Catherine   No.

Robert   Why not?

Catherine   Because in order for your friends to take you out you generally have to have friends.

Robert (*dismissive*)   Oh –

Catherine   It's funny how that works.

Robert   You have friends. What about that cute blonde, what was her name?

Catherine   What?

Robert   She lives over on Ellis Avenue – you used to spend every minute together.

Catherine   Cindy Jacobsen?

Robert   Cindy Jacobsen!

Catherine   That was in third grade, Dad. Her family moved to Florida in 1983.

Robert   What about Claire?

Catherine   She's not my friend, she's my sister. And she's in New York. And I don't like her.

Robert   I thought she was coming in.

Catherine   Not till tomorrow.

Beat.

Robert   My advice, if you find yourself awake late at night, is to sit down and do some mathematics.

Catherine   Oh please.

Robert   We could do some together.

Catherine   No.

Robert   Why not?

Catherine   I can't think of anything worse. You sure you don't want any?

Robert   Yeah, thanks.

You used to love it.

Catherine   Not any more.

Robert   You knew what a prime number was before you could read.

Catherine   Well now I've forgotten.

Robert (*hard*)   Don't waste your talent, Catherine.

Beat.

Catherine   I knew you'd say something like that.

Robert   I realize you've had a difficult time.

Catherine   Thanks.

Robert   That's not an excuse. Don't be lazy.

Catherine   I haven't been lazy, I've been taking care of you.

Robert   Kid, I've seen you. You sleep till noon, you eat junk, you don't work, the dishes pile up in the sink. If you go out it's to buy magazines. You come back with a stack of magazines this high – I don't know how you read that crap. And those are the good days. Some days you don't get up, you don't get out of bed.

Catherine   Those are the good days.

Robert   Bullshit. Those days are lost. You threw them away. And you'll never know what else you threw away with them – the work you lost, the ideas you didn't have, discoveries you never made because you were moping in your bed at four in the afternoon.

You know I'm right.

Beat.

Catherine   I've lost a few days.

Robert   How many?

Catherine   Oh, I don't know.

Robert   I bet you do.

Catherine   What?

Robert   I bet you count.

Catherine   Knock it off.

Robert   Well do you know or don't you?

Catherine   I don't.

Robert   Of course you do. How many days have you lost?

Catherine   A month. Around a month.

Robert   Exactly.

Catherine   Goddamn it, I don't –

Robert   HOW MANY?

Catherine   33 days.

Robert   Exactly?

Catherine   I don't know.

Robert   Be precise, for Chrissake.

Catherine   I slept till noon today.

Robert   Call it 33 and a quarter days.

Catherine   Yes, all right.

Robert   You're kidding!

Catherine   No.

Robert   Amazing number!

Catherine   It's a depressing fucking number.

Robert   Catherine, if every day you say you've lost were a year, it would be a very interesting fucking number.

Catherine   33 and a quarter years is not interesting.

Robert   Stop it. You know exactly what I mean.

Catherine (*conceding*)   1729 weeks.

Robert   1729. Great number. The smallest number expressible –

Catherine   – expressible as the sum of two cubes in two different ways.

Robert   12 cubed plus 1 cubed = 1729.

Catherine   And ten cubed plus 9 cubed. Yes, we've got it, thank you.

Robert   You see? Even your depression is mathematical. Stop moping and get to work. The kind of potential you have –

Catherine   I haven't done anything good.

Robert   You're young. You've got time.

Catherine   I do?

Robert   Yes!

Catherine   By the time you were my age you were famous.

Robert   By the time I was your age I'd already done my best work.

Beat.

Catherine   What about after?

Robert   After what?

Catherine   After you got sick.

Robert   What about it?

Catherine   You couldn't work then.

Robert   No, if anything I was sharper.

Catherine (*she can't help it: she laughs.*)   Dad.

Robert   I was. Hey, it's true. The clarity – that was the amazing thing. No doubts.

Catherine   You were happy?

Robert   Yeah, I was busy.

Catherine   Not the same thing.

Robert   I don't see the difference. I knew what I wanted to do and I did it.

If I wanted to work a problem all day long I did it.

If I wanted to look for information – secrets, complex and tantalizing messages – I could find them all around me: in the air. In a pile of fallen leaves some neighbor raked together. In box scores in the paper, written in the steam coming up off a cup of coffee. The whole world was talking to me.

If I just wanted to close my eyes, sit quietly on the porch and listen for the messages, I did that.

It was wonderful.

Beat.

Catherine   How old were you?

When it started.

Robert   Mid-twenties.

Twenty-three, four.

Beat.

Is that what you're worried about?

Catherine   I've thought about it.

Robert   Just getting a year older means nothing, Catherine.

Catherine   It's not just getting older.

Robert   It's me.

Beat.

Catherine   I've thought about it.

Robert   Really?

Catherine   How could I not?

Robert   Well if that's why you're worried you're not keeping up with the medical literature. There are all kinds of factors. It's not simply something you inherit. Just because I went bughouse doesn't mean you will.

Catherine   Dad . . .

Robert   Listen to me. Life changes fast in your early twenties and it shakes you up. You're feeling down. It's been a bad week. You've had a lousy couple years, no one knows that better than me. But you're gonna be okay.

Catherine   Yeah?

Robert   Yes. I promise you. Push yourself. Don't read so many magazines. Sit down and get the machinery going and I swear to God you'll feel fine. The simple fact that we can talk about this together is a good sign.

Catherine   A good sign?

Robert   Yes!

Catherine   How could it be a good sign?

Robert   Because! Crazy people don't sit around wondering if they're nuts.

Catherine   They don't?

Robert   Of course not. They've got better things to do. Take it from me. A very good sign that you're crazy is an inability to ask the question, "Am I crazy?"

Catherine   Even if the answer is Yes?

Robert   Crazy people don't ask. You see?

Catherine   Yes.

Robert   So if you're asking . . .

Catherine   I'm not.

Robert   But if you were, it would be a very good sign.

Catherine   A good sign . . .

Robert   A good sign that you're fine.

Catherine   Right.

Robert   You see? You've just gotta think these things through.

Now come on, what do you say? Let's call it a night, you go up, get some sleep, and then in the morning you can –

Catherine   Wait. No.

Robert   What's the matter?

Catherine   It doesn't work.

Robert   Why not?

Catherine   It doesn't make sense.

Robert   Sure it does.

Catherine   No.

Robert   Where's the problem?

Catherine   The problem is you are crazy!

Robert   What difference does that make?

Catherine   You admitted – You just told me that you are.

Robert   So?

Catherine   You said a crazy person would never admit that.

Robert   Yeah, but it's . . . oh. I see.

Catherine   So?

Robert   It's a point.

Catherine   So how can you admit it?

Robert   Well. Because I'm also dead.

Beat.

Aren't I?

Catherine   You died a week ago.

Robert   Heart failure. Quick. The funeral's tomorrow.

Catherine   That's why Claire's flying in from New York.

Robert   Yes.

Catherine   You're sitting here. You're giving me advice. You brought me champagne.

Robert   Yes.

Beat.

Catherine   Which means . . .

Robert   For you?

Catherine   Yes.

Robert   For you, Catherine, my daughter, who I love very much . . .

It could be a bad sign.

They sit together for a moment.

Hal *enters. He carries a backpack and a jacket, folded. He lets the door go and it bangs shut.*

Catherine *sits up with a jolt.*

Catherine   What?

Hal   Oh, God, sorry – did I wake you?

Catherine   What?

Hal   Were you asleep?

Beat. **Robert** *is gone.*

Catherine   You scared me for Chrissake. What are you doing?

Hal   I'm sorry. I didn't realize it had gotten so late. I'm done for the night.

Catherine   Good.

Hal   Drinking alone?

She realizes she is holding the champagne bottle. She puts it down quickly.

Catherine   Yes.

Hal   Champagne, huh?

Catherine   Yes.

Hal   Celebrating?

Catherine   No. I just like champagne.

Hal   It's festive.

Catherine   What?

Hal   Festive. (*He makes an awkward "party" gesture.*)

Catherine   Do you want some?

Hal   Sure.

Catherine (*gives him the bottle*)   I'm done. You can take the rest with you.

Hal   Oh. No thanks.

Catherine   Take it, I'm done.

Hal   No, I shouldn't. I'm driving.

Well. I can let myself out.

Catherine   Good.

Hal   When should I come back?

Catherine   Come back?

Hal   Yeah. I'm nowhere near finished. Maybe tomorrow?

Catherine   We have a funeral tomorrow.

Hal   God, you're right, I'm sorry. I was going to attend, if that's all right.

Catherine   Yes.

Hal   What about Sunday? Will you be around?

Catherine   You've had three days.

Hal   I'd love to get in some more time up there.

Catherine   How much longer do you need?

Hal   Another week. At least.

Catherine   Are you joking?

Hal   No. Do you know how much stuff there is?

Catherine   A week?

Hal   I know you don't need anybody in your hair right now. Look, I spent the last couple days getting everything sorted out. It's mostly notebooks. He dated them all; now that I've got them in order I don't have to work here. I could take some stuff home, read it, bring it back.

Catherine   No.

Hal   I'll be careful.

Catherine   My father wouldn't want anything moved and I don't want anything to leave this house.

Hal   Then I should work here. I'll stay out of the way.

Catherine   You're wasting your time.

Hal   Someone needs to go through your Dad's papers.

Catherine   There's nothing up there. It's garbage.

Hal   There are a hundred and three notebooks.

Catherine   I've looked at those. It's gibberish.

Hal   Someone should read them.

Catherine   He was crazy.

Hal   Yes, but he wrote them.

Catherine   He was a graphomaniac, Harold. Do you know what that is?

Hal   I know. He wrote compulsively. Call me Hal.

Catherine   There's no connection between the ideas. There's no ideas. It's like a monkey at a typewriter. 103 notebooks full of bullshit.

Hal   Let's make sure they're bullshit.

Catherine   I'm sure.

Hal   I'm prepared to look at every page. Are you?

Catherine   No. I'm not crazy.

Beat.

Hal   Well, I'm gonna be late . . . Some friends of mine are in this band. They're playing at a bar up on Diversey. Way down the bill, they're probably going on around two, two-thirty. I said I'd be there.

Catherine   Great.

Hal   They're all in the math department. They're really good. They have this great song, you'd like it, called "i" – lowercase I. They just stand there and don't play anything for three minutes.

Catherine   "Imaginary Number."

Hal   It's a math joke.

You see why they're way down the bill.

Catherine   Long drive to see some nerds in a band.

Hal   God I hate when people say that. It is not that long a drive.

Catherine   So they are nerds.

Hal   Oh they're raging geeks. But they're geeks who, you know, can dress themselves . . . hold down a job at a major University . . . Some of them have switched from glasses to contacts. They play sports, they play in a band, they get laid surprisingly often, so in that sense they sort of make you question the whole set of terms Geek, nerd, wonk, dweeb, dilbert, paste-eater.

Catherine   You're in this band, aren't you?

Hal   Okay, yes. I play drums. You want to come? I never sing, I swear to God.

Catherine   No thanks.

Hal   All right. Look, Catherine, Monday: what do you say?

Catherine   Don't you have a job?

Hal   Yeah, I have a full teaching load this quarter plus my own work.

Catherine   Plus band practice.

Hal   I don't have time to do this but I'm going to. If you'll let me.

Beat.

I loved your Dad.

I don't believe a mind like his can just shut down. He had lucid moments. He had a lucid year, a whole year four years ago.

Catherine   It wasn't a year. It was more like nine months.

Hal   A school year. He was advising students . . . I was stalled on my Ph.D. I was this close to quitting. I met with your Dad and he put me on the right track with my research. I owe him.

Catherine   Sorry.

Hal   Look. Let me – You're 25, right?

Catherine   How old are you?

Hal   It doesn't matter. Listen:

Catherine   Fuck you, how old are you?

Hal   I'm 28, all right? When your Dad was younger than both of us he made major contributions to three fields: game theory, algebraic geometry, and nonlinear operator theory. Most of us never get our heads around one. He basically invented the mathematical techniques for studying rational behavior, and he gave the astrophysicists plenty to work over too. Okay?

Catherine   Don't lecture me.

Hal   I'm not. I'm telling you if I came up with one-tenth of the shit your Dad produced I could write my own ticket to any math department in the country.

Beat.

Catherine   Give me your backpack.

Hal   What?

Catherine   Give me your backpack.

Hal   Why?

Catherine   I want to look inside it.

Hal   What?

Catherine   Open it and give it to me.

Hal   Oh come on.

Catherine   You're not taking anything out of this house.

Hal   I wouldn't do that.

Catherine   You're hoping to find something upstairs that you can publish.

Hal   Sure.

Catherine   Then you can write your own ticket.

Hal   What? No! It would be under your Dad's name. It would be for your Dad.

Catherine   I don't believe you. You have a notebook in that backpack.

Hal   What are you talking about?

Catherine   Give it to me.

Hal   You're being a little bit paranoid.

Catherine   PARANOID?

Hal   Maybe a little.

Catherine   Fuck you, Hal. I KNOW you have one of my notebooks.

Hal   I think you should calm down and think about what you're saying.

Catherine   I'm saying you're lying to me and stealing my family's property.

Hal   And I think that sounds paranoid.

Catherine   Just because I'm paranoid doesn't mean there isn't something in that backpack.

Hal   You just said yourself there's nothing up there. Didn't you?

Catherine   I –

Hal   Didn't you say that?

Catherine   Yes.

Hal   So what would I take?

Right?

Beat.

Catherine   You're right.

Hal   Thank you.

Catherine   So you don't need to come back.

Hal   Please. Someone should know for sure whether –

Catherine   I LIVED WITH HIM.

I spent my life with him. I fed him. Talked to him. Tried to listen when he talked. Talked to people who weren't there . . . Watched him shuffling around like a ghost. A very smelly ghost. He was filthy. I had to make sure he bathed. My own father.

Hal   I'm sorry. I shouldn't have . . .

Catherine   After my mother died it was just me here. I tried to keep him happy no matter what idiotic project he was doing. He used to read all day. He kept demanding more and more books. I took them out of the library by the carload. We had hundreds upstairs. Then I realized he wasn't reading: he believed aliens were sending him messages through the Dewey Decimal numbers on the library books. He was trying to work out the code.

Hal   What kind of messages?

Catherine   Beautiful mathematics. Answers to everything. The most elegant proofs, perfect proofs, proofs like music.

Hal   Sounds good.

Catherine   Plus fashion tips, knock-knock jokes – I mean it was NUTS, okay?

Hal   He was ill. It was a tragedy.

Catherine   Later the writing phase: scribbling, 19, 20 hours a day . . . I ordered him a case of notebooks and he used every one.

I dropped out of school . . .

I'm glad he's dead.

Hal   I understand why you'd feel that way.

Catherine   Fuck off.

Hal   You're right. I can't imagine dealing with that. It must have been awful. I know you –

Catherine   You don't know me. I want to be alone. I don't want him around.

Hal (*confused*)   Him? I don't –

Catherine   You. I don't want you here.

Hal   Why?

Catherine   He's dead.

Hal   But I'm not –

Catherine   He's dead; I don't need any proteges around.

Hal   There will be others.

Catherine   What?

Hal   You think I'm the only one? People are already working over his stuff. Someone's gonna read those notebooks.

Catherine   I'll do it.

Hal   No, you –

Catherine   He's my father, I'll do it.

Hal   You can't.

Catherine   Why not?

Hal   You don't have the math. It's all just squiggles on a page. You wouldn't know the good stuff from the junk.

Catherine   It's all junk.

Hal   If it's not we can't afford to miss any through carelessness.

Catherine   I know mathematics.

Hal   If there were anything up there it would be pretty high-order. It would take a professional to recognize it.

Catherine   I think I could recognize it.

Hal (*patient*)   Cathy . . .

Catherine   WHAT?

Hal   I know your Dad taught you some basic stuff, but come on.

Catherine   You don't think I could do it.

Hal   I'm sorry: I know that you couldn't.

Beat.

Catherine *angrily snatches his backpack.*

Hal   Hey! Oh come on. Give me a break.

She opens the backpack and rifles through it.

Catherine *removes items one by one. A water bottle. Some workout clothes. An orange. Drumsticks. Nothing else.*

She puts everything back in and returns it.

Beat.

Catherine   You can come tomorrow.

Beat. They are both embarrassed.

Hal   The University health service is uh very good.

My Mom died a couple years ago and I was pretty broken up. Also my work wasn't going that well . . . I went over and talked to this doctor. I saw her for a couple months and it really helped.

Catherine   I'm fine.

Beat.

Hal   Also exercise is great. I run along the lake a couple of mornings a week. It's not too cold yet. If you wanted to come sometime I could pick you up. We wouldn't have to talk . . .

Catherine   No thanks.

Hal   All right.

I'm gonna be late for the show. I better go.

Catherine   Okay.

Beat.

Hal   It's seriously like 20 minutes up to the club. We go on, we play, we're terrible but we buy everyone drinks afterward to make up for it. You're home by 4, 4:30, tops . . .

Catherine   Good night.

Hal   Good night.

Hal *starts to exit. He has forgotten his jacket.*

Catherine   Wait, your coat.

Hal   No, you (don't have to) –

She picks up his jacket. As she does a composition book that was folded up in the coat falls to the floor.

Beat. **Catherine** *picks it up, trembling with rage.*

Catherine   I'm PARANOID?

Hal   Wait.

Catherine   You think I should go JOGGING?

Hal   Just hold on.

Catherine   Get out!

Hal   Can I please just –

Catherine   Get the fuck out of my house.

Hal   Listen to me for a MINUTE.

Catherine (*waving the book*)   You stole this!

Hal   Let me explain!

Catherine   You stole it from ME, you stole it from my FATHER –

Hal *snatches the book*

Hal   I want to show you something, will you calm down?

Catherine   Give it back.

Hal   Just wait a minute.

Catherine   I'm calling the police.

She picks up the phone and dials.

Hal Don't. Look, I borrowed the book, all right? I'm sorry, I just picked it up before I came downstairs and thought I'd–

Catherine (*on phone*) Hello?

Hal I did it for a reason.

Catherine Hello, Police? I – Yes, I'd like to report a robbery in progress.

Hal I noticed something – something your father wrote. All right? Not math, something he wrote. Here, let me show you.

Catherine A ROBBERY.

Hal Will you put the fucking phone down and listen to me?

Catherine (*on phone*) Yes, I'm at 5724 South –

Hal It's about you. See? YOU. It was written about you. Here's your name: CATHY. See?

Catherine South . . .

She pauses. She seems to be listening. **Hal** *reads:*

Hal "A good day. Some very good news from Catherine."

I didn't know what that referred to, but I thought you (might) . . .

Catherine When did he write this?

Hal I think four years ago. The handwriting is steady. It must have been during his remission.

There's more.

A moment. **Catherine** *hangs up the phone.*

"Machinery not working yet but I am patient."

"The machinery" is what he called his mind, his ability to do mathematics.

Catherine I know.

Hal (*reads*) "I know I'll get there. I am an auto mechanic who after years of greasy work on a hopeless wreck turns the ignition and hears a faint cough. I am not driving yet but there's cause for optimism. Talking with students helps. So does being outside, eating meals in restaurants, riding busses, all the activities of 'normal' life.

"Most of all Cathy. The years she has lost caring for me. I almost wrote 'wasted.' Yet her refusal to let me be institutionalized – her keeping me at home, caring for me herself, has certainly saved my life. Made writing this possible. Made it possible to imagine doing math again. Where does her strength come from? I can never repay her.

"Today is her birthday: she is 21. I'm taking her to dinner."

Dated September 4th.

That's tomorrow.

Catherine   It's today.

Hal   You're right.

She takes the book.

I thought you might want to see it. I shouldn't have tried to sneak it out. Tomorrow I was going to – it sounds stupid now. I was going to wrap it.

Happy birthday.

Hal *exits.*

Catherine *is alone. She puts her head in her hands. She weeps.*

Eventually she stops, wipes her eyes.

From off: A POLICE SIREN, drawing closer.

Catherine   Shit.

FADE.

Scene Two

The next morning.

Claire *drinks coffee from a mug.*

She has brought bagels and fruit out to the porch on a tray. She arranges them on two plates.

She notices the champagne bottle lying on the floor. She picks it up and sets it on a table.

Catherine enters. Her hair is wet from a shower.

Claire   Better. Much.

Catherine   Thanks.

Claire   Feel better?

Catherine   Yeah.

Claire   You look a million times better. Have some coffee.

Catherine   Okay.

Claire   How do you take it?

Catherine   Black.

Claire   Have a little milk. (*She pours.*) Want a banana? It's a good thing I brought food: there was nothing in the house.

Catherine   I've been meaning to go shopping.

Claire   Have a bagel.

Catherine   No. I hate breakfast.

Beat.

Claire   You didn't put on the dress.

Catherine   Didn't really feel like it.

Claire   Don't you want to try it on? See if it fits?

Catherine   I'll put it on later.

Beat.

Claire   If you want to dry your hair I have a hair drier.

Catherine   Nah.

Claire   Did you use that conditioner I brought you?

Catherine   No, shit, I forgot.

Claire   It's my favorite. You'll love it, Katie. I want you to try it.

Catherine   I'll use it next time.

Claire   You'll like it. It has Jojoba.

Catherine   What is "Jojoba"?

Claire   It's something they put in for healthy hair.

Catherine   Hair is dead.

Claire   What?

Catherine   It's dead tissue. You can't make it "healthy."

Claire   Whatever, it's something that's good for your hair.

Catherine   What, a chemical?

Claire   No, it's organic.

Catherine   Well it can be organic and still be a chemical.

Claire   I don't know what it is.

Catherine   Haven't you ever heard of organic chemistry?

Claire   It makes my hair feel, look, and smell good. That's the extent of my information about it. You might like it if you decide to use it.

Catherine   Thanks, I'll try it.

Claire   Good.

If the dress doesn't fit we can go downtown and exchange it.

Catherine   Okay.

Claire   I'll take you to lunch.

Catherine   Great.

Claire   Maybe Sunday before I go back. Do you need anything?

Catherine   Like clothes?

Claire   Or anything. While I'm here.

Catherine   Nah, I'm cool.

Beat.

Claire   I thought we'd have some people over tonight. If you're feeling okay.

Catherine   I'm feeling okay, Claire, stop saying that.

Claire   You don't have any plans?

Catherine   No.

Claire   I ordered some food. Wine, beer.

Catherine   We are burying Dad this afternoon.

Claire   I think it will be all right. Anyone who's been to the funeral and wants to come over for something to eat, can. And it's the only time I can see any old Chicago friends. It'll be nice. IF it's okay with you.

Catherine   Yes, sure.

Claire   It's been a stressful time. It would be good to relax in a low-key way.

Mitch says Hi.

Catherine   Hi Mitch.

Claire   He's really sorry he couldn't come.

Catherine   Yeah, he's gonna miss all the fun.

Claire   He wanted to see you. He sends his love. I told him you'd see him soon enough.

We're getting married.

Catherine   No shit.

Claire   Yes! We just decided.

Catherine   Yikes.

Claire   Yes!

Catherine   When?

Claire   January.

Catherine   Huh.

Claire   We're not going to do a huge thing. His folks are gone too. Just City Hall, then a big dinner at our favorite restaurant for all our friends. And you, of course, I hope you'll be in the wedding.

Catherine   Yeah. Of course. Congratulations, Claire, I'm really happy for you.

Claire   Thanks, me too. We just decided it was time. His job is great. I just got promoted . . .

Catherine   Huh.

Claire   You will come?

Catherine   Yes, sure. January? I mean I don't have to check my calendar or anything. Sure.

Claire   That makes me very happy.

Beat. From here on **Claire** *treads gingerly.*

Claire   How are you?

Catherine   Okay.

Claire   How are you feeling about everything?

Catherine   About "everything"?

Claire   About Dad.

Catherine   What about him?

Claire   How are you feeling about his death? Are you all right?

Catherine   Yes, I am.

Claire   Honestly?

Catherine   Yes.

Claire   I think in some ways it was the "right time." If there is ever a right time. Do you know what you want to do now?

Catherine   No.

Claire   Do you want to stay here?

Catherine   I don't know.

Claire   Do you want to go back to school?

Catherine   I haven't thought about it.

Claire   Well there's a lot to think about.

How do you feel?

Catherine   Physically? Great. Except my hair seems kind of unhealthy, I wish there were something I could do about that.

Claire   Come on, Catherine.

Catherine   What is the point of all these questions?

Beat.

Claire   Katie, some policemen came by while you were in the shower.

Catherine   Yeah?

Claire   They said they were "checking up" on things here. Seeing how everything was this morning.

Catherine (*neutral*)   That was nice.

Claire   They told me they responded to a call last night, and came to the house.

Catherine   Yeah?

Claire   Did you call the police last night?

Catherine   Yeah.

Claire   Why?

Catherine   I thought the house was being robbed.

Claire   But it wasn't.

Catherine   No. I changed my mind.

Beat.

Claire   First you call 911 with an emergency and then you hang up on them –

Catherine   I didn't really want them to come.

Claire   So why did you call?

Catherine   I was trying to get this guy out of the house.

Claire   Who?

Catherine   One of Dad's students.

Claire   Dad hasn't had any students for years.

Catherine   No, he WAS Dad's student. Now he's – he's a mathematician.

Claire   Why was he in the house in the first place?

Catherine   Well he's been coming here to look at Dad's notebooks.

Claire   In the middle of the night?

Catherine   It was late. I was waiting for him to finish and last night I thought he might have been stealing them.

Claire   Stealing the notebooks.

Catherine   YES. So I told him to go.

Claire   Was he stealing them?

Catherine   Yes. That's why I called the police –

Claire   What is this man's name?

Catherine   Hal. Harold. Harold Dobbs.

Claire   The police said you were the only one here.

Catherine   He left before they got here.

Claire   With the notebooks?

Catherine   No, Claire, don't be stupid, there are over a hundred notebooks. He was only stealing ONE, but he was stealing it so he could give it BACK to me, so I let him go so he could play with his band on the north side.

Claire   His band?

Catherine   He was late. He wanted me to come with him but I was like Yeah, right.

Beat.

Claire (*gently*)   Is "Harold Dobbs" your boyfriend?

Catherine   No!

Claire   Are you sleeping with him?

Catherine   What? Euughh! No! He's a math geek!

Claire   And he's in a band? A rock band?

Catherine   No a marching band. He plays trombone. Yes a rock band!

Claire   What is the name of his band?

Catherine   How should I know?

Claire   "Harold Dobbs" didn't tell you the name of his rock band?

Catherine   No. I don't know. Look in the paper. They were playing last night. They do a song called "Imaginary Number" that doesn't exist.

Beat.

Claire   I'm sorry, I'm just trying to understand: is "Harold Dobbs"–

Catherine   Stop saying "Harold Dobbs."

Claire   Is this . . . person . . .

Catherine   HAROLD DOBBS EXISTS.

Claire   I'm sure he does.

Catherine   He's a mathematician at the University of Chicago. Call the fucking math department.

Claire   Don't get upset. I'm just trying to understand! I mean if you found out some creepy grad student was trying to take some of Dad's papers and you called the police I'd understand, and if you were out here partying, drinking with your boyfriend, I'd understand. But the two stories don't go together.

Catherine   Because you made up the "boyfriend" story. I was here ALONE.

Claire   Harold Dobbs wasn't here?

Catherine   No, he – YES, he was here, but we weren't partying!

Claire   You weren't drinking with him?

Catherine   No!

Claire (*she holds up the champagne bottle*)   This was sitting right here. Who were you drinking champagne with?

Catherine *hesitates.*

Catherine   With no one.

Claire   Are you sure?

Catherine   Yes.

Beat.

Claire   The police said you were abusive.

Catherine *doesn't say anything.*

They said you're lucky they didn't haul you in.

Catherine   These guys were assholes, Claire. They wouldn't go away. They wanted me to fill out a report . . .

Claire   Were you abusive?

Catherine   This one cop kept spitting on me when he talked. It was disgusting.

Claire   Did you use the word "dickhead"?

Catherine   Oh I don't remember.

Claire   Did you tell one cop . . . to go fuck the other cop's mother?

Catherine   NO.

Claire   That's what they said.

Catherine   Not with that phrasing.

Claire   Did you strike one of them?

Catherine   They were trying to come in the house!

Claire   Oh my God.

Catherine   I might have PUSHED him a little.

Claire   They said you were either drunk or disturbed.

Catherine   They wanted to come in here and SEARCH MY HOUSE –

Claire   YOU called THEM.

Catherine   Yes but I didn't actually WANT them to come. But they did come and then they started acting like they owned the place, pushing me around, calling me "girly," smirking at me, laughing: they were assholes.

Claire   These guys seemed perfectly nice. They were off-duty and they took the trouble to come back here at the end of their shift to check up on you. They were very polite.

Catherine   Well people are nicer to you.

Beat.

Claire   Katie. Would you like to come to New York?

Catherine   Yes, I told you, I'll come in January.

Claire   You could come sooner. We'd love to have you. You could stay with us. It'd be fun.

Catherine   I don't want to.

Claire   Mitch has become an excellent cook. It's like his hobby now. He buys all these gadgets. Garlic press, olive oil sprayer . . . Every night there's something new. Delicious, wonderful meals. The other day he made vegetarian chili!

Catherine   What the fuck are you talking about?

Claire   Stay with us for a while. We would have so much fun.

Catherine   Thanks, I'm okay here.

Claire   Chicago is dead. New York is so much more fun, you can't believe it.

Catherine   The "fun" thing is really not where my focus is at the moment.

Claire   I think New York would be a really fun and . . . safe . . . place for you to –

Catherine   I don't need a safe place and I don't want to have any fun! I'm perfectly fine here.

Claire   You look tired. I think you could use some downtime.

Catherine   Downtime?

Claire   Katie, please. You've had a very hard time.

Catherine   I'm PERFECTLY OKAY.

Claire   I think you're upset and exhausted.

Catherine   I was FINE till you got here.

Claire   Yes, but you –

Hal (*from off*)   Catherine?

Claire   Who is that?

A beat. **Hal** *enters.*

Hal   Hey, I –

Catherine *stands and points triumphantly at him.*

Catherine   HAROLD DOBBS!

Hal (*confused*)   Hi.

Catherine   OKAY? I really don't need this, Claire. I'm fine, you know, I'm totally fine, and then you swoop in here with these questions, and "Are you okay?" and your soothing tone of voice and "Oh, the poor policemen" – I think the police can handle themselves! – and bagels and bananas and jojoba and "Come to New York" and vegetarian CHILI, I mean it really pisses me off so just save it.

Beat.

Claire (*smoothly, to* **Hal***.*)   I'm Claire. Catherine's sister.

Hal   Oh, hi. Hal. Nice to meet you.

Uncomfortable beat.

I . . . hope it's not too early. I was just going to try to get some work done before the uh – if uh, if . . .

Claire   Yes!

Catherine   Sure, okay.

Hal *exits. A moment.*

Claire   That's Harold Dobbs?

Catherine   Yes.

Claire   He's cute.

Catherine (*disgusted*)   Eugh.

Claire   He's a mathematician?

Catherine   I think you owe me an apology, Claire.

Claire   We need to make some decisions. But I shouldn't have tried to start first thing in the morning. I don't want an argument.

Beat.

Maybe Hal would like a bagel?

Beat. **Catherine** *doesn't take the hint. She exits. After a moment of indecision* **Claire** *takes a banana and a bagel and goes inside.*

FADE.

Scene Three

Night.

Inside the house a party is in progress. Loud music from a not-very-good but enthusiastic band.

Catherine *is alone on the porch. She wears a flattering black dress.*

Inside, the band finishes a number. Cheers, applause.

After a moment **Hal** *comes out. He wears a dark suit. He has taken off his tie. He is sweaty and revved-up from playing. He holds two bottles of beer.*

Catherine *regards him. A beat.*

Catherine   I feel that for a funeral reception this might have gotten a bit out of control.

Hal   Aw come on. It's great. Come on in.

Catherine   I'm okay.

Hal   We're done playing, I promise.

Catherine   No, thanks.

Hal   Do you want a beer?

Catherine   I'm okay.

Hal   I brought you one.

Beat. She hesitates.

Catherine   Okay. (*She takes it, sips.*) How many people are in there?

Hal   It's down to about forty.

Catherine   Forty?

Hal   Just the hard-core partyers.

Catherine   My sister's friends.

Hal   No, mathematicians. Your sister's friends left hours ago.

The guys were really pleased to be asked to participate. They worshipped your Dad.

Catherine   It was Claire's idea.

Hal   It was good.

Catherine (*concedes*)   The performance of "Imaginary Number" was . . . sort of . . . moving.

Hal   Good funeral. I mean not "good," but –

Catherine   No. Yeah.

Hal   Can you believe how many people came?

Catherine   I was surprised.

Hal   I think he would have liked it. (*She looks at him.*) Sorry, it's not my place to –

Catherine   No, you're right. Everything was better than I thought.

Beat.

Hal   You look great.

Catherine (*indicates the dress*)   Claire gave it to me.

Hal   I like it.

Catherine   It doesn't really fit.

Hal   No, Catherine, it's good.

A moment. Noise from inside.

Catherine   When do you think they'll leave?

Hal   No way to know. Mathematicians are insane. I went to this conference in Toronto last fall. I'm young, right? I'm in shape, I thought I could hang with the big boys. Wrong. I've never been so exhausted in my life. 48 straight hours of partying, drinking, drugs, papers, lectures . . .

Catherine   Drugs?

Hal   Yeah. Amphetamines, mostly. I mean I don't. Some of the older guys are really hooked.

Catherine   Really?

Hal   Yeah, they think they need it.

Catherine   Why?

Hal   They think math's a young man's game. Speed keeps them racing, makes them feel sharp. There's this fear that your creativity peaks around 23 and it's all downhill from there. Once you hit fifty it's over, you might as well teach high school.

Catherine   That's what my father thought.

Hal   I dunno. Some people stay prolific.

Catherine   Not many.

Hal   No, you're right. Really original work – it's all young guys.

Catherine   Young guys.

Hal   Young people.

Catherine   But it is men, mostly.

Hal   There are some women.

Catherine   Who?

Hal   There's a woman at Stanford, I can't remember her name.

Catherine   Sophie Germain.

Hal   Yeah? I've probably seen her at meetings, I just don't think I've met her.

Catherine   She was born in Paris in 1776.

Beat.

Hal   So I've definitely never met her.

Catherine   She was trapped in her house.

The French Revolution was going on, the Terror. She had to stay inside for safety and she passed the time reading in her father's study. The Greeks . . . Later she tried to get a real education but the schools didn't allow women. So she wrote letters. She wrote to Gauss. She used a man's name. Uh, "Antoine-August Le Blanc." She sent him some proofs involving a certain kind of prime number, important work. He was delighted to correspond with such a brilliant young man.

Dad gave me a book about her.

Hal   I'm stupid. Sophie Germain, of course.

Catherine   You know her?

Hal   Germain Primes.

Catherine   Right.

Hal   They're famous. Double them and add 1, and you get another prime. Like 2. 2 is prime, doubled plus one is 5: also prime.

Catherine   Right. Or $92,305 \times 2^{16,998} +1$.

Hal (*startled*)   Right.

Catherine   That's the biggest one. The biggest one known . . .

Beat.

Hal   Did he ever find out who she was? Gauss.

Catherine   Yeah. Later a mutual friend told him the brilliant young man was a woman.

He wrote to her: "A taste for the mysteries of numbers is excessively rare, but when a person of the sex which must encounter infinitely more difficulties than men to familiarize herself with these thorny researches, succeeds nevertheless in penetrating the most obscure parts of them, then without a doubt she must have the noblest courage, quite extraordinary talents and superior genius."

(*Now self-conscious*) I memorized it . . .

Hal *stares at her. He suddenly kisses her, then stops, embarrassed. He moves away.*

Hal   Sorry. I'm a little drunk.

Catherine   It's okay.

Uncomfortable beat.

Catherine   I'm sorry about yesterday. I wasn't helpful. About the work you're doing. Take as long as you need upstairs.

Hal   You were fine. I was pushy.

Catherine   I was awful.

Hal   No. My timing was terrible. Anyway, you're probably right.

Catherine   What?

Hal   About it being junk.

Catherine (*nods*)   Yes.

Hal   I read through a lot of stuff today, just skimming. Except for the book I stole –

Catherine   Oh, God, I'm sorry about that.

Hal   No, you were right.

Catherine   I shouldn't have called the police.

Hal   It was my fault.

Catherine   No.

Hal   The point is that book – I'm starting to think it's the only lucid one, really. And there's no math in it.

Catherine   No.

Hal   I mean, I'll keep reading, but if I don't find anything in a couple of days . . .

Catherine   Back to the drums.

Hal   Yeah.

Catherine   And your own research.

Hal   Such as it is.

Catherine   What's wrong with it?

Hal   It's not exactly setting the world on fire.

Catherine   Oh come on.

Hal   It sucks, basically.

Catherine   Harold.

Hal   My papers get turned down. For the right reasons – my stuff is trivial. The big ideas aren't there.

Catherine   It's not about big ideas. It's work. You've got to chip away at a problem.

Hal   That's not what your Dad did.

Catherine   I think it was, in a way. He'd attack a question from the side, from some weird angle, sneak up on it, grind away at it. He was slogging. He was just so much faster than anyone else that from the outside it looked magical.

Hal   I don't know.

Catherine   I'm just guessing.

Hal   Plus the work was beautiful. You can read it for pleasure. It's streamlined: no wasted moves, like a 95-mile-an-hour fastball. It's just . . . elegant.

Catherine   Yeah.

Hal   And that's what you can never duplicate. At least I can't.

It's okay. At a certain point you realize it's not going to happen, you readjust your expectations. I enjoy teaching.

Catherine   You might come up with something.

Hal   I'm 28, remember? On the downhill slope.

Catherine   Have you tried speed? I've heard it helps.

Hal (*laughs*)   Yeah.

Beat.

Catherine   So, Hal.

Hal   Yeah?

Catherine   What do you do for sex?

Hal   What?

Catherine   At your conferences.

Hal   Uh, I uh –

Catherine   Isn't that why people hold conferences? Travel. Room service. Tax-deductible sex in big hotel beds.

Hal (*laughs, nervous*)   Maybe. I don't know.

Catherine   So what do you do? All you guys.

Beat. Is she flirting with him? Hal is not sure.

Hal   Well we are scientists.

Catherine   So?

Hal   So there's a lot of experimentation.

Catherine (*laughs*)   I see.

Beat. **Catherine** *goes to him. She kisses him. A longer kiss. It ends.* **Hal** *is surprised and pleased.*

Hal   Huh.

Catherine   That was nice.

Hal   Really?

Catherine   Yes.

Hal   Again?

Catherine   Yes.

Kiss.

Hal   I always liked you.

Catherine   You did?

Hal   Even before I knew you. I'd catch glimpses of you when you visited your Dad's office at school. I wanted to talk to you but I thought, No, you do not flirt with your doctoral adviser's daughter.

Catherine   Especially when your adviser's crazy.

Hal   Especially then.

Kiss.

Catherine   You came here once. Four years ago. Remember?

Hal   Sure. I can't believe you do. I was dropping off a draft of my thesis for your Dad. Jesus I was nervous.

Catherine   You looked nervous.

Hal   I can't believe you remember that.

Catherine   I remember you.

I thought you seemed . . . not boring.

FADE.

Scene Four

The next morning.

Catherine *alone on the porch, in a robe.* **Hal** *enters, half-dressed. He walks up behind her quietly. She hears him and turns.*

Hal   How long have you been up?

Catherine   A while.

Hal   Did I oversleep?

Catherine   No.

Beat. Morning-after awkwardness.

Hal   Is your sister up?

Catherine   No. She's flying home in a couple hours. I should probably wake her.

Hal   Let her sleep. She was doing some pretty serious drinking with the theoretical physicists last night.

Catherine   I'll make her some coffee when she gets up.

Beat.

Hal   Sunday mornings I usually go out. Get the paper, have some breakfast.

Catherine   Okay.

Beat.

Hal   Do you want to come?

Catherine   Oh. No. I ought to stick around until Claire leaves.

Hal   All right.

Do you mind if I stay?

Catherine   No. You can work if you want.

Hal (*taken aback*)   Okay.

Catherine   Okay.

Hal   Should I?

Catherine   If you want to.

Hal   Do you want me to go?

Catherine   Do you want to go?

Hal   I want to stay here with you.

Catherine   Oh . . .

Hal   I want to spend the day with you if possible. I'd like to spend as much time with you as I can unless of course I'm coming on WAY too strong right now and scaring you in which case I'll begin backpedaling immediately . . .

She laughs. Her relief is evident; so is his.

Hal   How embarrassing is it if I say last night was wonderful?

Catherine   It's only embarrassing if I don't agree.

Hal   Uh, so . . .

Catherine   Don't be embarrassed.

They kiss.

After a moment **Catherine** *breaks off.*

She hesitates, making a decision. Then she takes a chain from around her neck. There is a key on the chain. She tosses it to **Hal***.*

Catherine   Here.

Hal   What's this?

Catherine   It's a key.

Hal   Ah.

Catherine   Try it.

Hal   Where?

Catherine   Bottom drawer of the desk in my Dad's office.

Hal   What's in there?

Catherine   There's one way to find out, professor.

Hal   Now?

Catherine *shrugs.*

Hal *laughs, unsure if this is a joke or not.*

Hal   Okay.

He kisses her quickly then goes inside.

Catherine *smiles to herself. She is happy, on the edge of being giddy.*

Claire *enters, hungover. She sits down, squinting.*

Catherine   Good morning.

Claire   Please don't yell please.

Catherine   Are you all right?

Claire   No.

(*She clutches her head.*) Fucking physicists.

Catherine   What happened?

Claire   Thanks a lot for leaving me all alone with them.

Catherine   Where were your friends?

Claire   My stupid friends left – it was only 11 o'clock! – they all had to get home and pay their babysitters or bake bread or something. I'm left alone with these lunatics . . .

Catherine   Why did you drink so much?

Claire   I thought I could keep up with them. I thought they'd stop. They didn't. Oh God.

Catherine   Do you want some coffee?

Claire   In a minute.

That BAND.

Catherine   Yeah.

Claire   They were terrible.

Catherine   They were okay. They had fun. I think.

Claire   Well as long as everyone had fun.

Your dress turned out all right.

Catherine   I love it.

Claire   You do.

Catherine   Yeah, it's wonderful.

Claire   I was surprised you even wore it.

Catherine   I love it, Claire. Thanks.

Claire (*surprised*)   You're welcome. You're in a good mood.

Catherine   Should I not be?

Claire   Are you kidding? No. I'm thrilled.

I'm leaving in a few hours.

Catherine   I know.

Claire   The house is a wreck. Don't clean it up yourself. I'll hire someone to come in.

Catherine   Thanks. You want your coffee?

Claire   No, thanks.

Catherine (*starting in*)   It's no trouble.

Claire   Hold on a sec, Katie. I just . . .

Claire *takes a breath.*

I'm leaving soon. I –

Catherine   You said. I know.

Claire   I'd still like you to come to New York.

Catherine   Yes: January.

Claire   I'd like you to move to New York.

Catherine   Move?

Claire   Would you think about it? For me?

You could stay with me and Mitch at first. There's plenty of room. Then you could get your own place. I've already scouted some apartments for you, really cute places.

Catherine   What would I do in New York?

Claire   What are you doing here?

Catherine   I live here.

Claire   You could do whatever you want. You could work, you could go to school.

Catherine   I don't know, Claire. This is pretty major.

Claire   I realize that.

Catherine   I know you mean well. I'm just not sure what I want to do. I mean to be honest you were right yesterday. I do feel a little confused. I'm tired. It's been a pretty weird couple of years. I think I'd like to take some time to figure things out.

Claire   You could do that in New York.

Catherine   And I could do it here.

Claire   But it would be much easier for me to get you set up in an apartment in New York, and –

Catherine   I don't need an apartment, I'll stay in the house.

Claire   We're selling the house.

Beat.

Catherine   What?

Claire   We – I'm selling it.

Catherine   When?

Claire   I'm hoping to do the paperwork this week. I know it seems sudden.

Catherine   No one was here looking at the place, who are you selling it to?

Claire   The University. They've wanted the block for years.

Catherine   I LIVE HERE.

Claire   Honey, now that Dad's gone it doesn't make sense. It's in bad shape. It costs a fortune to heat. It's time to let it go. Mitch agrees, it's a very smart move. We're lucky, we have a great offer –

Catherine   Where am I supposed to live?

Claire   Come to New York.

Catherine   I can't believe this.

Claire   It'll be so good. You deserve a change. This would be a whole new adventure for you.

Catherine   Why are you doing this?

Claire   I want to help.

Catherine   By kicking me out of my house?

Claire   It was my house too.

Catherine   You haven't lived here for years.

Claire   I know that. You were on your own. I really regret that, Katie.

Catherine   Don't.

Claire   I know I let you down. I feel awful about it. Now I'm trying to help.

Catherine   You want to help now?

Claire   Yes.

Catherine   Dad is dead.

Claire   I know.

Catherine   He's dead. Now that he's dead you fly in for the weekend and decide you want to help? YOU'RE LATE. Where have you been?

Claire   I –

Catherine   Where were you five years ago? You weren't helping then.

Claire   I was working.

Catherine   I was here. I lived with him alone.

Claire   I was working 14 hour days. I paid every bill here. I paid off the mortgage on this three bedroom house while I was living in a studio in Brooklyn.

Catherine   You had your life. You got to finish school.

Claire   You could have stayed in school!

Catherine   How?

Claire   I would have done anything – I told you that. I told you a million times to do anything you wanted.

Catherine   What about Dad? Someone had to take care of him.

Claire   He was ill. He should have been in a full-time professional care situation.

Catherine   He didn't belong in the nuthouse.

Claire   He might have been better off.

Catherine   How can you say that?

Claire   This is where I'm meant to feel guilty, right?

Catherine   Sure, go for it.

Claire   I'm heartless. My own father.

Catherine   He needed to be here. In his own house, near the University, near his students, near everything that made him happy.

Claire   Maybe. Or maybe some real, professional care would have done him more good than rattling around in a filthy house with YOU looking after him.

I'm sorry, Catherine, it's not your fault. It's my fault for letting you do it.

Catherine   I was right to keep him here.

Claire   No.

Catherine   What about his remission? Four years ago. He was healthy for almost a year.

Claire   And then he went right downhill again.

Catherine   He might have been worse in a hospital.

Claire   And he MIGHT have been BETTER. Did he ever do any work again?

Catherine   No.

Claire   NO.

And you might have been better.

Catherine (*keeping her voice under control*)   Better than what?

Claire   Living here with him didn't do you any good. You said that yourself.

You had so much talent . . .

Catherine   You think I'm like Dad.

Claire   I think you have some of his talent and some of his tendency toward . . . instability.

Beat.

Catherine   Claire, in addition to the "cute apartments" that you've "scouted" for me in New York, would you by any chance also have devoted some of your considerable energies toward scouting out another type of –

Claire   NO.

Catherine   – living facility for your bughouse little sister?

Claire   NO! Absolutely not. That is not what this is about.

Catherine   Don't lie to me, Claire, I'm smarter than you.

Beat.

Claire   The resources . . . I've investigated –

Catherine   Oh my god.

Claire   If you WANTED to, all I'm saying is the doctors in New York and the people are the BEST, and they –

Catherine   FUCK YOU.

Claire   It would be entirely up to you. You wouldn't LIVE anywhere, you can –

Catherine   I hate you.

Claire   Don't yell, please, calm down.

Catherine   I HATE YOU. I –

Hal *enters, holding a notebook.* **Claire** *and* **Catherine** *stop suddenly.*

Beat.

Claire   What are you (doing here?) . . .

She looks at **Catherine***.* **Hal** *is nearly speechless. He stares at* **Catherine***.*

Hal   How long have you known about this?

Catherine   A while.

Hal   Why didn't you tell me about it?

Catherine   I wasn't sure I wanted to.

Beat.

Hal   Thank you.

Catherine   You're welcome.

Claire   What's going on?

Hal   God, Catherine, thank you.

Catherine   I thought you'd like to see it.

Claire   What is it?

Hal   It's incredible.

Claire   What IS it?

Hal   Oh, uh, it's a result. A proof. I mean it looks like one. I mean it is one, a very long one, I haven't read it all of course, or checked it, I don't even know if I could check it, but if it is what I think it is it's a very –

Claire   What does it prove?

Hal   It looks like it proves a theorem, a mathematical theorem about prime numbers, something mathematicians have been trying to demonstrate since . . . since there were mathematicians, basically. Most people thought it couldn't be done.

Claire   Where did you find it?

Hal   In your father's desk. Cathy told me about it.

Claire   You know what this is?

Catherine   Sure.

Claire   Is it good?

Catherine   Yes.

Hal   It's historic. If it checks out.

Claire   What does it say?

Hal   I don't know yet exactly. I've just read the first few pages.

Claire   But what does it mean?

Hal   It means that during a time when everyone thought your Dad was crazy . . . or barely functioning . . . he was doing some of the most important mathematics in the world. If it checks out it means you publish instantly. It means media all over the world are going to want to talk to the person who found this notebook.

Claire   Cathy.

Hal   Cathy.

Catherine   I didn't find it.

Hal   Yes you did.

Catherine   No.

Claire   Well did you find it or did Hal find it?

Hal   I didn't find it.

Catherine   I didn't find it.

I wrote it.

<u>CURTAIN</u>

Act Two

Scene One

Robert *is alone on the porch.*

He sits quietly, enjoying a drink, the quiet, the September afternoon. A notebook nearby, unopened. He closes his eyes, apparently dozing.

It is four years earlier than the events in Act One.

Catherine *enters quietly. She stands behind her father for a moment.*

Robert   Hello.

Catherine   How did you know I was here?

Robert   I heard you.

Catherine   I thought you were asleep.

Robert   On an afternoon like this? No.

Catherine   Do you need anything?

Robert   No.

Catherine   I'm going to the store.

Robert   What's for dinner?

Catherine   What do you want?

Robert   Not spaghetti.

Catherine   All right.

Robert   Disgusting stuff.

Catherine   That's what I was going to make.

Robert   I had a feeling. Good thing I spoke up. You make it too much.

Catherine   What do you want?

Robert   What do you have a taste for?

Catherine   Nothing.

Robert   Nothing at all?

Catherine   I don't care. I thought pasta would be easy.

Robert   Pasta, oh God don't even say the word "pasta." It sounds so hopeless, like surrender: "Pasta would be easy." Yes, yes it would. Pasta. It doesn't mean anything. It's just a euphemism people invented when they got sick of eating spaghetti.

Catherine   Dad, what do you want to eat?

Robert   I don't know.

Catherine   Well I don't know what to get.

Robert   I'll shop.

Catherine   No.

Robert   I'll do it.

Catherine   No, Dad, rest.

Robert   I wanted to take a walk anyway.

Catherine   Are you sure?

Robert   Yes. What about a walk to the Lake? You and me.

Catherine   All right.

Robert   I would love to go to the Lake. Then on the way home we'll stop at the store, see what jumps out at us.

Catherine   It's warm. It would be nice, if you're up for it.

Robert   You're damn right I'm up for it. We'll work up an appetite. Give me ten seconds, let me put this stuff away and we're out the door.

Catherine   I'm going to school.

Beat.

Robert   When?

Catherine   I'm gonna start at Northwestern at the end of the month.

Robert   Northwestern?

Catherine   They were great about my credits. They're taking me in as a sophomore. I wasn't sure when to talk to you about it.

Robert   Northwestern?

Catherine   Yes.

Robert   What's wrong with Chicago?

Catherine   You still teach there. I'm sorry, it's too weird, taking classes in your department.

Robert   It's a long drive.

Catherine   Not that long, half an hour.

Robert   Still, twice a day . . .

Catherine   Dad, I'd live there.

Beat.

Robert   You'd actually want to live in Evanston?

Catherine   Yes. I'll still be close. I can come home whenever you want.

You've been well – really well – for almost seven months. I don't think you need me here every minute of the day.

Beat.

Robert   This is all a done deal? You're in.

Catherine   Yes.

Robert   You're sure.

Catherine   YES.

Robert   Who pays for it?

Catherine   They're giving me a free ride, Dad. They've been great.

Robert   On tuition, sure. What about food, books, clothes, gas, meals out – do you plan to have a social life?

Catherine   I don't know.

Robert   You gotta pay your own way on dates, at least the early dates, say the first three, otherwise they expect something.

Catherine   The money will be fine. Claire's gonna help out.

Robert   When did you talk to Claire?

Catherine   I don't know, a couple weeks ago.

Robert   You talk to her before you talk to me?

Catherine   There were a lot of details to work out. She was great, she offered to take care of all the expenses.

Robert   This is a big step. A different *city* –

Catherine   It's not even a long distance phone call.

Robert   It's a huge place. They're serious up there. I mean serious. Yeah the football's a disaster but the math guys don't kid around. You haven't been in school. You sure you're ready? You can get buried up there.

Catherine   I'll be all right.

Robert   You're way behind.

Catherine   I know.

Robert   A year, at least.

Catherine   Thank you, I KNOW. Look, I don't know if this is a good idea. I don't know if I can handle the work. I don't know if I can handle any of it.

Robert   For Chrissake Catherine, you should have talked to me.

Catherine   Dad. Listen. If you ever . . . if for any reason it ever turned out that you needed me here full time again – ·

Robert   I WON'T. That's not (*what I'm talking about*) –

Catherine   I can always take a semester off, or –

Robert   No. Stop it. I just – the end of the month? Why didn't you say something before?

Catherine   Dad, come on. It took a while to set this up, and until recently, until very recently, you weren't –-

Robert   You just said yourself I've been fine.

Catherine   Yes, but I didn't know – I hoped, but I didn't know, no one knew if this would last. I told myself to wait until I was sure about you. That you were feeling okay again. Consistently okay.

Robert   So I'm to take this conversation as a vote of confidence? I'm honored.

Catherine   Take it however you want. I was believed you'd get better.

Robert   Well thank you very much.

Catherine   Don't thank me. I had to. I was living with you.

Robert   All right, that's enough, Catherine. Let's stay on the subject.

Catherine   This is the subject! There were library books upstairs stacked up to the ceiling, do you remember that? You were trying to decode messages –

Robert   The fucking books are gone, I took them back myself.

Why do you bring that garbage up?

Knocking off.

Beat. **Catherine** *goes inside to answer the door.*

She returns with **Hal***. He carries a manila envelope. He is nervous.*

Robert   Mr. Dobbs.

Hal   Hi. I hope it's not a bad time.

Robert   Yes it is, actually, you couldn't have picked worse.

Hal   Oh I uh

Robert   You interrupted an argument.

Hal   I'm sorry. I can come back.

Robert   It's all right. We needed a break.

Hal   Are you sure?

Robert   Yes. The argument was about dinner. We don't know what to eat. What's your suggestion?

A beat while **Hal** *is on the spot.*

Hal   Uh, there's a good pasta place not too far from here.

Robert   NO!

Catherine (w/Robert)   That is a BRILLIANT idea.

Robert   Oh dear Jesus God no.

Catherine (w/Robert)   What's it called? Give me the address.

Robert   No! Sorry. Wrong answer but thank you for trying.

Hal *stands there, looking at both of them.*

Hal   I can come back.

Robert   Stay. (*To* **Catherine**) Where are you going?

Catherine   Inside.

Robert   What about dinner?

Catherine   What about him?

Robert   What are you doing here, Dobbs?

Hal   My timing is horrible. I am really sorry.

Robert   Don't be silly.

Hal   I'll come to your office.

Robert   Stop. Sit down. Glad you're here. Don't let the dinner thing throw you, you'll bounce back.

(*To* **Catherine**.) This should be easier. Let's back off the problem, let it breathe, come at it again when it's not looking.

Catherine   Fine.

(*Exiting.*) Excuse me.

Robert   Sorry, I'm rude. Hal, this is my daughter Catherine.

(*To* **Catherine**.) Don't go, have a drink with us. Catherine, Harold Dobbs.

Catherine   Hi.

Hal   Hi.

Robert   Hal is a grad student. He's doing his Ph.D, very promising stuff. Unfortunately for him his work coincided with my return to the department and he got stuck with me.

Hal   No, no, it's been – I've been very lucky.

Catherine   How long have you been at U of C?

Hal   Well I've been working on my thesis for –

Robert   Hal's in our "Infinite" program. As he approaches completion of his dissertation, time approaches infinity. Would you like a drink, Hal?

Hal   Yes I would.

And uh, with all due respect . . .

He hands **Robert** *the envelope.* **Robert** *surprised.*

Robert   Really?

He opens it and looks inside.

You must have had an interesting few months.

Hal (*cheerfully*)   Worst summer of my life.

Robert   Congratulations.

Hal   It's just a draft. Based on everything we talked about last spring.

Robert *pours a drink.* **Hal** *babbles:*

I wasn't sure if I should wait till the quarter started, or if I should give it to you now, or hold off, do another draft, but I figured fuck it I, I mean I just . . . let's just get it over with, so I thought I'd just come over and see if you were home, and –

Robert   Drink this.

Hal   Thanks.

He drinks.

I decided, I don't know, if it feels done, maybe it is.

Robert   Wrong. If it feels done there are major errors.

Hal   Uh, I –

Robert   That's okay, that's good, we'll find them and fix them. Don't worry. You're on your way to a solid career, you'll be teaching younger, more irritating versions of yourself in no time.

Hal   Thank you.

Robert   Catherine's in the math department at Northwestern, Hal.

Catherine *looks up, startled.*

Hal   Oh, who are you working with?

Catherine   I'm just starting this fall. Undergrad.

Robert   She's starting in . . . three weeks?

Catherine   A little more.

Beat.

Robert   They have some good people at Northwestern. O'Donohue. Kaminsky.

Catherine   Yes.

Robert   They will work your ass off.

Catherine   I know.

Robert   You'll have to run pretty hard to catch up.

Catherine   I think I can do it.

Robert   Of course you can.

Beat.

Hal   You must be excited.

Catherine   I am.

Hal   First year of school can be great.

Catherine   Yeah?

Hal   Sure, all the new people, new places, getting out of the house.

Catherine (*embarrassed*)   Yes.

Hal (*embarrassed*)   Or, no, I –

Robert   Absolutely, getting the hell out of here, thank God, it's about time. I'll be glad to see the back of her.

Catherine   You will?

Robert   Of course. Maybe I want to have the place to myself for a while, did that ever occur to you? (*To* **Hal**.) It's awful the way children sentimentalize their parents. (*To* **Catherine**.) We could use some quiet around here.

Catherine   Oh don't worry, I'll come back. I'll be here every Sunday cooking up big vats of spaghetti to last you through the week.

Robert   And I'll drive up, strut around Evanston, embarrass you in front of your classmates.

Catherine   Good. So we'll be in touch.

Robert   Sure. And if you get stuck with a problem, give me a call.

Catherine   Okay. Same to you.

Robert   Fine. Make sure to get me your number. (*To* **Hal**.) I'm actually looking forward to getting some work done.

Hal   Oh, what are you working on?

Robert   Nothing.

Beat.

Nothing at the moment.

Which I'm glad of, really. This is the time of year when you don't want to be tied down to anything. You want to be outside. I love Chicago in September. Perfect skies. Sailboats on the water. Cubs losing. Warm, the sun still hot . . . with the occasional blast of Arctic wind to keep you on your toes, remind you of winter. Students coming back, bookstores full, everybody busy.

I was in a bookstore yesterday. Completely full, students buying books . . . browsing . . . Students do a hell of a lot of browsing, don't they? Just browsing. You see them shuffling around with their backpacks, goofing off, taking up space. You'd call it loitering except every once in a while they pick up a book and flip the pages: "Browsing." I admire it. It's an honest way to kill an afternoon. In the back of a used bookstore, or going through a crate of somebody's old record albums – not looking for anything, just looking, what the hell, touching the old bookjackets, seeing what somebody threw out, seeing what they underlined . . . maybe you find something great, like an old thriller with a painted cover from the 40s, or a textbook one of your professors used when he was a student – his name is written in it very carefully . . . Yeah, I like it. I like watching the students. Wondering what they're gonna buy, what they're gonna read. What kind of ideas they'll come up with when they settle down and get to work . . .

I'm not doing much right now. It does get harder. It's a stereotype that happens to be true, unfortunately for me – unfortunately for you, for all of us.

Catherine   Maybe you'll get lucky.

Robert   Maybe I will.

Maybe you'll pick up where I left off.

Catherine   Don't hold your breath.

Robert   Don't underestimate yourself.

Catherine   Anyway.

Beat.

Robert   Another drink? Cathy? Hal?

Catherine   No thanks.

Hal   Thanks, I really should get going.

Robert   Are you sure?

Hal   Yes.

Robert   I'll call you when I've looked at this. Don't think about it till then. Enjoy yourself, see some movies.

Hal   Okay.

Robert   You can come by my office in a week. Call it –

Hal   The 11th?

Robert   Yes, we'll . . .

Beat. He turns to **Catherine**. *Grave:*

I am sorry. I used to have a pretty good memory for numbers.

Happy birthday.

Catherine   Thank you.

Robert   I am so sorry. I'm embarrassed.

Catherine   Dad, don't be stupid.

Robert   I didn't get you anything.

Catherine   Don't worry about it.

Robert   I'm taking you out.

Catherine   You don't have to.

Robert   We are going out. I didn't want to shop and cook. Let's go to dinner. Let's get the hell out of this neighborhood. What do you want to eat? Let's go to the North Side. Or Chinatown. Or Greektown. I don't know what's good anymore.

Catherine   Whatever you want.

Robert   Whatever you want goddamnit, Catherine, it's your birthday.

Beat.

Catherine   Steak.

Robert   Steak. Yes.

Catherine   First beer, really cold beer. Really cheap beer.

Robert   Done.

Catherine   That Chicago beer that's watery with no flavor and you can just drink gallons of it.

Robert   They just pump the water out of Lake Michigan and bottle it.

Catherine   It's so awful.

Robert   I have a taste for it myself.

Catherine   Then the steak, grilled really black, and creamed spinach.

Robert   I remember a place. If it's still there I think it will do the trick.

Catherine   And desert.

Robert   That goes without saying. It's your birthday, hooray. And there's the solution to our dinner problem. Thank you for reminding me Harold Dobbs.

Catherine (*To* **Hal**)   We're being rude. Do you want to come?

Hal   Oh, no, I shouldn't.

Robert   Why not? Please, come.

Catherine   Come on.

A tiny moment between **Hal** *and* **Catherine**. **Hal** *wavers, then:*

Hal   No, I can't, I have plans. Thank you though. Happy birthday.

Catherine   Thanks. Well. I'll let you out.

Robert   I'll see you on the 11th, Hal.

Hal   Great.

Catherine   I'm gonna change my clothes, Dad. I'll be ready in a sec.

Hal *and* **Catherine** *exit.*

A moment.

It's darker. **Robert** *looks out at the evening.*

Eventually he picks up the notebook and a pen. He sits down. He opens to a blank page. He writes.

Robert   "September fourth.

A good day . . ."

He continues to write.

FADE.

Scene Two

Morning. An instant after the end of Act One: **Catherine**, **Claire**, *and* **Hal**.

Hal   You wrote this?

Catherine   Yes.

Claire   When?

Catherine   I started after I quit school. I finished a few months before Dad died.

Claire   Did he see it?

Catherine   No. He didn't know I was working on it. It wouldn't have mattered to him anyway, he was too sick.

Hal   I don't understand – you did this by yourself?

Catherine   Yes.

Claire   It's in Dad's notebook.

Catherine   I used one of his blank books. There were a bunch of them upstairs.

Beat.

Claire (*To* **Hal**)   Tell me exactly where you found this?

Hal   In his study.

Catherine   In his desk. I gave him the –

Claire (*To* **Catherine**)   Hold on. (*To* **Hal**.) Where did you find it?

Hal   In the bottom drawer of the desk in the study, a locked drawer: Catherine gave me the key.

Claire   Why was the drawer locked?

Catherine   It's mine, it's the drawer I keep my private things in. I've used it for years.

Claire (*To* **Hal**)   Was there anything else in the drawer?

Hal   No.

Catherine   No, that's the only –

Claire   Can I see it?

Hal *gives* **Claire** *the book. She pages through it.*

Beat.

I'm sorry, I just . . . (*To* **Catherine**.) The book was in the . . . You told him where to find it . . . You gave him the key . . . You wrote this incredible thing and you didn't tell anyone?

Catherine   I'm telling you both now. After I dropped out of school I had nothing to do. I was depressed, really depressed, but at a certain point I decided Fuck it, I don't need them. It's just math, I can do it on my own. So I kept working here. I worked at night, after Dad had gone to sleep. It was hard but I did it.

Beat.

Claire   Catherine, I'm sorry but I just find this very hard to believe.

Catherine   Claire. I wrote. The proof.

Claire   I'm sorry, I –

Catherine   Claire . . .

Claire   This is Dad's handwriting.

Catherine   It's not.

Claire   It looks exactly like it.

Catherine   It's my writing.

Claire   I'm sorry –

Catherine   Ask Hal, he's been looking at Dad's writing for weeks.

Claire *gives* **Hal** *the book. He looks at it.*

Beat.

Hal   I don't know.

Catherine   Hal, come on.

Claire   What does it look like?

Hal   It looks . . . I don't know what Catherine's handwriting looks like.

Catherine   It LOOKS like THAT.

Hal   Okay. It . . . okay.

Beat. He hands the book back.

Claire   I think – you know what? I think it's early, and people are tired, and not in the best state to make decisions about emotional things, so maybe we should all just take a breath . . .

Catherine   You don't believe me?

Claire   I don't know. I really don't know anything about this.

Catherine   Never mind. I don't know why I expected you to believe me about ANYTHING.

Claire   Could you tell us the proof? That would show it was yours.

Catherine   You wouldn't understand it.

Claire   Tell it to Hal.

Catherine (*taking the book*)   We could talk through it together. It might take a while.

Claire (*taking the book*)   You can't use the book.

Catherine   For God's sake it's forty pages long. I didn't MEMORIZE it. It's not a muffin recipe.

This is stupid. It's my book, my writing, my key, my drawer, my proof. Hal, tell her!

Hal   Tell her what?

Catherine   Whose book is that?

Hal   I don't know.

Catherine   What is the matter with you? You've been looking at his other stuff, you know there's nothing even remotely like this!

Hal   Look, Catherine –

Catherine   We'll go through the work together. We'll sit down – if Claire will PLEASE let me have my book back –

Claire (*giving her the book*)   All right, talk him through it.

Hal   That might take days and it still wouldn't show that she wrote it.

Catherine   Why not?

Hal   Your Dad might have written it and explained it to you later. I'm not saying he did, I'm just –

Catherine   Come on! He didn't do this, he couldn't have. He didn't do any mathematics at all for years. Even in the good year he couldn't work: you KNOW that. You're supposed to be a scientist.

Beat.

Hal   You're right. Okay. Here's my suggestion. I know three or four guys at the department, very sharp, disinterested people who knew your father, knew his work. Let me take this to them.

Catherine   WHAT?

Hal   I'll tell them we've found something, something potentially major, we're not sure about the authorship; I'll sit down with them. we'll go through the thing carefully –

Claire   Good.

Hal   – and figure out exactly what we've got. It would only take a couple of days, probably, and then we'd have a lot more information.

Claire   I think that's an excellent suggestion.

Catherine   You can't.

Claire   Catherine.

Catherine   No! You can't take it.

Hal   I'm not "taking" it.

Catherine   This is what you wanted.

Hal   Oh come on, Jesus.

Catherine   You don't waste any time, do you? No hesitation. You can't wait to show them your brilliant discovery.

Hal   I'm trying to determine what this is.

Catherine   I'm telling you what it is.

Hal   You don't know!

Catherine   I WROTE IT.

Hal   IT'S YOUR FATHER'S HANDWRITING.

Beat.

(*Pained.*) At least it looks an awful lot like the writing in the other books. Maybe your writing looks exactly like his, I don't know.

Catherine (*softly*)   It does look like his.

I didn't show this to anyone else. I could have. I wanted you to be the first to see it. I didn't know I wanted that until last night. It's ME. I trusted you.

Hal   I know.

Catherine   Was I wrong?

Hal   No. I –

Catherine   I should have known she wouldn't believe me but why don't you?

Hal   This is one of his notebooks. The exact same kind he used.

Catherine   I told you. I just used one of his blank books. There were extras.

Hal   There aren't any extra books in the study.

Catherine   There were when I started writing the proof. I bought them for him. He used the rest up later.

Hal   And the writing.

Catherine   You want to test the handwriting?

Hal   No. It doesn't matter. He could have dictated it to you for Chrissake. It still doesn't make sense.

Catherine   Why not?

Hal   I'm a mathematician.

Catherine   Yes.

Hal   I know how hard it would be to come up with something like this. I mean it's impossible. You'd have to be . . . you'd have to be your Dad, basically. Your Dad at the peak of his powers.

Catherine   I'm a mathematician too.

Hal   Not like your Dad.

Catherine   Oh he's the only one who could have done this?

Hal   The only one I know.

Catherine   Are you sure?

Hal   Your father was the most –

Catherine   Just because you and the rest of the geeks worshipped him doesn't mean he wrote this proof, Hal!

Hal   He was the BEST. My generation hasn't produced anything like him. He revolutionized the field twice before he was 22. I'm sorry, Catherine, but you took some classes at Northwestern for a few months.

Catherine   My education wasn't at Northwestern. It was living in this house for 25 years.

Hal   Even so, it doesn't matter. This is too advanced. I don't even understand most of it.

Catherine   You think it's too advanced.

Hal   Yes.

Catherine   It's too advanced for YOU.

Hal   You could not have done this work.

Catherine   But what if I did?

Hal   Well what if?

Catherine   It would be a real disaster for you, wouldn't it? And for the other geeks who BARELY finished their Ph.D's, who are marking time doing LAME research, bragging about the conferences they go to – WOW – playing in an AWFUL band, and whining that they're intellectually past it at 28, BECAUSE THEY ARE.

Beat.

Hal *hesitates, then abruptly exits.*

Beat.

Catherine *is furious and so upset she looks dazed.*

Claire   Katie.

Let's go inside.

Katie?

Catherine *opens the book and tries to rip out the pages, destroy it.* **Claire** *goes to take it from her. They struggle.* **Catherine** *gets the book away.*

They stand apart, breathing hard.

After a moment, **Catherine** *throws the book to the floor.*

She exits.

FADE.

Scene Three

The next day. The porch is empty. Knocking off. No one appears. After a moment **Hal** *comes around the side of the porch and knocks on the back door.*

Hal   Catherine?

Claire *enters.*

I thought you were leaving.

Claire   I had to delay my flight.

Beat.

Hal   Is Catherine here?

Claire   I don't think this is a good time, Hal.

Hal   Could I see her?

Claire   Not now.

Hal   What's the matter?

Claire   She's sleeping.

Hal   Can I wait here until she gets up?

Claire   She's been sleeping since yesterday. She won't get up. She won't eat, won't talk to me. I couldn't go home. I'm going to wait until she seems okay to travel.

Hal   Jesus, I'm sorry.

Claire   Yes.

Hal   I'd like to talk to her.

Claire   I don't think that's a good idea.

Hal   Has she said anything?

Claire   About you? No.

Hal   Yesterday . . . I know I didn't do what she wanted.

Claire   Neither of us did.

Hal   I didn't know what to say. I feel awful.

Claire   Why did you sleep with her?

Beat.

Hal   I'm sorry, that's none of your business.

Claire   Bullshit. I have to take care of her. It's a little bit harder with you jerking her around.

Hal   I wasn't jerking her around. It just happened.

Claire   Your timing was not great.

Hal   It wasn't my timing, it was both of our –

Claire   Why'd you do it? You know what she's like. She's fragile and you took advantage of her.

Hal   No. It's what we both wanted. I didn't mean to hurt her.

Claire   You did.

Hal   I'd like to talk to Catherine, please.

Claire   You can't.

Hal   Are you taking her away?

Claire   Yes.

Hal   To New York.

Claire   Yes.

Hal   Just going to drag her to New York.

Claire   If I have to.

Hal   Don't you think she should have some say in whether or not she goes?

Claire   If she's not going to speak what else can I do?

Hal   Let me try. Let me talk to her.

Claire   Hal, give up. This has nothing to do with you.

Hal   I know her. She's tougher than you think, Claire.

Claire   What?

Hal   She can handle herself. She can handle talking to me – maybe it would help. Maybe she'd like it.

Claire   Maybe she'd LIKE it? Are you out of your mind? You're the reason she's up there right now! You have NO IDEA what she needs. You don't know her! She's my sister. Jesus, you fucking mathematicians: you DON'T THINK. You don't know what you're doing. You stagger around creating these catastrophes and it's people like me who end up flying in to clean them up.

Beat.

She needs to get out of Chicago, out of this house. I'll give you my number in New York. You can call her once she's settled there. That's it, that's the deal.

Hal   Okay.

Beat. **Hal** *doesn't move.*

Claire   I don't mean to be rude but I have a lot to do.

Hal   There's one more thing. You're not going to like it.

Claire   Sure, take the notebook.

Hal (*startled*)   I –

Claire   Hold on a sec, I'll get it for you.

She goes inside and returns with the notebook. She gives it to **Hal**.

Hal   I thought this would be harder.

Claire   Don't worry, I understand. It's very sweet you want to see Catherine but of course you'd like to see the notebook too.

Hal (*huffy*)   It's – No, it's my responsibility – as a professional I can't turn my back on the necessity of the –

Claire   Relax. I don't care. Take it. What would I do with it?

Hal   You sure?

Claire   Yes, of course.

Hal   You trust me with this?

Claire   Yes.

Hal   You just said I don't know what I'm doing.

Claire   I think you're a little bit of an idiot but you're not dishonest. Someone needs to figure out what's in there. I can't do it. It should be done here, at Chicago: my father would like that. When you decide what we've got let me know what the family should do.

Hal   Thanks.

Claire   Don't thank me, it's by far the most convenient option available. I put my card in there, call me whenever you want.

Hal   Okay.

Hal *starts to exit.* **Claire** *hesitates, then:*

Claire   Hal.

Hal   Yeah?

Claire   Can you tell me about it? I'm just curious.

Hal   It would take some time. How much math have you got?

Beat.

Claire   I'm a currency analyst. It helps to be very quick with numbers. I am. I probably inherited about one-one thousandth of my father's ability. It's enough.

Catherine got more, I'm not sure how much.

FADE.

Scene Four

Winter. About three and a half years earlier.

Robert *is on the porch. He wears a T shirt. He writes in a notebook.*

After a moment we hear **Catherine***'s voice from off.*

Catherine   Dad?

Catherine *enters wearing a parka. She sees her father and stops.*

Catherine   What are you doing out here?

Robert   Working.

Catherine   It's December. It's 30 degrees.

Robert   I know.

Catherine *stares at him, baffled.*

Catherine   Don't you need a coat?

Robert   Don't you think I can make that assessment for myself?

Beat.

Catherine   Aren't you cold?

Robert   Of course I am! I'm freezing my ass off!

Catherine   So what are you doing out here?

Robert   Thinking! Writing!

Catherine   You're gonna freeze.

Robert   It's too hot in the house. The radiators dry out the air. Also the clanking – I can't concentrate. If the house weren't so old we'd have central air heating but we don't so I have to come out here to get any work done.

Catherine   I'll turn off the radiators. They won't make any noise. Come inside, it isn't safe.

Robert   I'm okay.

Catherine   I've been calling. Didn't you hear the phone?

Robert   It's a distraction.

Catherine   I didn't know what was going on. I had to drive all the way down here.

Robert   I can see that.

Catherine   I had to skip class. (*She brings him a coat and he puts it on.*) Why don't you answer the phone?

Robert   Well I'm sorry, Catherine, but it's question of priorities and work takes priority, you know that.

Catherine   You're working?

Robert   Goddamnit I am working! I say "I" – The machinery. The machinery is working, Catherine, it's on full blast. All the cylinders are firing, I'm on fire. That's why I came out here, to cool off. I haven't felt like this for years.

Catherine   You're kidding.

Robert   No!

Catherine   I don't believe it.

Robert   I don't believe it either! But it's true, it started about a week ago, I woke up, came downstairs, made a cup of coffee and before I could pour in the milk it was like someone turned the light on in my head.

Catherine   Really?

Robert   Not the light, the whole POWER GRID. I LIT UP and it's like no time has passed since I was twenty one.

Catherine   You're kidding!

Robert   No! I'm back! I'm back in touch with the source – the fount, the – whatever the source of my creativity was all those years ago I'm in contact with it again. I'm SITTING on it. It's a geyser and I'm shooting right up into the air on top of it.

Catherine   My God.

Robert   I'm not talking about divine inspiration. It's not funneling down into my head and onto the page. It'll take work to shape these things; I'm not saying it won't be a tremendous amount of work. It WILL be a tremendous amount of work. It's not going to be easy. But the raw material is there. It's like I've been driving in traffic and now the lanes are opening up before me and I can accelerate. I see whole landscapes – places for the work to go, new techniques, revolutionary possibilities. I'm going to get whole branches of the profession talking to each other. I – I'm sorry, I'm being rude, how's school?

Catherine (*taken aback*)   Fine.

Robert   You're working hard?

Catherine   Sure.

Robert   Faculty treating you all right?

Catherine   Yes. Dad –

Robert   Made any friends?

Catherine   Of course. I –

Robert   Dating?

Catherine   Dad, hold on.

Robert   No details necessary if you don't want to provide them. I'm just interested.

Catherine   School's great. I want to talk about what you're doing.

Robert   Great, let's talk.

Catherine   This work.

Robert   Yes.

Catherine (*indicating the notebooks*)   Is it here?

Robert   Part of it, yes.

Catherine   Can I see it?

Robert   It's all at a very early stage.

Catherine   I don't mind.

Robert   Nothing's actually complete, to be honest. It's all in progress. I think we're talking years.

Catherine   That's okay. I don't care. Just let me see anything.

Robert   You really want to?

Catherine   Yes.

Robert   You're genuinely interested.

Catherine   Dad, of course!

Robert   Of course. It's your field.

Catherine   Yes.

Robert   You know how happy that makes me.

Beat.

Catherine   Yes.

Robert   I think there's enough here to keep me working the rest of my life.

Not just me.

I was starting to imagine I was finished, Catherine. Really finished. Don't get me wrong, I was grateful I could go to my office, have a life, but secretly I was terrified I'd never work again. Did you know that?

Catherine   I wondered.

Robert   I was absolutely fucking terrified.

Then I remembered something and a part of the terror went away. I remembered you.

Your creative years were just beginning. You'd get your degree, do your own work. You were just getting started.

If you hadn't gone into math that would have been all right. Claire's done well for herself. I'm satisfied with her.

I'm proud of you.

I don't mean to embarrass you. It's part of the reason we have children. We hope they'll survive us, accomplish what we can't.

Now that I'm back in the game I admit I've got another idea, a better one.

Catherine   What?

Robert   I know you've got your own work. I don't want you to neglect that. You can't neglect it. But I could probably use some help. Work with me. If you want to, if you can work it out with your class schedule and everything else, I could help you with that, make some calls, talk to your teachers . . .

I'm getting ahead of myself.

Well, Jesus, look, enough bullshit, you asked to see something. Let's start with this. I've roughed something out. General outline for a proof. Major result. Important. It's not finished but you can see where it's going. Let's see:

He selects a notebook.

Here.

He gives it to **Catherine***. She opens it and reads.*

Robert   It's very rough.

After a long moment **Catherine** *closes the notebook.*

A beat.

Catherine   Dad. Let's go inside.

Robert   The gaps might make it hard to follow. We can talk it through.

Catherine   You're cold. Let's go in.

Robert   Maybe we could work on this together. This might be a great place to start. What about it? What do you think? Let's talk it through.

Catherine   Not now. I'm cold too. It's really freezing out here. Let's go inside.

Robert   I'm telling you it's stifling in there, goddamn it. The radiators. Look, read out the first couple of lines. That's how we start: you read, and we go line by line, out loud, though the argument. See if there's a better way, a shorter way. Let's collaborate.

Catherine   No. Come on.

Robert   I've been waiting years for this. This is something I want to do. Come on, let's do some work together.

Catherine   We can't do it out here. It's freezing cold. I'm taking you in.

Robert   Not until we TALK ABOUT THE WORK.

Catherine   No.

Robert   GODDAMNIT CATHERINE OPEN THE GODDAMN BOOK AND READ ME THE LINES.

Beat.

Catherine *opens the book. She reads slowly, without inflection.*

Catherine   "Let X equal the quantity of all quantities of X. Let X equal the cold. It is cold in December. The months of cold equal November through February. There are four months of cold, and four of heat, leaving four months of indeterminate temperature. In February it snows. In March the Lake is a lake of ice. In September the students come back and the bookstores are full. Let X equal the month of full bookstores. The number of books approach infinity as the number of months of cold approaches four. I will never be as cold now as I will in the future. The future of cold is infinite. The future of heat is the future of cold. The bookstores are infinite and so are never full except in September . . ."

She stops reading and slowly closes the book.

Robert *is shivering uncontrollably.* **Catherine** *puts her arms around him and helps him to his feet.*

Catherine   It's all right. We'll go inside.

Robert   I'm cold.

Catherine   We'll warm you up.

Robert   Don't leave. Please.

Catherine   I won't.

Let's go inside.

FADE.

Scene Five

The present. A week after the events in Scene Three.

Claire *on the porch. Coffee in takeout cups. Claire takes a plane ticket out of her purse, checks the itinerary.*

A moment.

Catherine *enters with bags for travel.* **Claire** *gives her a cup of coffee.* **Catherine** *drinks in silence.*

Beat.

Catherine   Good coffee.

Claire   It's all right, isn't it?

We have a place where we buy all our coffee. They roast it themselves, they have an old roaster down in the basement. You can smell it on the street. Some mornings you can smell it from our place, four stories up. It's wonderful. "Manhattan's Best": some magazine wrote it up. Who knows. But it is very good.

Catherine   Sounds good.

Claire   You'll like it.

Catherine   Good.

Pause.

Claire   You look nice.

Catherine   Thanks, so do you.

Beat.

Claire   It's bright.

Catherine   Yes.

Claire   It's one of the things I do miss. All the space, the light.

You could sit out here all morning.

Catherine   It's not that warm.

Claire   Are you cold?

Catherine   Not really. I just –

Claire   It has gotten chilly. I'm sorry. Do you want to go in?

Catherine   I'm okay.

Claire   I just thought it might be nice to have a quick cup of coffee out here.

Catherine   No, it is.

Claire   Plus the kitchen's all put away. If you're cold –

Catherine   I'm not. Not really.

Claire   Want your jacket?

Catherine   Yeah, okay.

Claire *gives it to her.* **Catherine** *puts it on.*

Thanks.

Claire   It's that time of year.

Catherine   Yes.

You can feel it coming.

Beat.

Catherine *stares out at the yard.*

Claire   Honey, there's no hurry.

Catherine   I know.

Claire   If you want to hang out, be alone for a while –

Catherine   No. It's no big deal.

Claire   We don't have to leave for 20 minutes or so.

Catherine   I know. Thanks, Claire.

Claire   You're all packed.

Catherine   Yes.

Claire   If you missed anything it doesn't really matter. The movers will send us everything next month.

Catherine *doesn't move.*

Beat.

I know this is hard.

Catherine   It's fine.

Claire   This is the right decision.

Catherine   I know. .

Claire   I want to do everything I can to make this a smooth transition for you. So does Mitch.

Catherine   Good.

Claire   The actual departure is the hardest part. Once we get there we can relax. Enjoy ourselves.

Catherine   I know.

Beat.

Claire   You'll love New York.

Catherine   I can't wait.

Claire   You'll love it. It's the most exciting city.

Catherine   I know.

Claire   It's not like Chicago, it's really alive.

Catherine   I've read about that.

Claire   I think you'll truly feel at home there.

Catherine   You know what I'm looking forward to?

Claire   What?

Catherine   Seeing Broadway musicals.

Beat. **Claire** *isn't sure if* **Catherine** *is joking.*

Claire   Mitch can get us tickets to whatever you'd like.

Catherine   And Rockefeller Center in winter – all the skaters!

Claire   Well, you –

Catherine   Also, the many fine museums!

Beat.

Claire   I know how hard this is for you.

Catherine   Listening to you say how hard it is for me, is what's hard for me.

Claire   Once you're there you'll see all the possibilities that are available.

Catherine   Restraints, lithium, electroshock.

Claire   SCHOOLS. In the New York area alone there's NYU, Columbia –

Catherine   Bright college days! Football games, road trips, necking on the "quad."

Claire   Or if that's not what you want we can help you find a job. Mitch has terrific contacts all over town.

Catherine   Does he know anyone in the phone sex industry?

Claire   I want to make this as easy a transition as I can.

Catherine   It's going to be easy, Claire, it's gonna be so fucking easy you won't believe it.

Claire   Thank you.

Catherine   I'm going to sit quietly on the plane to New York. And live quietly in a cute apartment. And answer Doctor Von Heimlich's questions very politely.

Claire   You can see any doctor you like, or you can see no doctor.

Catherine   I would like to see a doctor called Doctor Von Heimlich: please find one. And I would like him to wear a monocle.

And I'd like him to have a very soft, very well-upholstered couch, so that I'll be perfectly comfortable while I'm blaming everything on you.

Claire's *patience is exhausted.*

Claire   Don't come.

Catherine   No, I'm coming.

Claire   Stay here, see how you do.

Catherine   I could.

Claire   You can't take care of yourself for FIVE DAYS.

Catherine   Bullshit!

Claire   You were NON-RESPONSIVE ALL WEEK. I had to cancel my flight. I missed a week of work – I was this close to taking you to the hospital! I couldn't believe it when you finally dragged yourself up.

Catherine   I was tired!

Claire   You were completely out of it, Catherine, you weren't speaking!

Catherine   I didn't want to talk to you.

Beat.

Claire   Stay here if you hate me so much.

Catherine   And do what?

Claire   You're the genius, figure it out.

Claire *is upset, near tears. She digs in her bag, pulls out a plane ticket, throws it on the table. She exits.*

Catherine *is alone.*

She can't quite bring herself to leave the porch.

A moment.

Hal *enters – not through the house, from the side. He is badly dressed and looks very tired. He is breathless from running.*

Hal   You're still here.

Catherine *is surprised. She doesn't speak.*

I saw Claire leaving out front. I wasn't sure if you –

He holds up the notebook.

This fucking thing . . . checks out.

I have been over it, twice, with two different sets of guys, old geeks and young geeks. It is weird. I don't know where the techniques came from. Some of the moves are very hard to follow. But we can't find anything wrong with it! There might be something wrong with it but we can't find it. I have not slept.

(*He catches his breath.*) It works. I thought you might want to know.

Catherine   I already knew.

Beat.

Hal   I had to swear these guys to secrecy. They were jumping out of their skins. See, one email and it's all over. I threatened them. I think we're safe, they're physical cowards.

Beat.

I had to see you.

Catherine   I'm leaving.

Hal   I know. Just wait for a minute, please?

Catherine   What do you want? You have the book. She told me you came by for it and she gave it to you. You can do whatever you want with it. Publish it.

Hal   Catherine.

Catherine   Get Claire's permission and publish it. She doesn't care. She doesn't know anything about it anyway.

Hal   I don't want Claire's permission.

Catherine   You want mine? Publish. Go for it. Have a press conference. Tell the world what my father discovered.

Hal   I don't want to.

Catherine   Or fuck my father, pass it off as your own work. Who cares? Write your own ticket to any math department in the country.

Hal   I don't think your father wrote it.

Beat.

Catherine   You thought so last week.

Hal   That was last week. I spent this week reading it.

I think I understand it, more or less. It uses a lot of newer mathematical techniques, things that were developed in the last decade. Elliptic Curves. Modular Forms. I think I learned more mathematics this week than I did in four years of grad school.

Catherine   So?

Hal   So the proof is very . . . hip.

Catherine   Get some sleep, Hal.

Hal   What was your father doing the last ten years? He wasn't well, was he?

Catherine   Are you done?

Hal   I don't think he would have been able to master those new techniques.

Catherine   But he was a genius.

Hal   But he was nuts.

Catherine   So he read about them later.

Hal   Maybe. The books he would have needed are upstairs.

Beat.

Your Dad dated everything. Even his most incoherent entries he dated. There are no dates in this.

Catherine   The handwriting –

Hal   – looks like your Dad's. Parents and children sometimes have similar handwriting, especially if they've spent a lot of time together.

Beat.

Catherine   Interesting theory.

Hal   I like it.

Catherine   I like it too. It's what I told you last week.

Hal   I know.

Catherine   You blew it.

Hal   I –

Catherine   It's too bad, the rest of it was really good. All of it: "I loved your Dad." "I always liked you." "I'd like to spend every minute with you . . ." It's killer stuff. You got laid AND you got the notebook! You're a genius!

Hal   I don't expect you to be happy with me. I just wanted . . . I don't know. I was hoping to discuss some of this with you before you left. Purely professional. I don't expect anything else.

Catherine   Forget it.

Hal   I mean we have questions. Working on this must have been astonishing. I'd love just to hear you talk about some of this.

Catherine   No.

Hal   You'll have to deal with it eventually, you know. You can't ignore it, you'll have to get it published. You'll have to talk to someone.

Take it, at least. Then I'll go. Here.

Catherine   I don't want it.

Hal   Come on, Catherine. I'm trying to correct things.

Catherine   You CAN'T. Do you hear me?

You think you've figured something out? You run over here so pleased with yourself because you changed your mind. Now you're certain. You're so . . . SLOPPY. You don't know anything. The book, the math, the dates, the writing, all that stuff you decided with your buddies, it's just evidence. It doesn't finish the job. It doesn't prove anything.

Hal   Okay, what would?

Catherine   NOTHING.

You should have trusted me.

Beat.

Catherine *gathers her things.*

Hal   So Claire sold the house?

Catherine   Yes.

Hal   Stay in Chicago. You're an adult.

Catherine   She wants me in New York. She wants to look after me.

Hal   Do you need looking after?

Catherine   She thinks I do.

Hal   You looked after your Dad for five years.

Catherine   So maybe it's my turn.

I kick and scream but I don't know. Being taken care of, it doesn't sound so bad. I'm tired.

And the house is a wreck, let's face it.

It was my Dad's house.

I don't think I should spend another winter here.

Beat.

Hal   There is nothing wrong with you.

Catherine   I think I'm like my Dad.

Hal   I think you are too.

Catherine   I'm . . . afraid I'm like my Dad.

Hal   You're not him.

Catherine   Maybe I will be.

Hal   Maybe. Maybe you'll be better.

Pause. He sets down the book. No reaction from her. He slowly starts to exit.

She looks down at the book, runs her fingers over the cover.

Catherine   It didn't feel "astonishing" or — what word did you use?

Hal stops.

Hal   Yeah, astonishing.

Catherine   Yeah. It was just connecting the dots.

Some nights I could connect three or four. Some nights they'd be really far apart, I'd have no idea how to get to the next one, if there was a next one.

Hal   He really never knew?

Catherine   No. I worked after midnight. He was usually in bed.

Hal   Every night?

Catherine   No. When I got stuck I watched TV. Sometimes if he couldn't sleep he'd come downstairs, sit with me. We'd talk. Not about math, he couldn't. About the movie we were watching. I'd explain the stories.

Or about fixing the heat. Decide we didn't want to. We liked the radiators even though they clanked in the middle of the night, make the air dry.

Or we'd plan breakfast, talk about what we were gonna eat together in the morning.

Those nights were usually pretty good.

I know . . . it works . . . But all I can see are the compromises, the approximations, places where it's stitched together. It's lumpy. Dad's stuff was way more elegant. When he was young.

Beat.

Hal   Talk me through it? Whatever's bothering you. Maybe you'll improve it.

Catherine   I don't know . . .

Hal   Pick anything. Give it a shot? Maybe you'll discover something elegant.

A moment.

Eventually she opens the book, turns the pages slowly, locates a section. She looks at him.

Catherine   Here:

She begins to speak.

<u>CURTAIN</u>

The Columnist

The Columnist opened on Broadway at Manhattan Theatre Club's Samuel J. Friedman Theatre on April 25, 2012, with the following cast and director:

Director: Daniel Sullivan
Joseph Alsop: John Lithgow
Susan Mary Alsop: Margaret Colin
Stewart Alsop: Boyd Gaines
Abigail: Grace Gummer
Halberstam: Stephen Kunken
Philip: Marc Bonan
Andrei: Brian J. Smith

Characters:

Joe Alsop
Young Man (Andrei)
Stewart Alsop
Susan Mary Alsop
Abigail
Halberstam
Philip

Act One

Scene One

A hotel room. Moscow, 1954.

Joe *(late 40s) in bed. A* **Young Man**, *Russian, mid 20s, getting dressed.*

Joe   Come back to bed.

Young Man   I have to go.

Beat. **Joe** *watches him dress.*

Joe   I've never had a communist before.

Young Man   Can you tell the difference?

Joe   I'm not sure. I'd need to go again to give you a definitive answer.

Young Man   I'm giving a tour at four o'clock.

Joe   Where?

Young Man   Red Square.

Joe   That's down the block. We have plenty of time.

Young Man   This is my afternoon break. My boss does not like it when I'm gone so long.

Joe   Your "boss"?

Young Man   Is it the wrong word? For someone who tells you what to do?

Joe   It's the right word. I thought you were all comrades here.

Young Man   We are, yes. But he tells me what to do.

Joe   What if I told you to come back to bed?

Young Man   You are not my comrade.

Joe   No, I'm your superior. I'm older than you and American and I have more money. Now do as I say.

Young Man   Go to hell.

Joe *chuckles, lights a cigarette.*

Joe   Your English is extremely good, you know that?

Young Man   I was sent to government language schools. I do tours in French and German also.

Joe   Do you have a family?

Young Man   A sister.

Joe   What does she do?

Young Man   She's a laundress.

Joe   Doesn't have your talent for languages.

Young Man   She was a great athlete.

Joe   Really? What sort?

Young Man   Skiing. She tried out for the National team. As a girl. She was nearly chosen.

Joe   Good for her.

Young Man   We had interviews with the sports officials. Quite an exciting time. They took us to dinner, breakfasts in hotels with other athletes and their families. Eggs, sausages, fresh tomatoes, coffee with cream, thick white bread. Then she had a disappointing race, and . . .

Joe   What happened?

Young Man   Well, the meals stopped. We had been given a new refrigerator. Men came and took it away. They didn't even bring the old one back. We had to use the neighbor's from across the hall for five months – they let us have one shelf. Finally, finally we got another refrigerator, an old one, worse than the one we started with.

Joe   No, I meant what happened at the race?

Young Man   What do you mean, what happened?

Joe   Well, did she fall on the course, or –

Young Man   No she didn't fall. She ran a good course. She just came a bit short of the required time is all. She was nervous. How would you feel?

Joe   That's awful.

Young Man   What is your job?

Joe   I'm a journalist.

Young Man   That's why you ask me so many questions.

Joe   I suppose so.

Young Man   Are you from New York?

Joe   Washington.

Young Man   Which is your newspaper?

Joe   Oh, I'm in hundreds.

Young Man   Hundreds?

Joe   Well. 190 at last count. I have a syndicated column. With my brother.

Young Man   How many newspapers do you have in America?

Joe   I don't know. Thousands I suppose.

Young Man   No.

Joe   Easily. Every major city has five or six. Morning, afternoon, evening. Even the smallest town has its own weekly. It's one of our great strengths.

Young Man   You write one thing, one "column," it goes into 190 newspapers.

Joe   Yes.

Young Man   And each of them pays you.

Joe   Yes.

Young Man   Are you rich?

Joe   Yes, by your standards.

Young Man   I'm beginning to think I should stay after all.

Joe   I won't pay you. That would tip things over into the sordid.

Young Man   I was joking. Don't insult me.

Joe   Sorry.

Beat.

Young Man   So what are you writing about here?

Joe   The menace you pose to us.

Young Man   Me?

Joe   You seem very nice. No, you collectively.

Young Man   And your readers in 190 newspapers, this is what they want to read? How scary we are?

Joe   We don't give two shits what they want to read. We tell them what they need to know.

Young Man   You and your brother. Is he here too?

Joe   We never travel together. One of us goes, one of us stays home and writes, we switch off . . . now you seem to be asking me all the questions.

Young Man   Maybe I should be a journalist. If we had more than one newspaper. And journalists.

Joe *laughs.*

Joe   Tell me something. Why on earth do they have you doing tours? An intelligent young man like you, with your languages . . . Why aren't you in, I don't know, the diplomatic corps?

Young Man   I have wondered this myself, very often. I applied once. I was rejected.

Joe   They don't tell you why?

Young Man   No. Maybe something to do with my sister, I don't know.

Joe   And you have no appeal in the matter?

Young Man   Of course not.

Joe   Barbaric country.

You'd like America.

Young Man   I would like to go there. It's impossible, of course.

Joe   Someday, when your Soviet masters give up on this idiotic "experiment" and rejoin the civilized world – assuming of course we haven't already blasted each other into clouds of radioactive vapor – you can come, and I'll show you Washington.

Young Man   How would you introduce me? To your friends?

Joe   As my linguist.

Young Man   Are you free in America? More than here?

Joe   Oh my God yes. Are you joking?

Young Man   I mean, about this.

He indicates the two of them, the bed.

Joe   Oh. No. With that it's much the same.

Beat.

Young Man   I'd like to see Washington. And the Grand Canyon.

Joe   Not convenient to one another, unfortunately, but they should both be seen, and in the company of a knowledgeable guide. The Grand Canyon I don't know much about, but nobody knows Washington like me. It's my territory. Everyone knows me, everyone fears me, so if you're with me you are guaranteed a good table at restaurants.

Young Man   Why do they fear you?

Joe   I simply have a well-deserved reputation for speaking my mind, loudly. Have you heard of Joe McCarthy?

Young Man   The fellow who says everyone in America is a communist? We like him.

Joe   Yes, well he's a contemptible thug and liar and a drunk, and he's causing considerable havoc right now. Everyone's quaking in fear of him. Except Stewart and me. We've been going after McCarthy with all guns blazing. Probably we're the only ones who could get away with it.

Young Man   I don't care very much about politics.

Joe   My boy, politics is life! Politics is human intercourse at its most sublimely ridiculous and intensely vital. You may as well say you don't care very much for sex.

Young Man   No, that I like.

Joe   Yes, I've noticed. Can't you spare me half an hour more?

Young Man   No, I'm sorry. I'm late already.

Young Man *goes into the bathroom.*

Joe   Have you ever been with an American before?

Young Man (*from off*)   No.

Joe   How do you know Atkinson?

Young Man   Atkinson?

Joe   The PAO.

Young Man   I'm sorry?

Joe   The Public Affairs Officer. At the Embassy.

Young Man *comes back in.*

Young Man   Your Embassy?

Joe   Yes.

Young Man   I'm sorry, I don't know him.

Joe   But he told me about you.

Young Man   I don't know what you're talking about.

Joe   He told me that he'd take care of things. He's – well, he's like us, you see.

Young Man *shakes his head.*

I told him I was hoping to find some company and he said he'd help. Peter *Atkinson*. At the United States Embassy. Quite tall, reddish hair thinning a bit . . .

Young Man   I don't know this man. I met you in the bar.

Joe   You came right up to me. I assumed Peter sent you.

Young Man   You offered to buy me a drink.

Joe   And you accepted so *readily*.

Young Man   Why should I not accept?

Joe   Well, because you're so young, and . . . and I'm . . . You can't blame me for assuming . . .

Young Man   My God. You thought I was . . . *procured* for you?

Joe   Your English really is splendid.

Young Man   Picked out for you? Like a prostitute? Is this the arrangement you have with your *Embassy*?

Joe   No, my God no, it's nothing *official*. Peter's an old friend and he's discreet and knows a man can get lonely in a foreign city. I ask for a warm body, he finds one.

Young Man   A warm body?

Joe   Oh dear. That doesn't sound right. Look, I'm just a bit confused –

Young Man   We had a conversation! I thought you were interested in what I had to say.

Joe   Please—

Young Man   Every day at work, I take the tourists around, I recite for them the history of this church or square, oh, Pushkin lived here, or Catherine the Great built this . . . You, in the bar, were the first one to ask about *me*. I've never been asked so many questions in my life. Why did you do that if you thought I was—

Joe   That didn't matter. I wanted to know you.

Young Man   Yes, this is what I appreciated.

Joe   I want to make sure I understand this correctly. Are you saying you came here because you *wanted* to?

Young Man   Yes.

Beat.

Joe   I'm sorry.

I'm not at all used to this.

Young Man   What's the matter?

Joe   Nothing.

Young Man   Are you all right?

Joe   Yes, of course.

Young Man   I have to leave now.

Joe   I don't know your name.

Young Man   It's Andrei.

Joe   Andrei. I'm Joe.

Young Man   Yes, I know. Joe Alsop.

Joe   How do you know?

Young Man   You said.

Joe   Did I?

Young Man   When we met in the bar. I have a very good memory.

Joe   Did you know who I was?

Young Man   No. But I will look for you in the newspaper from now on.

Joe   How can you read my columns over here?

Young Man   I can't. But when Pravda denounces your columns, I will say, Yes! Joe! I knew him.

Joe   Wonderful. I should like that.

They shake hands, awkwardly.

And thank you for . . . the loveliest afternoon I've had in a long, long time.

Joe *holds Andrei's hand. Beat.*

Young Man   I have to go.

Joe   Of course, of course.

Young Man *exits. Beat. Joe begins to get dressed.*

After a moment, a knock at the door. **Joe** *starts. He goes to the door.*

Andrei?

Voice (*off*)   Mr. Alsop?

Joe (*disappointed*)   Yes?

Voice   We would like to speak with you please.

Joe   Who is it?

Voice   Just let us in, Mr. Alsop.

Joe *hesitates, then starts to open the door.*

FADE

Scene Two

Alsop's house in Georgetown. January, 1961.

Stewart *(late 40s) in a tuxedo. He looks tired. Puts his feet up. Lights a cigarette. Loosens his tie.*

Susan Mary *enters. 40s, attractive. Robe and slippers. They look at each other, surprised.*

Susan Mary   Hello.

Stewart   Hi.

Joe said to come over.

Susan Mary   Is Tish here?

Stewart   Home with the kids.

Beat. He looks at her.

Susan Mary   What?

Stewart   Nothing.

Susan Mary   You're surprised.

Stewart   A little.

Susan Mary   He hasn't said anything.

Stewart   About what?

Susan Mary   No. I'd better let him tell you.

Stewart   Why?

Susan Mary   He's your brother.

Stewart   He really tells me very little.

Susan Mary   Yes well he's going to tell you to get your feet off his coffee table.

Stewart   What is this? It looks pretty fancy.

Susan Mary   He's been going to auctions.

Do you want something to drink?

Stewart   Don't go to any trouble. I can help myself.

Susan Mary   It's no trouble.

Joe *enters.*

Joe   There you are. I was afraid you went to bed.

Susan Mary   No. Are we expecting anyone else?

Joe   Not to my knowledge. There should be some champagne chilling, bring it in here would you my dear?

Susan Mary   Mm-hm.

She goes.

Stewart *looks at* **Joe**.

Joe   She keeps a dressing gown here, and some comfortable shoes, for late nights. I shouldn't let her?

Stewart   Just never known you to share the house with anyone.

Joe   It's hardly sharing the *house*. She's here two or three nights a week as it is, for parties. She's an ideal hostess. I have to have someone at the foot of the table.

Especially now. My God socially this place is going to become *electrifying*. Don't smoke that.

Smoke this.

Joe *gives him a cigar.* **Stewart** *examines it.*

Stewart   Wow. Thanks. Inside?

Joe   Tonight, yes.

Stewart   You are feeling good.

Joe   He's our kind of man, Stewart. Jack will make this country interesting again but more importantly he'll make the *town* interesting again. He's got that gleam in the eye that FDR had. I didn't realize how much I'd missed it. Eisenhower was so plodding and dreary. His Washington was like going to bed with a glass of warm milk and a woman in curlers.

Stewart   That's not bad. Have you used it?

Joe   It's all yours.

Stewart   Everyone would know it was you.

Joe   Kennedy . . . Kennedy's Veuve Cliquot, and a starlet on each arm. And one of them has a degree from the Sorbonne.

Stewart   That one needs work.

Joe   Oh stop affecting nonchalance. You feel the same way I do.

Stewart   I just don't think we should get carried away.

Joe   I do. I will. This one night, I will be carried away, and so will you goddamn it. Only get your feet off my coffee table. Or at least take off your shoes – Oh never mind. You know what? Put your feet up. Stand on the sofa, do whatever you want, tonight.

Stewart   I want to go to bed.

Joe   Then you're an ass. How many nights do we get like this? He's *our man*. A tough man and a thoughtful one too, the kind we've been dreaming of and waiting for. He's like Stevenson with balls. Brains and balls, finally, in one package! And beauty. And charm. And he owes us.

Stewart   Does he?

Joe   You're damn right he does. The "missile gap" – we gave that to him on a plate, hell you *named* it, and he beat Nixon to death with it.

Stewart   He barely squeaked by.

Joe   All the more reason then. Without me pushing the Johnson pick, and the missile gap pieces, he might well have fallen short. And don't think he doesn't know it. Don't think he won't remember that debt either and repay it, because that's the sort of man he is.

Stewart   We'll see.

Joe   Yes we will. We're going to see *everything*. We're in an extraordinary position, Stew, at an extraordinary time, this is *our moment*, so why do you look so goddamn depressed? Go home if you're not going to celebrate with me, for Chrissake.

Stewart   I'm just tired.

Joe   You have no sense of history.

Stewart   I have enough of a sense of history to know that when a man in a tuxedo smoking a cigar announces "this is our moment," he's generally fucked.

Joe   Then here's to being fucked.

It's a new day, Stew. We should revive the partnership.

Stewart   What?

Joe   Why not? Come back to the column. The Alsop brothers. Together again. What do you say?

Stewart   "No."

Joe   Foolish. Short-sighted.

Stewart   I'm happy at the *Post*.

Joe   The *Saturday Evening Post*. It's in decline. Becoming pablum for salesmen and housewives. Don't you want to write for the people who matter?

Stewart   I think housewives matter.

Joe   Don't be sentimental.

Stewart   I get to write nice long pieces at the *Post*, and the editors mostly stay out of my way. Okay, I don't have the impact I did when we wrote together . . .

Joe   So why wouldn't you want to come back?

Stewart   Because you're such a colossal pain in the ass.

Joe   Yes, but what else?

Stewart   You never paid me enough. Actually, I was never sure why *you* paid *me* at all.

Joe   We'll go 60-40 this time.

Stewart   That's mighty generous, Joe.

Joe   55-45. That's fair – you can keep your contract with the *Post*, the column is all I have.

Stewart   I can't do both. And I've got a family to support.

Joe   So have I.

Stewart   Who?

Joe   Susan Mary. And her daughter.

Stewart   What?

Joe   We're getting married.

Stewart   When?

Joe   Next month.

Beat.

Stewart   Congratulations.

Joe   Thank you.

I asked her last March, actually, and she turned me down. My fault, it was too soon after Bill's death. Then after Jack got the nomination I suppose I was emboldened, and I asked her again, and she said yes.

Stewart   That's terrific, Joe. I'm happy for you.

Joe   I'm happy for me. I can't believe my luck, honestly. She's everything I want. She's sparkling and bright and at home in the world. And she'll fit in here, beautifully. She already does. And her daughter has become very dear to me.

Stewart   I should have seen this coming.

Joe   Surely it can't be that much of a surprise. We've been friends for years.

Stewart   I didn't realize you'd become more than friends.

Joe   I didn't either, until suddenly I did.

Stewart   And does she know. . .?

Joe   What? Oh, of course. I told her myself. In a letter.

Stewart   What did she say?

Joe   It's not a major concern.

You haven't given me an answer. The column.

Stewart   I thought I did. Not in a million years.

Joe   You haven't given me a reason.

Stewart   Okay. Apart from the money . . . and the abuse . . . and the general indignity of working for my big brother at the age of 46 . . . I guess I just like where I am.

Joe   The Norman Rockwell Weekly.

Stewart   On the outside.

Joe   Why on earth would you want to be *there*?

Stewart   I guess I think that's where a reporter belongs.

Joe   That's *profoundly* wrong. You realize that, I hope. That is the stupidest goddamn thing I have ever heard in my *life*. Forget it. I rescind the offer.

Susan Mary *enters with a bottle of champagne and glasses. She's changed out of the robe.*

Susan Mary   There's a tub of ice in the kitchen. It's filled with bottles.

Joe   Yes, I asked Jose to set some to chill.

Susan Mary   He's brought up a case from the basement. How much are you planning on celebrating tonight?

Joe   To excess.

Stewart   Congratulations.

Susan Mary   Here's to the President.

Stewart   I'm drinking to you.

Susan Mary   Good. You told him.

Joe *nods.*

(*to* **Stewart**) We weren't going to announce it until after the Inauguration.

Joe   We didn't want to hog the limelight from Jack.

Susan Mary   He's joking.

Stewart   I'm not sure he was.

Joe   Oh fuck you, Stew, of course I was.

Susan Mary   Joe.

Joe   Sorry.

She gives **Stewart** *a sympathetic look.*

Susan Mary (*she takes a glass*)   Shouldn't you tell Jose we don't need so much?

Joe   We may have visitors.

Susan Mary   It's two in the morning, Joe.

Joe   The balls are just letting out.

Susan Mary   Who did you invite?

Joe   No one.

Susan Mary   Are we having a party or not?

Joe   If people drop in for a drink, on this *historic* evening, I want to be prepared. You never know who might want a night cap.

Susan Mary   Oh God. This is my life now, isn't it? I was going to have a hot bath.

Joe   The hell you were. (*to* **Stewart**) She stays up later than I do. I never met a woman more enamored of the social whirl.

Susan Mary   I thought you were the one who wanted to get home.

(*to* **Stewart**) We couldn't get a cab on Pennsylvania Avenue, he was in absolute hysterics.

Joe   It was snowing. I was cold. Was I that bad?

Susan Mary   You were awful.

Joe   What if our guests had beat me home?

Susan Mary   If anyone were coming they'd have been here by now.

(*to* **Stewart**) He can't stand to think his house isn't the center of the Universe tonight.

Joe   Wherever *you* are, my dear, is the center of *my* universe, and I would be perfectly happy were it just the three of us tonight, but I have laid in supplies just in case.

Abigail, *14, enters.*

Abigail   What's going on? Are you having a party?

Joe   Yes.

Susan Mary   No. We're just saying goodnight. Go back to bed.

Joe   Do not go back to bed. Stew, you know Susan Mary's-daughter-soon-to-be-my-step-daughter Abigail? Abigail, my brother Stewart.

Stewart   Hello.

Abigail   Hi. Do I call him Uncle Stewart?

Joe   No.

Stewart   She can if she wants.

Abigail   Can I have some champagne?

Susan Mary   No.

Joe   Of course. (*Goes to pour it.*) In fact you must. I don't understand why you were even in bed –

Susan Mary   It's the middle of the night.

(*to* **Stewart**) We've been staying here during the week . . . it's closer to her school . . .

Abigail   I've got an exam tomorrow.

Joe   An *exam*? They give you an exam the morning after the *Inauguration*? How are they supposed to concentrate?

Abigail   I don't know. Half the girls' parents were going to parties. Some of the girls were having their *own* parties.

Susan Mary   At their age. Isn't that ridiculous?

Abigail   You're so stodgy.

Joe   She certainly is.

Susan Mary   One's at a hotel. With an orchestra. We got an engraved invitation. Can you imagine?

Abigail   You're supposed to go dressed like Jackie. They got a singer who sounds *exactly* like Nat King Cole. I can't believe I'm missing it.

Susan Mary   Imagine. Buying Chanel suits for schoolgirls.

Abigail   You could have loaned me one of yours.

Susan Mary   Over my dead body.

Joe   And your pearls. The long strand.

Abigail   Oh, the long strand!

Susan Mary (*to* **Joe**)   Stop causing trouble. Go to bed, Abby. Don't give her that, Joe, she's going to be exhausted.

Joe   Champagne is revitalizing.

Stewart   That is not actually true.

Joe *gives* **Abigail** *a glass of champagne.*

Joe   What's the exam?

Abigail   Latin.

Susan Mary   It's her worst subject.

Joe   Not for long. You'll study with me. I happen to be a fervent and dedicated Latinist. I can still give you *reams* of Virgil. Won all the prizes at Groton.

Stewart   That *is* true.

Joe   I helped Stew.

Stewart   Got a D in Latin. Would have been an F without him.

Joe   Which established the template for the rest of his career. I've been all that's standing between him and humiliating failure for 20 years.

Stewart   Oh fuck you, Joe.

(*Beat. to* **Abigail**) Excuse me.

Susan Mary   It's all right.

Stewart   I'm very sorry.

Susan Mary   It's not your fault. Honestly, Joe.

Joe (*mild*)   Sorry. (*Indicates his glass.*) High spirits.

Anyway. We'll have your marks up in no time. You will find me a patient if relentless instructor. We shall commence daily tutorials in the first full day of the Kennedy administration. Now drink.

Abigail *looks to her mother, who nods.* **Abigail** *drinks.*

Susan Mary   Stewart, now, about the wedding. Don't say anything to Tish. I want to tell her myself. Promise?

Stewart   Of course. What kind of thing are you planning?

Joe   We haven't discussed the actual event yet –

Susan Mary   And *we* won't be discussing it. I'm handling it, thanks, and it'll be simple, simple.

Joe   I am in your hands.

Susan Mary   Good.

Stewart   You are a very lucky man.

Abigail *has drained her glass.*

Abigail   My teacher says Kennedy's all flash.

Joe   What?

Abigail   That he's just a lucky pretty boy who gets by on charm and his daddy's money.

Stewart   What sort of Latin teacher is this?

Joe   No wonder you're failing. The man sounds like a boob.

Abigail   She's a woman.

Joe   Let me guess. Sixtyish. Mannish hands. Trace of a mustache. Flask in her desk drawer. Virgin, possibly lesbian.

Susan Mary   Joe –

Joe   Voted for Wendall Wilkie.

Abigail   Who's Wendall Wilkie?

Joe   My God, Susan, what sort of education is this child receiving?

Stewart   Who's the first President you remember?

Abigail   Truman.

Joe   Really?

Susan Mary   She was born in 1946, Joe.

Joe   So more or less your entire political consciousness, your understanding of the modern presidency itself, has been shaped by . . . *Dwight Eisenhower?*

Abigail   I guess so.

Joe   Oh you poor child. Come, sit with Uncle Joe. Have some more champagne. (*before* **Susan** *can say "No"*) *Yes*. You cannot imagine how different this city was when I first came in the late 1930s. You could hardly call it a city. It was a town. Everybody knew each other. A young reporter knew everyone, every Senator, every cabinet head. I knew everyone, and not because of family connections, either. It was a town. People knew you walking down the street. Cousin Eleanor invited us to the White House for scrambled eggs. Her scrambled eggs were appalling, really dreadful, but she made them herself, and the President mixed the martinis and handed them around, and that's how business was done, and you talked and laughed and learned and listened, and there was a marvelous sense of excitement and of new beginnings. And now – you have the enormous good fortune to be living in the same sort of era. Jackie won't be serving scrambled eggs of course – thank *God*, it's going to be infinitely more glamorous and sophisticated . . . but once again it's a time of youth and excitement and energy, "vigor," as our new man in the White House likes to say. Oh, there will be setbacks, and disappointments. I'm sure we'll have our hearts broken sixteen different ways. But watch. Jack understands the Soviets. He'll know how to deal with them. He'll do something about civil rights. He'll do something about Indochina. (*to* **Stewart**) That's coming – you watch. The communists will keep the pressure on, they'll keep testing us, in Laos –

Stewart   Not Laos.

Joe   No, perhaps not, but possibly – or possibly Viet Nam . . . and Jack will do what needs to be done. And if he doesn't *know* what needs to be done, I'll tell him. Or if he knows but wavers, he will hear from me then too.

(*to* **Stewart**) And he could be hearing from *you*, if you had any sense. Fifty-fifty? My name would still come first, it's alphabetical . . .

Stewart *looks at* **Joe**. *Beat. He puts down his glass.*

Stewart   Good night, everyone.

(*he kisses* **Susan Mary**) Congratulations again.

Susan Mary   Thank you.

Stewart (*to* **Abigail**)   I'm sorry you missed your parties. There'll be others.

Abigail   I know.

Stewart *exits.* **Joe** *watches him go.*

Beat. The room is quiet. **Susan Mary** *collects the glasses. The evening appears to be over.*

Abigial   Some party.

Joe *looks a bit forlorn.* **Susan Mary** *notices, goes to him.*

Susan Mary   Don't be too disappointed.

Joe   Don't be silly.

He puts his arm around her. Kisses her forehead.

Abigail   Eaugh. Now I am going to bed.

The phone rings. **Susan Mary** *goes to answer it.*

Susan Mary (*to* **Abigail**)   Good.

Hello? I'm sorry? (*to* **Joe**) It's for you.

Abigail *goes to the window.* **Joe** *takes the phone.*

Joe   Hello?

Abigail   Hey. There's a crowd across the street. What's going on?

Joe *shushes her.*

Joe (*on phone*)   Yes. Of course. It's no difficulty at all. Well thank you very much indeed for calling.

He hangs up. Beat.

Susan Mary   Joe?

Joe (*to* **Susan Mary**)   Open a few more bottles. (*to* **Abigail**) You may want to change your clothes.

<u>FADE</u>

Scene Three

A bar in Saigon. September, 1963.

Stewart *with a glass of beer.* **Halberstam** *(late 20s) approaches him. He carries a sheet of teletype paper.*

Halberstam   I heard you were in town.

Stewart   I just got in yesterday.

Halberstam   Welcome to Saigon. Good of you to join us.

Stewart   Thanks. Have we met?

Halberstam   Halberstam. The *Times*.

Stewart   I read your stuff. Good to meet you. Stew Alsop.

Beat.

Halberstam   I looked for you over at the Caravelle.

Stewart   This is more my kind of place.

Halberstam   Mine too. Wouldn't drink the beer, though.

Stewart   Tastes okay to me.

Halberstam   They don't wash the glasses. You need something stronger if you want to kill the hepatitis.

Stewart *smiles.*

Stewart   Can I get us both something?

Halberstam   No thanks. What are you working on?

Stewart   Piece for the *Post*.

Halberstam   Fine paper.

Stewart   *The Saturday Evening Post.*

Halberstam   Oh. Well. They publish some good things.

Stewart   We sneak it in, when we can. Between the recipes.

Halberstam   State of the conflict, that kind of thing? "Kennedy's Next Test" . . . "Turning Back the Red Tide" . . .

Stewart   Depends on what I see, I suppose.

Halberstam   Uh huh. Who's showing you around?

Stewart   I'm finding my own way around.

Halberstam   Good for you.

Stewart   Thanks.

Halberstam   Not like your brother.

Stewart   Sorry?

Halberstam   He was just in town last week.

Stewart   I wasn't aware.

Halberstam   You guys don't travel together?

Stewart   No. Why would we?

Halberstam   I thought –

Stewart   Why were you looking for me at the Caravelle, Mr. Halberstam?

Halberstam   I was delegated.

Stewart   By whom?

Halberstam   By my colleagues. After we read Joe's latest.

We get it a little late over here, when *Stars and Stripes* picks it up, but some of the wire service guys made sure I saw this one right away. I dunno, maybe I should be flattered . . .

Stewart   You'll have to help me out. I haven't read it.

Halberstam   Don't you guys work together?

Stewart   Not formally, not for a long time.

Halberstam   But informally?

Stewart   Mr. Halberstam, if my brother wrote something that's bothering you –

Halberstam   He blames *us*.

Stewart   For what?

Halberstam   For everything. The whole situation here. He blames *us*, his fellow reporters. And here I thought we were all in the same business.

Stewart   As I say, I haven't read it, but I'm sure he doesn't mean to –

Halberstam (*reads*)   "The constant pressure of the *reportorial crusade*" – that's me and my colleagues, if I'm not mistaken – "against the Vietnamese government has helped mightily" – Mightily! – "to transform President Diem from a courageous, quite viable national leader into a man afflicted with galloping persecution mania, seeing plots around every corner."

Stewart   Joe wrote this?

Halberstam *hands him the paper. Beat.*

Stewart   I see.

Halberstam   *We* drove him crazy. President Diem, the poor, courageous, noble friend of the USA, has been driven round the bend by assholes like me and the nasty things we write in American newspapers.

Stewart   This is new?

Halberstam   It just came out. He must have filed it before he left the country.

Stewart   Maybe you should take it up with him.

Halberstam   I'd like to but he *left*. He's already gone.

Stewart   Well, I really don't see what you –

Halberstam   He doesn't know the country. He breezes over here for a *week*, he stays with Lodge at the Embassy, he gets his Army car and driver, Harkins puts a helicopter at his disposal, he gets whatever he wants.

Meanwhile the rest of us are killing ourselves here, living in hovels, earning crap, and taking literally *endless* shit back home for trying to tell a sliver of a fraction of the truth about this fucked-up place.

And Joe saunters in with his pressed suits and his cigarette holder and his phony fucking Andover WASP Harvard accent. He waltzes into Diem's palace – easy, since the two of you have been sucking up to him for years. And during his exclusive *two-day* interview, he *somehow* manages to notice that the fucking *head of the country*, the guy we're killing and dying for, Our Man in Vietnam – Joe *notices* that this man is not only a corrupt and incompetent and hopeless loser and dope, but also by the way *actually insane* – He *notices* this . . . and then blames . . . the press! We did it! It's all our fault!

Beat.

Stewart   The accent's real.

Halberstam   What?

Stewart   I don't think you can hold him responsible for that. It's how we were brought up.

Halberstam   Is that all you have to say?

Stewart   Joe does know the country. He knows it very well.

Halberstam   He was here for a *week*.

Stewart   He's been coming here since 1954. So have I. We covered Dien Bien Phu together. Joe's been coming to Asia since before the War. He was in a Japanese prison camp when you were in grade school.

Halberstam   Well things have changed here since 1954.

Stewart   Yes. They washed the glasses then.

Halberstam   Jesus. I knew there was no point.

Halberstam *turns to go.*

Stewart   Just a moment. The offer of a drink still stands if you'd like to discuss this calmly.

Halberstam   Forget it. I'm sending a cable.

Stewart   To whom?

Halberstam   My editor, okay? He knows your brother. He can stand up for his staff for once.

Stewart   And say what, exactly?

Halberstam   That we are not the enemy! There's half a dozen hard working guys over here who don't appreciate being smeared in our own papers by some preening D.C. socialite with a press pass.

Stewart   David, take my advice. Don't go picking fights with Joe Alsop.

Halberstam   He picked the fight with *us*.

Stewart   No. Joe's playing on a different field. The same things Joe's writing in his column he's telling Kennedy in person.

(*Checks his watch.*) He's probably with him now, patiently explaining that, after a thorough investigation, he can say with confidence that except for the little problem of Diem we are on the right track over here, and you kids who say differently are juvenile, deluded malcontents. At *best*.

Halberstam   Yeah, well Kennedy doesn't run the assignment desk at the New York Times.

Stewart   Do you know where Kennedy went on inauguration night? After all the balls, after Jackie went home to rest, when he just wanted to relax, get a little drunk, his first night as President? He went to Joe's house.

Halberstam   What is that, some kind of country club threat?

Stewart   I'm just trying to make sure you understand what –

Halberstam   I *understand* that Joe Alsop wouldn't last five seconds if someone pushed back on his bullshit. We all know what the story is with him.

Stewart   Excuse me?

Beat.

Halberstam   Look, it's not exactly a state secret. He uses a *cigarette holder*, for Chrissake.

Stewart   My brother is a very happily married man.

Halberstam   Oh come on, Stewart. I'm sorry but everybody knows about the pictures.

Stewart   I don't have any idea what you're talking about.

Halberstam   I know guys who've seen them.

Beat.

Stewart   Who?

Halberstam   People. They've circulated. A bit.

Stewart   But *you* haven't seen them. These "pictures."

Halberstam   It's a well-known thing. It's . . . newspaper lore. The roll of film from the Moscow hotel room . . . The great Cold Warrior who got set up and blackmailed by the KGB. It's why he's so strident now, he knows he's compromised.

Stewart *considers this calmly.*

Stewart   Who do you know that's seen them?

Halberstam   I've heard from a bunch of different people. FBI guys, mostly.

Stewart   "FBI guys."

Halberstam   Evidently Hoover has the negatives.

Stewart   And you believe that?

Halberstam   I . . . it . . .

Stewart   The KGB sends its dirty photos to Hoover.

Halberstam   No, but –

Stewart   My brother's "compromised," so he's *harder* on the Soviets?

Gossip. Spiteful, envious sleaze that doesn't even make sense on its face. I thought you were a better reporter than that.

Stewart *puts down his drink.*

Do you know, for a moment there I was actually going to defend you to Joe?

But now I think I'd better just say good afternoon, and go fuck yourself.

FADE

Scene Four

Joe*'s study. November, 1963.* **Abigail** *(now 16) in a chair with schoolbooks in her lap.* **Joe** *perched on his desk.*

Joe   Again.

Abigail   Dividimus muros et moenia pandimus urbis. Accingunt omnes operum pedibusque rotarum subiciunt lapsus, et stuppea vincula collo intendunt; scandit fatalis machina muros feta armes.

Joe   Very good. Only it's *operi* not *operum*, and *armis* not *armes*. But otherwise, you're doing splendidly.

Abigail (*packing up her books*)   Thanks Joe.

Joe   Where are you going? We have to review your vocabulary.

Abigail   Not today.

Joe   Yes today. Don't you have a quiz Friday?

Abigail   Yeah, but I'll do fine.

Joe   Last week you got a B, I think we could do a little better than that.

Abigail   But I have to be somewhere at two.

Joe   Where?

Abigail   Somewhere.

Joe   Where?

Abigail   Joe. Come on.

Joe   I have not tutored you assiduously for the past two years to watch you slack off now. I had to reschedule or postpone *multiple* important interviews to preserve today's session. Shall I read you the list?

Abigail   No.

Joe   Two United States congressmen. An undersecretary of defense. A top Senate staffer. The First Lady of the United States.

Abigail   What?

Joe   You heard me.

Abigail   You canceled with *Jackie* to help me practice my Latin vocab.

Joe   Yes.

Abigail   Liar.

Joe   Prove it.

Abigail   They're not even in town, I read about it.

Joe   Very good. The others were real; that last was an exaggeration designed to suggest the importance I attach to your education.

Abigail   Thanks, but don't bullshit me, Joe.

Joe   I take it back. You have learned some new vocabulary.

Abigail   You use language like that all the time.

Joe   I am not a fifteen year old girl.

Abigail   Neither am I. I'm sixteen.

She gets up. She's wearing a skirt that stops above the knees.

Joe   Dear God. What are you wearing?

Abigail   What? Nothing.

Joe   I can see that. Were the bottom four inches torn off in some sort of garment-rending incident?

Abigail   It's just a skirt. This is what people are wearing.

Joe   It's an abomination. It doesn't even cover your knees. Has your mother seen you in it?

Abigail   What? I don't know. I guess.

Joe   Don't you dare leave the house like that. Where are you going anyway?

Abigail   None of your business.

Joe   A social occasion?

Abigail   Maybe.

Joe   A date?

Abigail   It's just a bunch of friends going out.

Joe   Male and female friends? That would account for the acres of thigh you're exhibiting.

Abigail   Oh for God's sake –

The phone rings.

Better get that. Could be the Queen of England.

Joe   *Do not leave this room.*

(*On phone.*) Hello? Scotty! No, it's a perfectly good time, thanks for calling back. This won't take long. I just have one question and it's entirely public-spirited: When are you going to fire those irresponsible children you've got reporting for you in Southeast Asia?

Of course I'm serious.

If I didn't think it were an appropriate question I wouldn't ask it. I –

Susan Mary *enters.*

Sorry, just a moment.

(*to* **Susan Mary**) *Knock*, Susan. Is that really too much to ask? I'm working.

Susan Mary   I'm sorry, Joe. I just have a quick –

Joe holds up a hand to stop her.

Joe   I'm sorry, Scotty. I simply refuse to believe you and the paper wouldn't be far better off having them cover something more suited to their experience and abilities, such as high school athletics or one of the sleepier state legislatures . . .

Susan Mary   What are you wearing?

Abigail   Nothing.

Susan Mary   You're not going out in that.

Joe   That's what I told her. Now will you both please leave? I am trying to conduct a conversation.

Abigail   A minute ago you ordered me to stay.

Joe   Now I am ordering you to go and change, and then come back for the rest of the lesson. Scotty, I'm sorry, I . . . Hello? Scotty?

He's lost the call.

Oh for God's sake, now look what's happened. Susan, really, I've asked not to be interrupted while I'm working.

Susan Mary   I thought you were having a lesson.

Abigail   We're finished.

Joe   No, we still have to do your vocabulary. After you change your clothes.

Susan Mary   Yes, you really should change, Abby.

Abigail   I can't believe you're siding with *him*.

Susan Mary   I'm not siding with anybody. I do think the skirt is a little much. Especially for November.

Abigail   My legs don't get cold! Please. Everyone gets to wear them out except me. My coat is long enough, it doesn't matter anyway.

Susan Mary   If it doesn't matter just put on a longer skirt.

Abigail   Agh, I hate you both.

Abigail *stomps out.*

Susan Mary   She's really become impossible.

Joe   Nonsense. She's just stretching her wings a bit. You shouldn't be so rigid.

Susan Mary   *I'm* rigid? You just said –

Joe *is dialing the phone.*

Joe   I am the step-parent. It's my job to be waspish and brutal, thus opening up the space for you to appear sympathetic and accommodating.

Susan Mary   You think I should let her wear the skirt?

Joe   She's right, they are all wearing them now, God help us. And she's worked awfully hard on her Latin.

(*on the phone*) Yes. Joe Alsop for James Reston please. We were accidentally disconnected.

Susan Mary   Joe, I wanted to talk to you about –

Joe   Susan, I am on a phone call.

Susan Mary   A call you made after you knew I wanted to speak with you.

Joe   Can't it wait?

Susan Mary   It *can* wait, but I was hoping we could –

Joe *holds his hand up.*

Joe   Scotty. I'm sorry, I think we were accidentally disconnected.

Well why would you do that?

Pause.

All right, I'll tell you precisely where I "get off." First of all, I do not see you and I as "rivals," that is a stupidly blinkered view of our business, we are all in this together and we have to look out for one another and for the greater journalistic good. Secondly, your boys over there –

They *are* boys, goddamn it, they *are* boys! Does Sheehan even have his driver's license? And if you let me know the date of Halberstam's bar mitzvah, I'll be sure to send him something nice –

Hello?

Shit.

He hangs up.

Joe   Susan, can we talk about this after dinner? I have an awful lot of work.

Susan Mary   It's about the trip.

Joe   Which trip?

Susan Mary   We talked about this. The London trip. Remember?

Joe   Oh. Yes. When are you going?

Susan Mary   We're going together, Joe.

Joe   When?

Susan Mary   That's what I'm here to - You really don't remember any of this.

Joe   No, of course I do. Just remind me of the reason?

Susan Mary   To see old friends, Abby has her winter break coming up, it'd be wonderful for her, *we've* never been . . .

Joe   Of course we've been.

Susan Mary   Not *together*. Don't you think it would be fun?

Joe   I'm sure it would be fun. Am I supposed to book passage on the Queen Mary right now?

Susan Mary   We could talk about where we'd like to stay. You could look at your calendar. You could give me some dates that you have free –

Joe   Yes, well there's the difficulty, I mean it's very hard to imagine having any sort of break coming up. I've never been so swamped. Now if you're talking about the summer, all right, but our dinners alone into New Year –

Susan Mary   We can cancel some of those.

Joe   Cancel?

Susan Mary   I'm not going to wait until the *summer*, Joe. I'm just talking about a little trip so we can spend some time together.

Joe   We're together every night.

Susan Mary   With a dozen or more guests.

Joe   With friends.

Susan Mary   Yes, and our *friends* will understand if we wanted to take a little break now and then.

Joe   But I don't want to take a little break.

Susan Mary   But I do. That's what I'm trying to tell you.

Joe   But you haven't said *why*.

Susan Mary   Yes I have. Because there are other things I want to do.

Joe   My God, Susan, what else *have* you to do apart from sit at the end of my table and be fascinated by whatever is being said by the person on your right? How taxing can it be?

Beat.

Susan Mary   It's a pleasure. And a privilege. That I wish to forego. For a few weeks of travel with my husband and daughter. How taxing could *that* be?

Joe   Oh now you're being ridiculous. If we can't discuss this rationally there's no point. Honestly, you surprise me. This is my work. Our work. This is what we do, you know that. Go and have a nap.

The phone rings. **Joe** *waits for her to go.*

Susan Mary   I'm not through with you.

Susan Mary *exits.* **Joe** *answers.*

Joe   How dare you hang up on me twice in a row, you miserable son of a bitch, when all I am trying to do is help you? You –

Oh hello, Stewart. I'm sorry. Welcome back. No, it's –

Congratulations for what?

Yes, it's been an interesting few weeks, they got rid of Diem all right, but not "just like I told them to," Stew. If you think I have that sort of influence on the South Vietnamese generals I can only say I'm flattered.

What about the White House?

Oh please. I *told* them no such thing, and they *did* no such thing.

Well even if we merely looked the other way while that very unpleasant man was removed –

All right, was "killed," don't be prissy Stewart, this isn't a girl scout picnic. The point is Jack had the guts thank God to either arrange, or allow to occur, the necessary change in leadership, and now finally our responsibility is clear, and the *way* is clear for real success over there.

Balls.

He is *not* looking for an excuse to get out. That is a ludicrous misreading of both the situation and the man. Promise me you won't write that anywhere, you'll just embarrass yourself. He's far more tough-minded than you give him credit for, or than you yourself seem to be at the moment, if you don't mind my saying so.

Fine, I'll set you straight over dinner. Love to Tish.

He hangs up. **Abigail** *comes in, coat on, still wearing the skirt.*

Abigail   She said I could wear it.

Joe   I disapprove.

She folds her arms. He picks up a piece of paper.

Joe   "Courage; vivacity."

Abigail   Animus.

Joe   "To uncover or lay bare."

She giggles. He rolls his eyes.

Abigail   Aperio.

Joe   Yes. "Grasping, or obstinate."

Abigail   Tenax?

Joe   Good. "Immortal." Too easy.

Abigail   Immortalis.

Joe   "Evasiveness."

Abigail   Ter . . . *shit*!

Joe   Or "reluctance" . . .

Abigail   Tergiversatio!

Joe   Bravo. Finally: how fitting. "Skilled, expert."

Abigail   Peritus.

Joe   Satisfactory. Go and flaunt yourself in the streets.

Abigail *goes.*

Abigail.

She stops. He takes out his wallet and gives her a few bills.

For an extra . . . Pepsi cola, or pizza, or whatever you kids are eating. And take a cab home.

Abigail   Thanks Joe.

She kisses him quickly on the cheek. The phone rings. **Abigail** *exits.*

Joe   Hello. Hello Scotty.

Pause.

I accept your apology. Though I don't believe I've ever hung up on you.

Well I don't recall any of that, but I appreciate your calling back. Nevertheless I am right about this, Scotty, and you are wrong. Your boys– *Your boys* scurry around out in the underbrush over there interviewing every whining malcontent and defeatist in the Army rank and file they can find, and calling their bitching and moaning the "truth," meanwhile all but calling the men at the top, the men in charge, the men who *know*, *liars*, and I call that undermining American interests. And I am here to tell you for your own damn good to reassign them, or maybe you'd prefer to wait until after we lose Vietnam the way we lost China, and what comes next, tell me that? Yes you're damn right I "subscribe" to the domino theory, I *named* the damned theory, and I'll – listen to me: the President thinks you should reassign them too. You bet your ass we spoke about it and he agrees with me, and as soon as he gets back I am going to urge him again to call you – I think it certainly *is* his goddamn business, I don't know what on earth his business *is* if not –

Going after me too? I'm quaking. What did Halberstam say? I don't give a good goddamn, you brought it up. What are they saying about me? *What are they saying about me?*

Don't you *dare — Hello?*

Scotty *has hung up.* **Susan Mary** *enters.*

Susan Mary   Joe –

Joe (*fury*)   For Chrissake, *do you ever knock?*

Susan Mary   Joe.

He looks at her. She looks stricken.

From off – a choked sob from **Abigail**.

Joe   Is that Abby? Is she all right? Did you two argue?

Susan Mary   Come into the living room.

Joe   Why? What's the matter? What's going on?

Susan Mary   It's . . . You need to come look at the television.

Joe *gets up and follows her from the room.*

The phone begins to ring.

FADE

Scene Five

Joe'*s study. That night.* **Joe** *typing.* **Stewart** *writing on a yellow pad.* **Joe** *finishes, takes the page out of the typewriter and hands it to* **Stewart**. *He reads.*

Stewart   Damn it.

Joe   It can be improved.

Stewart   Maybe. Third graf.

Joe   Third fourth and fifth, I should think.

Stewart   Nah, don't touch the fifth.

Joe   Let me see yours.

Stewart   I got nothing.

Joe   Let me see.

Stewart *shows him the pad.*

No, you really don't have anything do you?

Stewart   I shouldn't have come over here.

Joe   I'm glad you did. Sit down. Do you want to use my portable?

Stewart   I should get home. The kids were hysterical. They don't understand what's going on but they see everybody in tears so they're a mess too.

Joe   Is Tish all right?

Stewart   She's a rock. She's having anyone who wants to come. Feeding the whole neighborhood. Nobody wants to be alone tonight.

And my editor wants a profile of Johnson by tomorrow morning.

Joe   So?

Stewart   I can't work tonight.

Joe   Nonsense. On a night like this there's nothing you can do but work.

He puts another sheet of paper into the typewriter and begins typing.

Susan Mary *comes in with coffee.*

Susan Mary   I gave Jose and Maria the night off. And tomorrow too.

Joe   That's fine.

Stewart   How's Abigail?

Susan Mary   She went out. There's some sort of vigil forming on the Mall. I thought it was right to let her go.

Stewart   How are you?

Susan Mary   I can't stop this ridiculous crying.

I feel so useless. I can't stand doing nothing. I was in France after the War. I helped the Red Cross, we had *responsibilities*. I helped people find their families after they'd come out of the camps . . . I was good at it. I can't watch any more television. The goddamn television, I hate it. I've called all my friends on the phone. I can't stand hearing their dead voices.

Joe   We must all try to keep busy in the coming weeks and months.

Susan Mary   I don't want to be busy, I want to be necessary.

She wells up.

Joe *holds out a handkerchief without looking up from his typewriter.* **Stewart** *hands her one too.* **Stewart***'s is closer.* **Susan Mary** *takes it.*

Stewart *puts an arm around her to comfort her. She falls into his arms, holding him very tightly, needing this.* **Stewart** *is surprised.* **Joe** *doesn't look up.*

Susan Mary *collects herself, pulls away.*

Susan Mary   I'm going out.

Stewart   Where?

Susan Mary   To find Abby.

Joe   You'll never find her. There'll be thousands.

Susan Mary   That's not the point. I want to be there.

Stewart   Maybe I'll go too.

Joe   You have work to do.

Stewart   It is work.

(*to* **Susan Mary**) Do you mind if we swing by the house? I want to take my kids.

Susan Mary   Of course not.

Joe   They're too young.

Stewart   I want them to be there. No. I just want them with me.

Beat.

You should come too.

Joe   I haven't the time.

He keeps typing.

Stewart   All right.

Beat.

I'll call you later, Joe.

Stewart *looks at him, then exits.*

Beat.

Susan Mary   Joe?

Joe   Yes?

Susan Mary   Stop typing.

Joe *stops. Beat.*

Are you all right?

Joe   Yes.

Susan Mary   He was also your friend.

Joe   I don't have time to think about that right now.

Susan Mary   Will you come with us?

He shakes his head.

Joe . . .

She goes to him. Tries to embrace him. He lets her, briefly, then pulls away. **Susan** *moves away. She exits.*

Joe *starts to change pages in his typewriter. Sees the handkerchief and starts to put it back in his pocket.*

Suddenly lets out a single sob. Swallows it.

Then carefully wipes his face, folds the handkerchief.

He puts another page in the typewriter and begins typing again, with greater intensity.

END OF ACT ONE

Act Two

Scene One

New York, 1965. An auditorium, backstage.

Halberstam *studying some papers.* **Stewart** *enters.*

Halberstam   Hello. This is a surprise. To what do I owe the – Are you coming to my talk? I'm honored.

Stewart   No. I need to speak with you.

Halberstam   Well. We could get a drink after, I guess.

Stewart   No, now. Your talk can wait.

Halberstam   No it can't. Excuse me.

Stewart   David.

Halberstam   *Excuse me.* You're welcome to go out front and listen. I'll be taking questions after.

Stewart   I got your package.

Beat.

Halberstam   I'm sorry?

Stewart   That was a goddamn shitty thing to do. Is that how you people do things now? Is this how you prove a point?

Halberstam   What?

Stewart   A friend at the AP brought it to me. He took me to lunch, he didn't know what to say, he's a church-going man, he was *mortified*. You put him in a terrible position. I thought a lot of things about you David but I didn't think you were a coward. You should have had the guts to put your name on it.

Halberstam   I have no idea what you're talking about, Stewart.

Stewart   Bullshit. You ought to be ashamed of yourself. You set yourself up as some sort of righteous, truth-telling . . . it turns my stomach. These kids out there might fall for it but I don't.

Stewart *starts to go.*

Halberstam   Stewart.

Stewart *stops and stares at him.*

They didn't come from me.

Stewart   Who then?

Halberstam   I don't know.

Stewart   I don't believe you.

Halberstam   Fine, but I got a set too.

Stewart   You did.

Halberstam   Four or five guys got sent the package. That I know of.

How many do you –

Stewart   Three.

Halberstam   Yeah, they're really circulating.

Stewart   Who sent them, David?

Halberstam   I told you, I don't know. How the hell should I know? Why would you think it was me?

Stewart   Or one of your cohorts. To . . . show me. To prove a point.

Halberstam   What point?

Stewart   That what you told me in Saigon about Joe was true.

Halberstam   You knew it was true.

Beat.

Stewart   All right. Then . . . to push back. Against Joe. A warning shot.

Halberstam   Now that makes a little more sense. But no. I don't think so. Come on. Give us a little more credit.

Stewart   I'd like to.

Halberstam   No one I know had even seen the photographs before a few days ago.

Stewart   That's not what you told me in Saigon. You said you knew people who had seen them.

Halberstam   Okay, so I was exaggerating a little bit. There were rumors, but it was just guys winding each other up. Like those stories in high school about the cheerleader and the whole football team. Somehow you never actually met anyone with first-hand knowledge.

Stewart   Not any more.

Beat.

Halberstam   Yeah well I think you owe me an apology. You barge in here, I'm about to give a speech –

Stewart   I'm sorry.

Who do you think sent them out?

Halberstam   Well who had them? I dunno. The Russians, I guess?

Stewart (*mock-dramatic*)   The *KGB*.

Halberstam   Maybe. Or our guys? I just don't know.

Stewart   Not our guys.

Halberstam   Why not?

Stewart   Who?

Halberstam   FBI? CIA?

Stewart   No. How would they have obtained them, to begin with.

Halberstam   Lots of ways.

Stewart   What would be the point of throwing them around?

Halberstam   Maybe the Administration asked them to.

Stewart   Oh don't be ridiculous.

Halberstam   I've been reading your brother's stuff, Stewart. I doubt very much that Johnson enjoys being called a bed-wetting pinko sissy-boy every time he utters a halfway sensible word about Vietnam. Joe's really pushing it. He's taunting him. I used to enjoy reading his stuff. No, I did. I mean, I despised every word, but there was real skill there, real finesse. Now it's just piss and venom. Maybe he's not getting his phone calls returned so fast anymore. I don't know who *wouldn't* want to knock him down at this point.

Beat.

You look terrible.

Stewart   My cares are resting heavily upon me.

Halberstam   No, I mean it. You don't look good.

Stewart   Fuck you.

Halberstam   You want a cigarette?

Stewart   Yeah all right.

Halberstam *gives him one and lights it.* **Stewart** *drags, studies it.*

I don't know what to tell him.

Halberstam   About what?

Stewart   The pictures getting around.

Halberstam   He doesn't *know*?

Stewart   No. And he *won't*. Not if I can help it. It would kill him. It would just play into his paranoia.

And his family . . .

Don't . . . make it any worse, all right? Talk to your friends?

Beat.

Halberstam   I'll see what I can do.

Stewart   Thank you.

Halberstam   Don't thank me. Whatever you think of the younger generation, we're not sleaze merchants.

Stewart   I know that.

By the way. Congratulations. On the Prize.

Halberstam   It's all downhill from here.

Stewart   I doubt that very much.

(*He takes a long drag.*) I've always . . . coveted it.

Halberstam   It's not too late for you, Stew.

Stewart (*light*)   I think it may be, actually.

Halberstam   I have to go on.

Stewart *nods.* **Halberstam** *starts off.*

Stay and listen. You might learn something.

FADE

Scene Two

Joe's *study. November 1965.*

Joe *typing.* **Susan Mary** *opens the door.*

Joe   Working.

Susan Mary   You said after the last one you always want to make up the seating plan.

Joe *keeps typing;* **Susan Mary** *waits impatiently.*

Susan Mary   Joe. Do you –

Joe   Read me the list.

Susan Mary   Robert McNamara and wife.

Joe   All right.

Susan Mary   The Achesons.

Joe   Good.

Susan Mary   Two Senators. Fulbright and Church.

Joe   Church is a bore.

Susan Mary   His wife is lovely.

Joe   So together they make half a bore. I guess we can afford half.

Susan Mary   Stewart and Tish.

Joe   Yes.

Susan Mary   And Abigail . . .

Joe   You didn't tell me she was coming.

Susan Mary   Joe, I did, she has her winter break, she's taking the train down from Boston today.

Joe   You never said anything.

Susan Mary   I told you a dozen times. You weren't paying attention.

Joe   I wouldn't have scheduled a dinner if I'd known she was coming back today.

Susan Mary   Of course you would have.

Joe   Well I would have invited another guest at least. Now we have an odd number. Who are we going to put her next to?

Susan Mary   It's all right. She's bringing a friend, she said.

Joe   To stay?

Susan Mary   Yes. Just for the vacation.

Joe   Oh for God's sake, Susan, this isn't a flop house.

Susan Mary   It's only for a week or so.

Joe   There isn't a spare room. I don't want anybody on the couch. I'll have to tiptoe by her going into breakfast. The girl will have to sleep in Abigail's room. They can double up I suppose . . .

Susan Mary   It's not a girl.

Joe   Really?

Susan Mary *shakes her head.*

Joe   A boyfriend?

Susan Mary   She hasn't used the word, but I suppose yes, he must be.

Joe   Are they sleeping together?

Susan Mary   How on earth should I know?

Joe   You don't talk about these things with your daughter?

Susan Mary   No.

Joe   Is she a virgin?

Susan Mary   Joe.

Joe   What?

Susan Mary   Don't be prurient.

Joe   It's not prurient, it's parental. Don't tell me you've never wondered.

Susan Mary   I don't know. I've always assumed she was –

Joe   Oh that's absurd. She's 18 years old. Surely she's sleeping with this boy. Even in our era perfectly decent girls were experienced fornicators by her age, and young people today are far more wanton.

Susan Mary   I don't even want to think about it.

Joe   Well now we have to think about it. Do we let them share a room? Astounding that we're even asking the question. Social mores have broken down so completely . . .

Susan Mary   Then let's just put him on the couch and be done with it.

Joe   If we put him on the couch he'll be sneaking into her room in the middle of the night, bumping into furniture, keeping everyone awake . . .

Susan Mary   So what then? I just put him in her room, say Good night, have at it? I'd have to look at them at breakfast –

Joe   It is a dilemma. And what will the servants think?

Susan Mary   Please. You decide. It's your house.

Joe   It's your daughter. And it's your house too –

Susan Mary (*Dismissive sound.*)

Joe   What?

Susan Mary   Nothing.

Joe   Go on, you were about to say something.

Susan Mary   I just . . . In four years here I haven't bought a piece of furniture, or a *dish* . . . hung a picture on a wall . . .

Joe   Susan. If you're unhappy with the decor, by all means, change it.

Susan Mary   I'm not unhappy with the decor. That's not the –

Joe   I've put considerable care into the place, and never actually had my taste questioned before –

Susan Mary   Your *taste* is *impeccable*, Joe, you know I –

Joe   But if you think you can do better –

Susan Mary   I don't. I just – I never think of this as *my* house, is all I –

Joe   Surely that is your failing, not mine.

Beat.

Susan Mary (*flat*)   Surely it is.

Joe   I put an entire addition on the house just for you. Your room. It's what you said you wanted.

Susan Mary   I know. It's not your fault.

Joe   Evidently it is.

Susan Mary   No. You did everything right. I –

Joe   You said you needed your own room . . .

Susan Mary   I didn't. That wasn't –

Joe   You *didn't*? I don't see how I could possibly have misunderstood that, for God's sake, we looked at the architect's drawings together.

Susan Mary   Joe! I didn't want my own *room*, I wanted –

Joe   What?

Susan Mary   Nevermind. Let's drop it.

Joe   You began it.

Susan Mary   It's my fault.

I thought I didn't care about . . . all that. And I don't, really. I've never been one of those people who really needs that. Not even in my first marriage. I mean, it was perfectly nice, but after the children . . . And so I thought with you it wouldn't matter, that it might even be a relief not to . . .

But it is a *marriage*. And without the physical . . . element . . .

Joe   Without sex. Is that what you mean?

Susan Mary   Yes, of course.

Joe   You can say sex, can't you?

Susan Mary   Yes.

Joe   Shall we review the whole vocabulary set? Intercourse, erection, balls, cock, tits.

Susan Mary   Stop it.

Joe   I told you when I proposed what my situation was.

Susan Mary   I know. You were very honest.

Joe   You said you understood.

Susan Mary   I did. I do.

Joe   Then what is the problem?

Susan Mary   I thought it would change.

Joe   *It*, Madam?

Susan Mary   Your . . . nature. I thought I could . . .

Joe   Oh Susan, for God's sake.

Susan Mary   What?

Joe   Don't humiliate yourself.

Susan Mary   I'm trying to explain to you –

Joe   You thought what, exactly? That your feminine *wiles* . . . your Mata Hari-like erotic aura . . . the pulsing electric charge of your sensuality would magnetically flip the poles of my *nature*, as you call it? Dear God woman. You're attractive enough, but there are limits.

Susan Mary   Why do you have to be such a bastard?

Joe   Why do you have to be such a child? You knew exactly who I was because I was honest and I *told* you. You said yes anyway, because, you said, you loved me, and you wanted the life I could give you. And important men came to your dinner parties. And they're still coming. They're coming tonight, you'd better go get ready.

She starts to go, in tears.

And do put the young man in with your daughter, you're so concerned there's too little fucking in our house.

Susan Mary *slaps him. Beat.*

Joe   I'm sorry.

Beat.

That was unforgivable. I haven't been myself lately.

Susan Mary   Lately.

Joe   I'm sorry.

Susan Mary   It's been two years since Dallas.

Beat.

Joe   I feel like my life has been broken in half.

I don't enjoy anything anymore. Not the town. Not the work. Not even the damned parties. I –

A tap at the door. **Stewart** *enters.*

Stewart   Hello.

Joe *quickly resumes work.*

Working late?

Joe   I've been trying to finish a column, but there have been a number of distractions.

Stewart   I haven't seen you for a few weeks, I thought I'd say hello to my brother and sister-in-law before the company came.

If you mind I'll go walk around the damn block.

Susan Mary   Of course we don't mind. Hello Stewart.

Joe (*grim*)   I am in need of a drink.

Susan Mary   I'll get it.

Joe   I can get my own.

Joe *exits.*

Stewart   Maybe it's not a good time.

Susan Mary (*wiping her eyes*)   No, it's fine. We just . . .

Beat. **Stewart** *looks at her.*

Stewart   Tish claims she's got a suitcase all ready to go in the front hall closet, just in case. I'm pretty sure it's only a prop. Never had the nerve to check inside, though. Keeps me in line.

Maybe you should try it.

Susan Mary   Oh, mine is packed.

Stewart   That bad?

Susan Mary   No. Just the usual . . . squabbles.

(*attempt at brightness*) I have found myself looking at apartment listings, though. Glancing, really. Just for fun. They're putting up that new complex, the enormous one, have you seen it?

Stewart   Those are gonna be the ugliest buildings in Washington.

Susan Mary   Supposed to be awfully nice, inside. Some of my friends are looking at places there. I wouldn't mind living somewhere new, I've always lived in old houses.

Stewart   It'd be awfully quiet after the Center of the Universe.

Susan Mary   Quiet and obscure sounds all right to me sometimes.

He looks at her.

Susan Mary   I'm joking, Stewart, don't look so "concerned."

Stewart   I'm not.

Susan Mary   Good.

Now. How was the last test?

Stewart   Ugh. Tish?

Susan Mary   Of course. She keeps me posted.

Stewart   I told her to keep it quiet.

Susan Mary   From me? That's absurd.

Stewart   What about – (*indicates* **Joe**)

Susan Mary   Never, not unless you give the word, you know that. What have you found out?

Stewart   Nothing.

Susan Mary   Still?

Stewart   They have no idea what it is. If it's really anything. They're useless. They've been running the damn tests for nearly a year. I think it's all a lot of bullshit, actually.

Susan Mary   Let's hope so.

Stewart   I can't believe she *updates* you.

Susan Mary   I ask her to.

Maybe you should say something to Joe. He'd be upset if he got wind of it somehow, and you hadn't mentioned anything . . .

Stewart   Not yet.

Susan Mary   Why not? He can be very understanding, when he –

She stops. They laugh together. Beat.

Anyway, he's your brother.

Stewart   Yeah, and I don't want his sympathy.

This is a slip. Beat.

Susan Mary   So. They think it might be something that will . . . require sympathy.

Beat.

Stewart   Yes.

Beat.

Susan Mary   Oh.

She embraces him, really shocked.

She kisses his face. Then, surprising herself, his mouth.

Stewart *gently moves her away.*

Stewart   No. No.

Beat.

Susan Mary   I'm sorry.

Stewart   They're not sure of anything.

She nods.

Joe *enters.* **Susan Mary** *leaves quickly.*

Joe   She's irritable today.

Stewart   Mm.

Joe goes back to his desk.

Haven't seen you since I got back from New York.

Joe   How was New York?

Stewart   Fine. How was Vietnam?

Joe   That was a month and a half ago. Fine.

Beat.

Stewart   How many times have you been this year?

Joe   Twice.

Stewart   I need to get back. I haven't been since, God, '63.

Joe   You're still busy with your civil rights things?

Stewart   Yes. Believe it or not that issue's not quite resolved yet.

Joe   And how are the poor negroes doing?

Stewart   Read my pieces.

Joe   I'm a little behind in my reading.

Stewart   I'm not.

Beat.

You've been pretty tough on Johnson lately.

Joe   LBJ is a complicated fellow. He's physically intimidating but surprisingly sensitive to public accusations of weakness. It's been interesting testing the limits of his vulnerability.

Stewart   A little experiment.

Joe   He will do the right thing on Vietnam if I have anything to say about it. And I have great deal to say about it.

Stewart   Did you read Lippman last week?

Joe   No.

Stewart   "If Johnson continues to escalate, at least 50 per cent of the responsibility will be Joe Alsop's."

Joe   I would hope for at least that much.

Beat.

Stewart   I . . . went up to Columbia University while I was in New York. Pretty interesting.

Joe   Surveying the Nation's Youth?

Stewart   Just trying to keep my finger on the pulse.

Joe   For the *Post* or freelance?

Stewart   Freelance, if it turns into anything.

Joe   It sounds like a waste of time, frankly.

Stewart (*ignoring this*)   Some of these kids, you can't believe the stuff they're wearing now.

Joe   I've seen pictures.

Stewart   Like a gypsy circus. You can't tell the boys from the girls sometimes. Some of the boys are better looking, actually.

Joe   Oh dear. You're not turning fairy on us, are you Stewart?

Stewart (*mild*)   No.

Beat.

I heard David Halberstam speak.

Joe   Hm.

Stewart   He raked us over the coals.

Joe   Us?

Stewart   He used us as an example of what's wrong with "Elite opinion." He used the name Alsop as a kind of punch line. The dying WASP elite, he called us. The audience clapped, and laughed.

Joe   I'm glad they enjoyed themselves.

Stewart   They call us "The Establishment."

Joe   Well that's good, anyway.

Stewart   It's not a compliment.

Beat.

Halberstam –

Joe   Halberstam is pursuing a personal vendetta, because he believes that a year ago I tried to get him fired.

Stewart   Did you?

Joe   Yes.

Stewart   Why?

Joe   Why? What do you mean why? Because he's a defeatist and a disgrace to the profession.

Stewart   Jesus, Joe.

Joe   What?

Stewart   Who the hell do you think you are?

Joe   I know who *I* am. It's you I'm worried about. What on earth has gotten into you, Stewart? Listening to *college students*? Since when do you give two shits about the so-called *opinions* – i.e., the knee-jerk juvenile *fancies* – of a bunch of long-haired teenage radicals? I certainly don't. They don't know politics. They don't know history. They don't know *anything*. We don't write for them.

Stewart   Who do we write for?

Joe   The influential.

Stewart   You think those kids aren't influential? Have you visited the campuses lately?

Joe   No, I haven't been hanging around on college campuses, Stewart. I've been rather busy in some other places. Vietnam, for example.

Stewart   What did you see in Vietnam?

Joe   I saw brave kids risking their lives. I saw the endlessly resourceful military of a great and benevolent power in a twilight struggle for freedom against an inhuman enemy.

Stewart   Save that crap for the column. What did you really see?

Joe   The implication that I'd present a different picture to my brother in private than I would to my readers is deeply offensive to me.

Stewart   Did you get out in the field?

Joe   Of course I was out in the field. I *live* in the field. What are you *implying*, Stewart?

Stewart   I'm just saying. Halberstam, Sheehan, those guys, they're young guys and they're hot headed but they're smart and they're good –

Joe   They are *children*. They're in their *twenties* –

Stewart   They're professionals, Joe, just like we were professionals in *our* twenties, and they've been there for a pretty decent spell. And they don't want America to lose.

Joe   They very definitely *do* want America to lose.

Stewart   Oh come on. You can't believe that.

Joe   Have you seen the coverage? (*suddenly shouting*) Have you read the *fucking* stories?

Stewart   Easy. Joe . . .

Joe   I have just been going through the reports from Ia Drang. It's the subject of my next column. Do you know *anything at all* about Ia Drang?

Stewart   Of course I do. Don't shout at me.

Joe   450 Air Cav soldiers surrounded in a valley by over 2,000 North Vietnamese. *Two thousand*. Against our *four hundred fifty*. And we fight our way out. 250 Americans killed. Heartbreaking. Heartbreaking. But –

We killed *one thousand* North Vietnamese communist troops. My sources at the Pentagon say probably more. We *routed* them. We *obliterated* a massively superior force by a factor of *one half*. It was *astonishing*. It was *heroic*.

And *Sheehan* – do you want to know what he writes?

"American *casualties* . . . Americans' heaviest *death* toll . . . Americans sustain serious *losses* . . ."

Stewart   What would you call a fifty percent casualty rate?

Joe   We killed them by a factor of seven to one. *Seven to one*. I call that a massive victory. Would it have killed him to use the word *victory*? I think it would. Or *success* or *won*?

Stewart   I don't know. I don't know, Joe. I wish I had your certainty.

Joe   What is there to be uncertain about? A victory is a victory.

Stewart   Except when it's not.

Joe   *Except*, I suppose you mean, when certain correspondents *say* it's not, and the American people, who have no better source of information, *believe* them.

Stewart   So you'll be the better source of information.

Joe   *General Westmorland* is the better source. *Robert McNamara*. What better sources do you need? For God's sake, don't expertise and authority mean anything anymore? I have to stand up for these men and the damned hard work they do and for the *simple truth*, which they have maintained steadily, *courageously*, for many months, through sunny days and stormy, which is that we *must* win this war, we *will* win it, and *we are winning it now*.

Stewart   I heard Westmorland's gonna ask for 100,000 more troops next year.

Joe   I believe that is more or less correct.

Stewart   How come we need 100,000 more kids if we're winning now?

Joe   Do you want a debate, Stew? Is that what you want?

Stewart   What's the point? You don't listen to me. You don't listen to anyone. I don't know why you bother to go on these trips. You never change you mind, and you sit with the same old fossils peddling the same old crap –

Joe   Oh, this is spite. This is just sheer professional envy.

Stewart   *Don't,* Joe.

Joe   I can't see any other reason for this harangue.

Stewart   It's my name, not just yours. The Alsop *Brothers* –

Joe   I won't be blamed for sharing a name with you.

Stewart   We're linked whether we want it or not and I'm not gonna sit here at the end and watch you undo everything I've–

Joe   The *end*? The *end* of what? Nothing's at an *end*. Don't blame me because you're floundering in your career.

Stewart   I –

Joe   You could have stayed with me, you could have stayed with the column! I would have *helped* you. I'm helping you *now*. My damn *name, my* name, is all that's keeping *you* afloat.

Stewart   I don't want your help and I don't need your goddamn help you reckless arrogant prick.

Joe   "Reckless?"

Stewart   I –

Joe   Now arrogant I will accept, and the other as well, gladly, but I have never been *reckless* in my *life* –

Stewart   Oh come on, Joe. It's a miracle it hasn't all blown up in your face. Half the time when we were partners I was terrified that – I never said anything. It's none of my business how you run your life –

Joe   Just a moment. I thought we were talking about work. What does my "life" have to do with anything?

Stewart   It's – nothing. I'm sorry I said it.

Joe   Blown up in my face? What the hell do you think you're talking about?

Stewart   Nothing. Look, forget it. See you at dinner.

Joe   *Stewart.*

Stewart   Moscow.

Joe   Moscow?

Stewart   Yes.

Joe   Well . . .

Beat.

You've obviously heard certain rather scurrilous rumors. Ugly words, "blackmail," and so forth. I'm not surprised. I know they're out there of course. I wouldn't have thought my brother capable of believing them, let alone repeating them.

Stewart   Look, I –

Joe   Do you believe them?

Stewart *says nothing.*

Have you discussed them with my wife? I'm aware you're close.

Stewart   God no. Never.

Joe   Do you believe them?

Stewart *looks away.*

Stewart.

Beat.

I will *never* forgive you for this.

Beat.

A knock on the door. **Abigail** *enters. With her is* **Philip***. They both have a proto-hippie look.*

Abigail   Joe? Mom said you were – Oh hi, Stewart.

Stewart   Hi.

Abigail   I'd like you to meet my friend Phili –

Joe *suddenly points to* **Philip***.*

Joe   *You.* Sit down here now.

Philip   I –

Joe   *Sit down.*

Philip *sits.* **Joe** *makes a big show for* **Stewart** *of picking up a pad and pen and sits next to* **Philip** *on the couch.*

Now. I want you to tell me – and I'm going to write it *all down* –

What do you think about *everything*?

<u>FADE</u>

Scene Three

Winter, 1967. Outside a church.

Halberstam *in an overcoat.* **Joe** *enters, sees him, stops. Beat.*

Halberstam   I didn't expect the honor guard.

Joe   He was a soldier.

Halberstam   I didn't know that.

Joe   He parachuted into occupied France. He was decorated for it.

Beat.

I didn't know you were friends.

Halberstam   We weren't. We met a few times.

He never mentioned it?

Joe   No.

Halberstam *takes this in.*

Halberstam   First time in Vietnam in . . . '63, I guess it was.

Joe   Ah.

Halberstam   I'm afraid I sort of exploded at him.

Joe   Yes, you're famous for that.

Halberstam   He took it incredibly well. He just sort of . . . *listened* to me. Like I was an interesting phenomenon. Noteworthy, but not something to get emotional about. I just kept pushing . . . It was all I could do to get one "fuck you" out of him.

Joe   He was a reporter.

Halberstam   Yeah. That's right.

Joe   He told me, about his leukemia – "It's a very interesting experience. I just wish I weren't so personally involved."

Halberstam *smiles. Beat.*

Halberstam   Anyway. I'm sorry.

Beat.

Joe   I haven't seen your byline lately.

Halberstam   Working on a book.

Joe   What about?

Halberstam   How we got into this mess.

Joe   Am I in it?

Halberstam   I'm afraid you'll have to be.

Joe   Well. Spell my name correctly.

Halberstam *starts to go.*

Halberstam   Okay.

Joe   David?

Halberstam *turns.*

You didn't have to do it.

Halberstam   The least I could do.

Joe   I don't mean coming here.

Beat.

I used to be a pretty fair reporter myself. I wondered why my brother went to hear you lecture in New York. I learned why. And I learned what you did for me subsequently. Thank you.

Halberstam (*smiles*)   I don't know what you're talking about.

Halberstam *exits.*

Abigail *has entered. Full hippie attire.* **Joe** *turns and sees her. He goes to her, very pleased.*

Joe   Abby! I saw you in the church. I didn't think you'd be able to come.

Abigail   It's good to see you, Joe.

Joe   My God you look like Pocahontas. You should have called. You should have told me you were coming, I'd have made plans.

Abigail   No, come on. You have too much going on.

Joe   Don't be silly. How long can you stay?

Abigail   I can't.

Joe   What?

Abigail   I've got to be back at school tomorrow. Exams.

Joe   You'll at least let me take you to dinner.

Abigail   Can't. Mom's waiting for me in the car. I'm taking the bus right back.

Joe   Oh that's ridiculous.

Abigail   I was lucky to get away at all. I wanted to make sure and say Hi, though, before I –

Joe   Oh come on. Lunch, at least? Please. Nothing elaborate, we'll go somewhere casual. (*RE her clothes*) We'll have to, actually . . .

Abigail I'm sorry, Joe.

Joe *swallows his disappointment.*

Joe No apologies. It means the world that you came at all.

Beat.

Abigail How are you?

Joe Well, it wasn't entirely unexpected. After he told me he still had . . . a few months. That helps a bit. But it's still difficult. The younger sibling is just not meant to predecease the older, you know, it just seems . . . poorly managed, somehow.

Abigail Uh huh.

Joe We were partners for two decades, and close our entire lives. Mostly. He would never admit it . . . and nobody but I saw it . . . but we complemented each other, I think.

Abigail No, I saw it.

Joe You did?

Abigail That night a couple years ago. Remember? I was visiting from school?

Joe Which?

Abigail I brought that boy over.

Joe Yes. What was his name?

Abigail Philip.

Joe That's right, Philip. Your boyfriend.

Abigail Well. Semi-.

Joe What was wrong with him?

Abigail Nothing. He was very . . . mild. Anyway. You terrorized him. That interrogation.

Joe I interviewed him.

Abigail You spent an *hour*. You buttonholed him, you *probed* him *mercilessly* for his opinions about the war, "today's Youth," the whole geo-political deal. . . He was a *piano teacher*. He was quaking.

Joe His responses were reasonably cogent, as I recall.

Abigail Then we went into dinner and he's sitting next to *Robert McNamara*, and you repeat everything Philip said and make him repeat himself to the whole table, all those arrogant, articulate people, those professional talkers . . .

Joe He didn't do as well there.

Abigail   No. Stewart tried to defend him, though.

Joe   Yes, he did.

Abigail   He took his side, backed him up all the way. I loved him for that.

Joe   Still. The prosecution, I believe, won.

Did that have anything to do with why he didn't spend the night?

Abigail   *Possibly*, Joe. Possibly.

Joe   Oh dear.

Abigail   He took the next train back to Boston. He never spoke to me again.

Joe   Well, look, if I had known he was so sensitive, I –

Joe *sees she's laughing.*

It's good you can laugh about it now.

Abigail   I don't know how Mom lived with you.

Beat.

Joe   How is she?

Abigail   She's okay. Keeping busy.

Joe   I wasn't sure if I would see her here.

Abigail   Oh God of course. She loved Stewart.

Joe   I wish we could have had a word.

Abigail   She's just . . . it's so soon after . . .

Joe   I understand. Tell her I wouldn't mind hearing from her?

Abigail   No, Joe. She can't deal with all the legal stuff right now.

Joe   No, God no, I'm not trying to rush her along, it would be strictly for the sake of friendship.

We *were* friends, you know. Good friends. At the beginning. She kept me honest. Or tried at least.

Stewart tried too. And in return I abused him.

Abigail   I'm sure he didn't see it that way.

Joe   He saw so many things clearly.

Joe *weeps.* **Abigail** *tries to comfort him, awkward. Beat. He collects himself, dries his eyes with a handkerchief.*

Oh dear. I'm sorry.

Abigail   It's all right.

Joe   Abby, there's something I feel you should know. It might help you make sense of . . . I don't know, things, your youth, now that you're at an age when people try to take stock of their upbringing, understand their parents . . . I don't actually know if you ever considered me a *parent* but I certainly consider *myself* . . .

Abigail   Joe, of course, you know I do.

Joe   Yes well that's not even the point. The point is, you see, I'm not . . . your mother and I had a somewhat unconventional arrangement, and for a time at least a not unsuccessful one – or even particularly *unusual* one, I might add – but the fact remains that we . . . you see, I'm – and I haven't spoken about this to very many people, just your mother and Stewart, really, and now they're . . . but you're, as I say, family, and I want you to know, you deserve to know that that I . . .

Abigail   Joe. I know.

Joe   You don't even know what it is I'm going to say.

Abigail   Yes, I do.

Joe   She *told* you? I can't believe she –

Abigail   No. God, no, she never *said* anything. Mom? Are you kidding? She didn't even say anything when I got my first period, she just sent me to her doctor in a chauffeured car. No. She didn't have to. I mean, it's pretty obvious. I think probably everybody knows.

Joe (*stunned by this*)   Everybody?

Abigail   It's really not that big a thing.

She hugs him. He returns it, awkward.

Abigail   I have to go. My exam –

Joe   Yes, of course. What is it?

Abigail   Oh, I have three or four, they really pile up.

Joe   If it's Latin, you don't have a thing to worry about.

Abigail   It isn't Latin.

Joe   It isn't anything.

Abby. It was my school too. It isn't exam week. The term just started.

Abigail   Yeah. I . . . dropped out. I wanted to work full time. Against the war. I didn't think you'd want to hear that.

Joe   I see.

No. I admire your . . . willingness to act on conviction, however misguided.

Beat.

Write me?

She nods, then starts to go.

And if you run into him in Boston, say hello to poor Philip for me.

She smiles, briefly.

Abigail   I can't. He was drafted.

FADE

Scene Four

Washington. Summer 1968. The Mall.

A bearded **Man** *in his 30s, holding a magazine. Off, the sounds of a demonstration.* **Joe** *enters. He looks irritated and tired. He sits on a bench. The* **Man** *eventually sits down too, nods to Joe, begins glancing at his magazine.*

Joe   There used to be places in Washington DC where a man could sit and enjoy the afternoon without being subjected to *tribal drumming*.

Man   They've been there all morning.

Joe   They've been there all year. My God. Don't they have anything better to do?

Man   What's better to do?

Joe   Honest labor? Education? Travel? Auto-eroticism? *Anything*'s better. The *chanting*, my God. You can't escape it. I can hear it in the library.

Man   They're young. Students.

Joe   Do you know where students spent most of their time in my day? *In school.*

Man   Yes.

Joe   It's a quaint idea, I know. But these . . . "hippies," or "New Lefties," or SDS-ees, or whatever they're calling themselves this week, they don't have the slightest interest in –

He stops himself.

But now *I'm* disturbing *your* day. My apologies.

Man   It's no problem.

Beat. **Joe** *looks at him.*

Joe   Say that again.

Man   Sorry?

Joe   What you just said.

Man   "It's no problem"?

Beat.

Joe   You are Russian.

Man   Yes.

Joe   I knew it.

Man   Well, Soviet.

Joe   I heard the faintest trace of it.

Man *looks carefully at* **Joe**. **Joe** *goes back to his reading. Beat.*

Man   I worked hard to lose it. I pride myself on being completely unaccented.

Joe   Well that's impossible. No one, however fluent, can manage that.

Man   I listen to tapes. I try to pick the best voice.

Joe   Unquestionably, the finest American speaking voice of my lifetime belonged to Franklin Delano Roosevelt.

Man   Too WASPy.

Joe   I beg your pardon.

Man   I listen to Walter Cronkite.

Joe   No one should listen to Walter Cronkite.

Man   And Alistair Cooke, he has a nice quality.

Joe   Yes, I suppose he's all right.

Man   I like the way the English sound. I've gone back and forth. For a long time I couldn't decide who I wanted to sound like. I even considered Lennon.

Joe   Lenin?

Man   No, John Lennon. (*Beatles voice*) "Those in the cheap seats applaud. The rest of you just rattle your jewelry."

Joe *looks blank.*

He's one of the Beatles.

Joe   Oh, the Beatles, yes. Thank God that silly fad ran its course.

Man   Are you joking? They're great artists.

Joe   What?

Man   Have you heard *Sgt. Pepper's*?

Joe   What is that?

Man   It's a record album by the Beatles.

Joe   Oh. No, I haven't heard it.

Man   It came out a year ago.

Joe   I haven't even heard *of* it.

Man   You're joking.

Joe   No.

Man   It's brilliant! It's a symphony! How can you not have listened to it? I bought two so I can stack them on my turntable and don't have to get up and flip the record. Take my advice: buy two copies, get yourself a good pair of headphones, lie back, have a few glasses of wine – or something else – and you'll be transported. You'll blow your mind.

Joe   I don't think I'll be doing that.

Man   Too bad.

Beat.

Joe   Tell me, how did you come here? Did you defect?

Man   Defect? No, I work for the embassy.

Joe   You do?

Man   Yes, I'm an attaché.

Joe   You certainly seem to have embraced the West.

Man   The West will implode soon, a victim of its own internal contradictions, and the United States will be the first sucked into history's abyss.

Joe   Ah.

Man   Meanwhile . . .

Joe   Yes?

Man   Confidentially?

Joe   Please.

Man   I love it here.

Joe   Really?

Man   Ah, the music, the films, the food – breakfasts especially, the miracle of the "bottomless cup of coffee"! – the weather . . .

Joe   You love the weather in *Washington, D.C.*?

Man   You've been to Moscow.

Joe   As a matter of fact I have.

Man   So you understand. And I love the bookstores . . . You can't imagine how it feels walking into an American bookstore. Or just a newsstand. The *magazines* –

Joe   What is that you're reading?

Man   *Esquire*. Norman Mailer! Genius.

Joe   He's a thug.

Man   No, he's fantastic, he's like something out of Dostoyevsky, a mad monk, hysterical and obscene, I love him. And James Baldwin. And Truman Capote and Paul Newman and James Brown and Andy Warhol.

Joe   Everyone you just named I frankly despise.

Man   And those kids over there too.

Joe   Not all of them. My step-daughter's in there somewhere, apparently. Her I like. The remaining 99,99% of that writhing, fetid mass, yes, with particular venom.

Man   You know what? I think you hate America more than anyone at home does.

Joe   That's absurd. I love my country. I just don't care very much for many of the people in it right now.

Man *smiles. Beat.*

Joe   Tell me, how exactly do your bosses at the Embassy feel about your passion for the enemy?

Man   Not bosses. Comrades.

Joe *stares at him.*

And the top men I never deal with, and the mid-level officers are too busy buying hi-fis for their kids to listen to Simon and Garfunkel records to mind what we do in our spare time, as long as we behave sensibly during working hours, and don't . . .

Joe *is still staring, frozen.*

What?

Beat.

Joe   Andrei?

Andrei   Yes.

Joe   My God.

Andrei   I'm sorry. I shouldn't have gone on so long, I thought you would have known me right away.

Beat.

Joe   What is it you want from me?

Andrei   Nothing.

Joe   Please. This could hardly be an accidental meeting.

Andrei   You spend your mornings in the library. I see you here often, taking the air. It seemed silly never once to say hello.

Joe   Stop it. I'm not an idiot. Just tell me what you want and get it over with.

Andrei   Oh dear. I've done this badly. I didn't mean to alarm you. I wanted only to say hello.

Joe   I don't believe you.

Andrei   I guess I shouldn't be surprised. I read your work too. I never miss a column. You look for plots everywhere. Secret agendas.

Joe   And I usually find them.

Andrei   Is it really so impossible to imagine I don't have one?

Joe   Yes.

Andrei   How sad for you, then.

Beat.

Joe   You got your diplomatic posting.

Andrei   Yes.

Joe   How is your sister? The . . . skier, wasn't she?

Andrei   You have a remarkable memory. She is fine.

Joe   Really.

Andrei   I've been able to help her since . . . my new job. I am trying to arrange for her to visit me here. It's not easy, but I'm close to getting permission. I want to take her to ski in Colorado. I think she would love the Rocky Mountains.

Joe   Congratulations. You've done well for yourself.

Andrei (*Noncommittal sound.*)

Joe   Quite a change from your wayward youth.

Andrei   I don't think much about those days.

Joe   You entrapped me.

Beat.

Andrei   It was just a job.

Joe   How many of those "jobs" did you do?

Andrei   A few.

Joe   You were a contemptible little trick.

Andrei   And you were procuring a whore, what did you expect?

Joe   I suppose now you're some sort of spy. "Attaché" indeed.

Andrei   I *am* an attaché.

Joe   And what else?

Andrei   Nothing else. A music fan.

Joe   Don't insult me. You were a tour guide working for the KGB, now you're an embassy aide and nothing else?

Andrei   I never *worked* for them. If they asked I did a job. A half a dozen times at most. If you think I had a choice then you don't understand our system. I got out as soon as I could. I clawed my way into the diplomatic branch.

Joe   And they owed you after all the work you'd done.

Andrei   It wasn't like that.

Joe   Oh wasn't it.

Andrei   I earned my way.

Joe   On your knees.

Andrei   You don't understand. I took your advice. I used my languages. What *you* suggested. Fine, maybe I began that day the thing you thought I was. But I refused to remain one. And I am not one now. Don't you see? In a way I owe this life to you.

I came here to say thank you.

And "I'm sorry," too. For any . . . distress I may have caused.

Will you accept my apology?

Joe   You honestly came here expecting that I would?

Andrei   I didn't expect. I hoped.

Joe   Nevertheless I'll have to disappoint you.

Andrei   All right.

Then there's only one thing left to do.

Andrei *reluctantly opens his magazine, takes out a small envelope. He hands it to* **Joe**.

For you. Negatives.

I obtained them – well, never mind how.

They're yours now. You can burn them. You can do whatever you want.

Joe   Well, this is quite a risk you're taking.

Andrei   I feared it might be the only apology you would accept.

Beat.

Joe   I see.

Andrei   Goodbye, Joe. And thank you again.

Andrei *turns to go.*

Joe   Andrei, wait.

It's I who should be thanking you.

It's not every day a subject for a column drops into one's lap. I'd been struggling to find something for the next one and now you've come to my rescue.

Andrei   I don't understand.

Joe   "The new Soviet hypocrites." "A chance encounter on a park bench with a fickle Embassy aide – we'll just call him 'Andrei' – gave me new hope for America's not-so-distant triumph in the Cold War. . . Seduced by the very the pleasures of the West they claim to hate, these 'decadent-niks'" – something like that – "are secretly longing not for Stalingrad but for San Francisco" . . . it'll write itself. Not many do. I'm in your debt.

Beat.

Andrei   You can't.

Joe   Don't be silly, you've given me a splendid idea for the sort of piece that will be talked of all over town. Do you imagine I'm going to pass it up?

Andrei   They'll know it's me.

Joe   Not necessarily.

Andrei   Of course they will.

Joe   I'll only use your first name, A-N-D-R-E-I, and don't worry, I won't say anything that isn't scrupulously accurate. I liked the bit about your bosses buying hi-fis, for example.

Andrei   Please. I'll lose my job. I'll be ruined, humiliated –

Joe (*shouts*)   Don't talk to me about humiliation!

Andrei   I'm *sorry*. Should I say it again? I'm sorry about Moscow. That's why I brought you these –

Joe *throws the envelope back at him.*

Joe   I don't need *these*. They couldn't mean less to me. It's far too late and I don't give two shits about Moscow anymore. You did your worst there and you didn't lay a *glove* on me. Do you know what I did with those ridiculous photographs those thugs who came to my door showed me? I took them straight to our Ambassador. Then I went to the FBI, and the State Department. I said, here it is. Here's what I've done. Here's what I am. If my career's to end I want *you* to end it, not those depraved blackmailing psychopaths over there. And they *didn't* end it. And *that* is the difference between my country and yours. Christ you disgust me. You think you've got us beat. You think you've got us on the run in Vietnam, you've got our youth running riot in the streets, naked and stoned out of their minds, you think you're winning. Well not while I'm around, thank you very much. If you don't think I won't go absolutely to the limit to defend what I hold dear you don't know me very well, and you don't know this country very well.

Andrei   No.

Joe   Study the history! You thought you had us fixed with Cuba but JFK, a better man *by far* than any your country has ever produced *outfoxed* you, God bless his soul, and then after Dallas you probably thought you'd caught another break – maybe you were *involved* with Dallas – I scoffed at that at the time but now I'm not so sure – and you surely thought LBJ the big dumb cowboy would go easy on you but *I* bucked him up, by God, I stiffened his spine and even if he's not man enough to finish the job somebody else will, Nixon will, he will burn you bastards out of the jungles and *we will win* there, there and everywhere, God knows what miserable filthy tricks you'll stoop to next but we will match you stunt for stunt and *we will win*. So fuck Moscow, sir. And please enjoy your final afternoon at your Embassy or in the record shops or however you choose to spend it.

Beat.

Andrei   I suppose I cannot stop you.

Joe   No, you cannot.

Andrei   My sister –

Joe *shrugs*.

Andrei *goes*.

Joe *sits alone for a moment. Then slowly gets up.*

The set changes around him to his study.

Scene Five

Joe'*s study. Night.*

Joe *sits at his typewriter. He types purposefully for a bit. Then slows. Then stops.*

He pulls the paper out of the typewriter and reads what he's written. A long pause. Then he violently crumples the paper and tears it.

He takes a breath.

He picks up the phone, dials.

Joe   Hello. It's Alsop. The column tomorrow is going to be a bit late. I'm sorry, I just wanted to let you know.

Yes I thought I had a piece but I've changed my mind. It wasn't working. No, I know I've never been late before. I haven't been late in 25 years. That's precisely why you shouldn't be complaining now. I –

Yes I have other ideas, I have a *thousand* ideas for Chrissake, don't worry. I'll get you something. Yes. All right.

He hangs up.

He puts another sheet of paper in the typewriter.

He stares at it. He doesn't move.

A moment.

<u>CURTAIN</u>

Lost Lake

Lost Lake opened at Manhattan Theatre Club's City Center Stage 1 on November 11, 2014 with the following cast and director:

Director: Daniel Sullivan
Hogan: John Hawkes
Veronica: Tracie Thoms

The play was originally developed at the Eugene O'Neill Playwrights Conference in July 2013, directed by Wendy C. Goldberg and starring Frank Wood and Elsa Davis. It was presented at the Sullivan Project at the University of Illinois in February 2014, directed by Daniel Sullivan and starring Jake Weber and Opal Alladin.

Characters:

Veronica
Hogan

Setting:

The main room of a decrepit cabin on a lake.

Scene One

March. **Veronica**, *a black woman in her 30s wearing a winter coat, looking around.* **Hogan**, *a disheveled white man in his 40s/50s, with her.*

Hogan   So what do you think?

Veronica   It looks all right.

Beat.

Hogan   I know it's cold now. July-August you won't have to worry about that.

Veronica   Of course.

Hogan   Though the last couple weeks of August nights can get cool again, you might want to bring some extra blankets for the kids.

Veronica   Uh-huh.

Beat.

Hogan   How many kids?

Veronica   Two. Maybe three – the older one, my girl, wants to bring a friend. I haven't decided about that. It may just be her and her brother.

Hogan   They identical?

Veronica   What? No.

Hogan   They are twins, you said.

Veronica   No. They're two years apart. Boy and girl.

Hogan   I don't know why I thought they were twins.

Veronica   No. They're just . . . regular.

Beat.

Hogan   There's only one bed in the second room.

Veronica   That's all right. They can double up.

Hogan   It's pretty small. I might have a trundle I can get for you.

Veronica   Oh no, that's fine. One of them can sleep with me if we have to.

Hogan   Your husband won't mind?

Veronica   It's just me.

Hogan   Oh. Sorry.

Veronica   No.

But maybe an extra bed would be –

Hogan   No problem. I can call my brother, see if I can borrow his trundle. But if the third kid comes –

Veronica   I think I'm gonna have to tell my little girl that isn't happening.

Hogan   No, it'll still work. You put one in the single, one on the trundle and one on the couch in a sleeping bag or whatever. You'd have to bring up some extra linens is all.

Veronica   We'll figure that out.

Hogan   She wants to bring a friend, let her. They'll have a ball.

Veronica   We'll see.

Beat.

Hogan   Pretty gorgeous out there, huh? Even this time of year.

Veronica   Yes, it is.

Hogan   The dock will be fixed by June. It's almost done now. We finally got around to it.

Veronica   The dock?

Hogan   Yeah.

Veronica   Is there some kind of boat?

Hogan   Swimming dock.

Veronica   Oh. Yes.

Hogan   See out there?

Veronica   Yes. It's pretty far out.

Hogan   Nah. It's an easy swim. There's usually a diving board. That'll get put back on. I'm gonna paint the deck a nice fire engine red after I get the 15 years of Canada goose shit scrubbed off. You'll see the geese, they shit on everything.

Veronica   You're doing the work?

Hogan   I was the low bid.

Veronica   I see.

Hogan   Community association's been putting it off for years. Last summer a woman put her foot through a rotten plank. Had to go to the emergency room to get the splinters out. Finally I said look, give me fifteen hundred bucks, I'll have it ready by Memorial Day. I'm going to put in a second diving platform higher up. It's gonna be great. I made some sketches. It'll just be stationary but you'll still have the springboard on the opposite side. You'll never get your kids off it.

Veronica   They don't really swim.

Hogan   Why not?

Veronica   City kids.

Hogan   That's not good. They need to learn.

Veronica   That's one of the reasons we wanted to be up here.

Hogan   It's a life skill. You should get them lessons at the Y or someplace now. That way when they get up here they're ready.

Veronica   I don't know if we have time for that.

Hogan   It's only March. You got four months.

Veronica   Well, we'll see.

Hogan   Don't let them go out to the dock unless you're sure they can manage it.

Veronica   Of course not.

Hogan   Now there is a canoe I'll get out for you, which will require some bailing but it's more or less seaworthy, and I think two life jackets. But I believe only one paddle. I'll check the garage. If I can't find another one I'll ask my brother. But you'd still need a third life jacket if your little girl brings her friend. Or if you need it. Do you swim?

Veronica   Yes.

Hogan   Because some . . . city people don't.

Veronica   I do.

Hogan   Okay then. Any other questions?

Veronica   No. I think . . .

Beat. She looks around. Swallows her doubts.

All right. Let's do it.

Hogan   Great. You're really gonna enjoy it here.

Veronica   I hope so.

Hogan   You will.

Veronica   So how should we – how do you like to do this?

Hogan   Well we talked about the total on the email, that still works for you?

Veronica   Yes.

Hogan   So now I guess maybe just a deposit. To hold the rental.

Veronica   All right.

Hogan   What if we say half now and then half when you get here. And add maybe 500 on to the front end as a damage deposit, that I'll refund at the end if everything's ship shape.

Veronica   So you're saying half the total rental plus 500 now?

Hogan   Yes. And you'll get the 500 back at the end of the summer.

Veronica   Unless there's damage.

Hogan   There won't be. I'll put away anything fragile. There's nothing much you can hurt around here anyway even with kids.

Veronica   So maybe we don't need to do the damage deposit? I'm just –

Hogan   It's pretty standard.

Veronica   I'm just wondering if maybe – half plus the 500 now seems like a lot.

Hogan   Uh huh.

Veronica   I mean I could do half and half, but then maybe I'd ask you to waive the damage deposit, given that everything around here already looks pretty . . . broken in.

Hogan   I just thought *if* something got damaged, I don't even know what–

Veronica   Uh huh.

Hogan   It'd be easier – if it's already dealt with, so to speak, rather than negotiate it later –

Veronica   No, I understand, but maybe then a better way to do the rent would be third now, a third I can send you let's say in June, and then a third when we come up. Uh huh.

Hogan   And we'd still do the damage deposit.

Veronica   Yes. But maybe spread out over the first two payments.

Hogan   Two fifty, two fifty.

Veronica   Yes.

Hogan   Third payment when you get here.

Veronica   Yes.

Beat.

Hogan   Deal!

Veronica   Okay. Thank you.

Hogan   Thank you. You're a real wily negotiator, huh?

Veronica   I don't know about that.

Hogan   No, I like it! So all right. Any other questions?

Veronica   Do you have internet?

Hogan   No. That would require a dish and it's just not worth it to me. If I need to check my email I drive into town to the library. Cell phone service is spotty. If you stand by the window and kind of elevate yourself a little bit and hold your phone out at about a 45 degree angle sometimes a signal can be had – I don't even bother usually, I use the land line for calls at the house and the library for internet, like I said.

Veronica   I will need to get online a few times for work. How far is the library?

Hogan   10 minutes. It's only open 3 days a week but you don't even have to go in. When it's closed you can park outside with your laptop. People do it all the time. Oh – you'll need a car. I mean once you get up here. But you saw that.

Veronica   I'll rent a car for the week.

Hogan   You got that budgeted in.

Veronica   Yes.

Hogan   Well great, so everything is settled.

What sort of work do you do, you don't mind my asking?

Veronica   I'm a nurse practitioner.

Hogan   A nurse, huh?

Veronica   Practitioner, yes.

Hogan   Which means what?

Veronica   I can prescribe certain medications, perform certain procedures.

Hogan   Turn your head and cough, that kind of thing?

Veronica   I'm sorry?

Hogan   Sort of halfway to a doctor in other words.

Veronica   Sort of.

Hogan   Well that sounds good.

Beat.

So right – if you need to stay in touch with your office or hospital or whatever –

Veronica   Hospital.

Hogan   – Just give them this number the week you're here. We did say a week, didn't we?

Veronica   The third week in August.

Hogan   The last week's available too. Stay til Labor Day.

Veronica   I have to work.

Hogan   You only get one week of vacation?

Veronica   That's all I've been able to arrange.

Hogan   Then you really should get those kids swimming before they get up here.

Veronica   Maybe. We'll see.

Hogan   They'll spend the whole week watching other kids dive off the dock.

Veronica   We'll manage.

Hogan   Well if you change your mind the rest of August is available.

Veronica   Thank you, but I don't think we'll be able to do that.

Beat. She looks at an old hockey stick propped against the wall.

Hogan   I'll get all that stuff out of here before you come, naturally, pack up my clothes and so forth, the drawers will be free. When are you heading back to the city?

Veronica (*Takes out a bus schedule.*)   I think I can make the 3:30 bus.

Hogan   Today.

Veronica   Yes. If you could drop me back in front of the movie theater.

Hogan   Didn't you just come up this morning?

Veronica   I wanted to make sure I saw the place before –

Hogan   No, that's wise. Picking something off the internet, who the hell knows what you're going to get? If the pictures they put up are even real. Or the descriptions. The way people exaggerate you do have to watch out.

Veronica   Well, you certainly didn't exaggerate.

Hogan   I said "Rustic." That's what you're looking for, isn't it?

Veronica   Yes.

Hogan   I'll fix that shutter before you come up. And the dock will be done like I said. And I don't know if you looked in the shower but I'll get that section of ceiling patched and the wall repainted, I've been meaning to borrow some paint from my brother – he has a beautiful robin's egg blue from when he did his bathrooms. I just need a free weekend.

Veronica   I definitely would appreciate any . . .

Hogan   Little improvements –

Veronica   Yes – you plan to do. The kitchen seems fine.

Hogan   Don't use the two front burners on the stove, they only work on high and then they smoke. Those I doubt I'll be able to get to –

Veronica   Did you say you'll be moving your clothes out of here?

Hogan   Oh sure. I'll get all the drawers clear for you.

Veronica   You live here now.

Hogan   Yes. But I'll get everything cleared out.

What?

Veronica   Nothing. Sorry. I suppose I thought this was just a summer place.

Hogan   It is but lately I've been a full timer. A couple space heaters and you can get through a winter if it stays mild like it has this year. It's not so bad.

The Lake used to freeze over sometimes believe it or not. We played hockey out there when we were kids. That doesn't happen hardly ever anymore, the winters are so mild now. That's a collector's item. Big hockey fan. You?

Veronica   Where will you go when we're renting?

Hogan   My brother's. He's only about 45 minutes away. So I can be here quickly if anything comes up.

Veronica   I hate to kick you out of your house.

Hogan   Are you kidding? You're doing me a favor. I wish you'd do me a bigger favor and rent all summer.

Veronica   Your brother'd take you for the whole summer?

Hogan   That's a good point.

Beat.

Veronica   Well, Mr. Hogan . . .

Hogan   Yes. Terry.

Veronica   Let me get you that deposit.

She writes a check. Gives it to him.

Hogan   Thank you. (*Looks at it.*) Veronica.

Veronica   Okay.

They shake hands. Beat.

I'd better get to that bus stop.

FADE.

Scene Two

August. Sound of kids playing outside. **Hogan** *lets himself in the cabin. It has been straightened up. He notices a large library book. He picks it up, flips through it.* **Veronica** *enters. Summer clothes.*

Veronica   You got my messages.

Hogan   Why I'm here.

Veronica   Well good.

Hogan   Sorry about the delay. My phone died and I couldn't find the charger! You a birder?

Veronica   No. (*He shows her the book. It's a Field Guide to North American Birds.*) Oh. No, that's just for my son. He's into birds and wildlife right now, he's always asking their names, so.

Hogan   How old is he?

Veronica   Seven.

Hogan   Wow. Is he some kind of genius?

Veronica   No.

Hogan   Pretty heavy reading for a seven year old, isn't it? I mean this is like a hardcore scientific text.

Veronica   It's just in case he wants to look up one of the names. It's what the library had.

Hogan   Oh. Okay.

Veronica   So look –

Hogan   They're having a good time looks like! You got them some lessons?

Veronica   Yes.

Hogan   Where'd you get the inner tubes?

Veronica   I bought them in town.

Hogan   Great idea. You know I taught my own kid to swim out there. She could dive like a porpoise. You should have seen her go off the springboard. Fearless. She always asked, "Why isn't there a high platform? There should be a high-dive." She was right. That's one of the reasons I volunteered to do the dock. You think I was gonna make a profit on that? Forget it. The lumber alone . . . She's with her Mom now. In Florida. But we're still real close. We email . . .

Veronica   Uh-huh. So look, if you could do something about the hot water I'd appreciate it.

Hogan   I'll see what I can do.

Veronica   All right then.

Hogan   You know, even if they've had a few lessons if you're gonna be in here maybe you should put some water wings on them.

Veronica   I told them how far in they are allowed to go, and my children do what they're told. And they had ten lessons. A friend of mine who does physical therapy let us use the pool where she works after hours. I taught them myself.

Hogan   Okay, great.

Veronica   You said back in March the dock would be ready for the summer.

Hogan   I know.

Veronica   You said it'd be painted. There'd be a diving board. There's no diving board. There's hardly any dock. Half the planks are gone.

Hogan   I know it's not ideal.

Veronica   It's dangerous. My daughter's friend went out the first day, she nearly put her hand through a nail sticking right out of the side. I would have had to get her a tetanus shot. I had to ban them from the dock.

Hogan   The inner tubes were a good idea.

Veronica   Four inner tubes from the Kmart duct-taped together are a pretty poor substitute for a swimming dock. And it's sixty dollars I didn't plan to spend.

Hogan   It's nice your little girl's friend could come up at least.

Veronica   Mr. Hogan. I think you should reimburse me.

He says nothing.

You said the dock would be repaired; it isn't. We've been up here three days with no hot water. You did not provide the trundle bed you promised. I've had two nine year olds sleeping on a twin bed. You know I saw the place, I wasn't expecting the Four Seasons, but —

Hogan   I fixed the shutter.

Veronica   What shutter?

Hogan   That one, that was off its hinge.

Veronica   It's ornamental. What do I care about that? This is my vacation. It's been very frustrating.

Hogan   I understand.

Veronica   I hope so.

Hogan   I'm gonna take a look at the water heater right now. I'm sure I can get it going. It's probably just the pilot light.

Veronica   It's not the pilot light. I know how to check a pilot light. You've got some other problem.

Hogan   I'll take a look at it right away.

Veronica   Thank you.

Hogan   Is there anything else?

Veronica   You mean besides the dock, the bed, the hot water, the disconnected phone, and the dead tree branch over the walkway looks like it's about to fall and smash in one of my children's skulls any second?

Hogan   I was not aware about the phone.

Veronica   I had to use my cell phone. You were right about one thing, you got to be a circus acrobat to get a signal in this place. You know what? I really think it's only fair you consider refunding a portion of my rental fee.

Hogan   You haven't had a good time?

Veronica   We have had – we have managed to enjoy ourselves so far ——

Hogan   The weather's been gorgeous.

Veronica   It rained all day yesterday.

Hogan   Besides that.

Veronica   I made a decision not to let some of these disappointments ruin my vacation, but —

Hogan   That's the right attitude. And you know what? Kids don't care. Give them a little water to splash around in they're happy forever.

Veronica   Yes but I would like to be able to give them a hot bath afterward. *I'd* like to be able to take a bath. Call me greedy.

Hogan   I don't think you're greedy.

Veronica   Thank you.

Hogan   But I never did get your third payment. (*Beat.*) The last third we agreed you would give me when you arrived.

Veronica   I know.

Hogan   Do you have it?

Veronica   You're seriously asking for it now?

Hogan   If you don't mind. We can get that straight and then we can deal with any other issues.

Veronica   You got it backwards. I think we should deal with this first.

Hogan   You mean the refund.

Veronica   I don't want a full refund. We're here now, we're going to stay out the week.

Hogan   What do you want?

Veronica   I think you ought to refund, let's say three days' rent.

Hogan   Uh-huh.

Veronica   Assuming you can get everything else working. Not the dock of course, I can see that's a lost cause.

Hogan   There were structural problems with the dock I didn't anticipate.

Veronica   Uh-huh.

Hogan   I thought it was just the decking needed replacement. But it was one of the pilings too. They're sunk into concrete under the lake bed. This is a man-made lake. They probably did it before the lake was filled. So they had it easier. I'm not a Navy SEAL. I can't replace a piling that's sunk in four feet of concrete under fifteen feet of water.

Veronica   Maybe you should have figured that out before you took the job.

Hogan   Right, that is exactly what the Homeowner's Association said. Or rather their attorney. Which is why I am currently being sued by the Homewoner's Association.

Veronica   Well I'm sorry about that.

Hogan   Thanks. It's a huge pain in the ass.

Veronica   But it's not my problem.

Beat.

Hogan   I hate to argue about money.

Veronica   Mr. Hogan, I'm about to give lunch to my kids here —

Hogan   What are you having?

Veronica   Sandwiches. So I —

Hogan   What kind?

Veronica   I got baloney and peanut butter and jelly. Why? Do you want one?

Hogan   Sure. I haven't eaten.

Veronica   Okay, let me be clearer. I don't exactly feel like giving you lunch right now. I would like to resolve this.

Hogan   Look, what do you expect me to do? We said twelve hundred for the week. Now that is not a lot of money for a two-bedroom rental on a lake in this area two weeks before Labor Day. Now you want three days back. That's what, about five hundred bucks?

Veronica   More like six.

Hogan   Okay, whatever. I'm gonna deal with your hot water problem. I don't really see how a few days of cold showers, which is good for the circulation by the way – you're a nurse, you should know that – could be worth – how much did you say you wanted?

Veronica   Six hundred dollars.

Hogan   But you still owe *me* four hundred. Don't you? Minus whatever you paid for the inner tubes.

Veronica   Forget the inner tubes. I bought them, that's done.

Hogan   No, I'll reimburse you for those, I don't have a problem with that. I know you're especially upset about the inner tubes.

Veronica   I don't care about the damn inner tubes. I care about three days with no hot water.

Hogan   But you haven't paid rent for those three days!

Veronica   I —

Hogan   So why not just pay it?

Veronica   Because this house is shabby! All right? It's a shabby mess. I had to spend the whole first night cleaning. There's more bugs in this damn house than in my apartment in New York City.

Hogan   You're in nature, you're not in the goddamn city.

Veronica   Oh they're better bugs, is that what you're saying?

Hogan   If you were expecting an insect-free cabin in the woods I can't help you, that's all, I don't think we have anything to talk about.

Veronica   And I can't sleep up here! I'm out here in the woods all by myself a million miles from nowhere with three little children, I can't believe how creepy it is at night with the crickets and the frogs and hoot-owls and I don't know what.

Hogan   Well I'm sorry but that's what you paid for. Or partially paid for.

Veronica   Okay, look. Just give me two hundred dollars.

Hogan   How did you get two hundred now?

Veronica   Because! Six hundred dollars you owe me for the three days minus the last third of the rent, the difference is —

Hogan   All right, all right, all right, the hell with it.

He takes out his wallet and tosses bills toward her.

I got thirty-eight dollars on me which is all the cash I've got until my disability comes in Friday. Take it. Go on. Take it.

Veronica   I don't want your last thirty-eight dollars.

Hogan   Take it. It's fine. My brother'll tide me over. If Debbie lets him.

Veronica   Debbie?

Hogan   His wife. We don't get along.

Veronica   I can't imagine.

Hogan   She is not any easygoing person. I like a relaxed atmosphere. I don't like a lot of tension.

Veronica   Who does?

Hogan   Debbie. I think she feeds on it.

(*At the window.*) Oh hey, you know they're really swimming out there.

Veronica   They better not be swimming. (*She looks.*) Hey!

She goes outside.

Hogan   Yeah, I would say something about that.

Veronica (*outside*)   Hey! The three of you! I said I do not want you out farther than up to your belly buttons! Come on out. Come up on the beach now. Just get dried off now. I'm gonna be out there with your lunch in one minute! Thank you!

She comes back in.

Hogan   Kids.

Veronica *makes a frustrated sound.*

What'd you end up doing yesterday?

Veronica   What?

Hogan   While it was raining.

Veronica   Nothing. Took them bowling.

Hogan   Hey. Putnam Lanes? In town?

Veronica   I guess so. Yes.

Hogan   I haven't been in there for years. You still have to keep score yourself or do they have those automatic score-keepers now?

Veronica   It's automatic. On screens.

Hogan   That's too bad. That's a shame. A screen doing it all for you. I used to like taking home the score sheets. And you got those little stubby pencils . . . Remember?

Veronica   Bowling was not a big part of my childhood.

Hogan   Putnam Lanes. Can't beat that for keeping kids happy. I used to take my daughter there. I remember she was maybe eight or nine and she'd pick out an eight-pound ball —- this little girl! -— and stride right up the lane to the line and roll two or three strikes a game, and then write the little Xs in the box herself and add up her own score.

She's very (*Taps his head*). She's going to Columbia University in the fall. Did I tell you that? Full scholarship. Her mom just let me know. A little late, seeing as how she got in in April, I would have appreciated a word then, but — Anyway. I'm proud, I can't deny it. It's supposed to be a hell of a school. It's in your neck of the woods, isn't it?

Veronica   Sort of.

Hogan   Maybe I'll drive down there in the fall, check it out. I haven't been down to the city in a long time. Not since everybody had those "no radio" signs in their car windows. They don't do that anymore, do they?

Veronica   No.

Hogan   I'd like to see her play. She's gonna be on the soccer team. She was recruited and everything. Don't know where she gets it. Not from me. It's funny how kids just latch on to these things and go. Like your boy with his birds maybe.

Veronica   Well, who knows how long that'll last. Before birds it was old airplanes, like from World War II. He gets a new obsession every two weeks seems like. He's always on to the next thing so fast, it's hard for me to keep up.

Hogan   He got a father?

Beat.

Veronica   Yes. Both of my children do, actually.

Hogan   Oh hey. I didn't mean to, uh —

Veronica   And the father of both of my children passed away two years ago. All right?

Hogan   Oh jeez. Sorry.

Veronica   Thank you.

Beat.

Hogan   How?

Veronica   Hit and run. On the street in front of our building.

Hogan   Well shit.

Beat.

Veronica   Excuse me. I'm going to bring the children their lunch.

She exits.

Hogan   I'll see what I can do about the water heater.

Scene Three

That Evening. **Veronica** *alone. She looks troubled. She tries to settle down to read a paperback. Her cell phone rings.*

Veronica   Charles? Hi, thanks for calling me back. I'm fine. We're—Yes, everything is fine but I needed to tell you something, you'll probably hear it from Mia. There was a little incident today out on the lake. It — No, everything's fine, but she — Charles? Can you hear me? Charles? Sorry, is this better? I'm just losing you a little up here. Is that any better? Charles? Shit.

She moves to a different part of the room.

Hi. I'm sorry. The service up here — Yes, okay. Well look all it was was Mia was out swimming with my kids and she got out a little far and must have got a mouthful of water. Excuse me? No. No. I was out there with them, I was right on the shore. No I wasn't swimming. I was just watching them and I – Charles. Charles. I'm gonna tell you the whole story all right? Just hold on. She got out a little far and got a mouthful of water and went under a second so I jumped in and pulled her out, the whole thing wasn't more than maybe ten seconds and everything was fine after, I gave them all hot chocolate and everybody's good but I just wanted you to hear it from me right away. I don't think so. No, you don't have to come up. She's having a great time. Uh-huh.

Hogan *knocks and enters. He carries a carton of eggs.*

Well you did say she had passed her Red Cross test. Well actually she wasn't even out farther than she could stand, it was just one of those things where she opened her mouth at the wrong time and got a face-full of water and then got scared, it could've happened in the bathtub. I know, she swims better than my kids. She's asleep now. Ate a big supper, uh-huh. Hot dogs and baked beans. No, I got her the tofu dogs. Yeah I'll have her call you first thing. What? You're cutting out. Hello? – I'll have her call you in the morning —

(*She hangs up.*) Asshole.

Hogan   Uh-oh. Salty language! (*Beat.*) You need to call him back?

Veronica   What? No.

Hogan   He wasn't mad, was he?

Veronica   Sorry, do you want to tell me what you're doing back here?

Hogan   Just making sure everything's okay.

Veronica   Everything is fine.

Hogan   The water heater —

Veronica   It's fine! It was fine at four o'clock when you got done fixing it!

Hogan   Just because it was running before doesn't mean it stayed running long enough to heat up the tank. I thought you'd appreciate me coming back to check up on it. And I brought you some eggs.

He goes to put them in the fridge.

Veronica   Eggs?

Hogan   From my brother's.

Veronica   What, does he keep chickens or something?

Hogan   No.

Beat.

Veronica   I see you found some dry clothes.

Hogan   Yeah.

Veronica   Good thing you didn't clear out those drawers like you said, you got plenty of extra clothes around the place.

She gets settled again on the couch.

Hogan   What are you reading?

Veronica   Mystery.

Hogan   Any good?

Veronica   Yeah, I'd like to finish it.

Beat.

Hogan   He wasn't blaming you, was he? The dad.

Veronica   He was just concerned.

Hogan   Why'd you say "asshole" then?

Veronica   I didn't.

Hogan   Yeah you did.

Veronica   Oh whatever, he was just worried about his little girl.

Hogan   He wanted to come get her?

Veronica   What difference does it make?

Hogan   You think he doesn't trust you?

Veronica   I don't care if he trusts me or not.

Hogan   Seems like you do.

Veronica   He trusts me, he let me take his girl for the week. He's just one of those parents, you know, one of those parents.

Hogan   What kind?

Veronica   You know.

Hogan   White?

Veronica   What? No!

Hogan   Sorry.

Veronica   I mean, yes he is, but that's not what I mean.

Hogan   Uh-huh.

Veronica   I mean that kind of New York parent like, Oh she's got a nut allergy so if you have even one almond anywhere in the house it's an emergency. And makes his kid wear a helmet all the time. Pushing her on a swing at the playground. Like she's going sky-diving.

Hogan   Really? On a swing?

Veronica   Maybe not that. But like that.

Hogan   You were making peanut butter sandwiches earlier.

Veronica   I gave her plain jelly! She ain't gonna go into anaphylactic shock looking at the Skippy jar! And guess what? If she does I got an epi pen. I've got everything. I could perform open heart surgery with the kit I brought up here. I'm *equipped*. So don't go and sort of imply that . . .

Hogan   That what?

Veronica   Whatever. It doesn't matter. Oh and by the way. Something else you forgot to clear out your drawers before we got here, your magazines. My little boy found them. I put them in a bag by the door, you can take them when you go.

Hogan   What's the big deal? So I left some hunting and fishing magazines—

Veronica   It wasn't just hunting and fishing. You left something else mixed in there.

Hogan   Oh.

Veronica   Yeah, "Oh." So tonight I got a seven-year-old showing me —

Hogan   Yeah, okay, that is my fault.

Veronica   Thanks a lot.

Hogan   That is a little embarrassing, I'm sorry about that.

Veronica   You should be.

Hogan   Oh come on, it's not so strange. You're a nurse.

Veronica   What does that mean?

Hogan *shrugs.*

All right. If you don't mind, I'm gonna read my book and then I'm gonna go to bed so good *night*, for heaven's sake.

Hogan   Okay. I'll be out in the truck if you need anything.

He starts to go.

Veronica   Wait.

Hogan   What?

Veronica   Out in the *truck*?

Hogan   Way down the drive. Near the road. You can't see it from here.

Veronica   Is that where you've been while you were waiting to check the water heater? Sitting in your truck the whole time?

Hogan   Sort of.

Veronica   What do you mean sort of?

Hogan   Well since it's come up . . . I've sort of been sleeping out there.

Veronica   *What?*

Hogan   Debbie kicked me out.

My sister-in-law. I mean, she didn't so much kick me out as make it clear she didn't want me staying there at all while you were renting. And my brother's too pussy-whipped to say no. Can you believe that? My little brother.

Veronica   How long have you been out there?

Hogan   I guess more or less since you arrived.

Veronica   Oh my God.

Hogan   Did you know I was there?

Veronica   No I didn't know you were there!

Hogan   So what's the problem?

Veronica   I'm renting this place! Do you understand that? *I am renting this property.* You are not supposed to be *on the property*.

Hogan   Come on, I'm barely on the property.

Veronica   No. I am sick of this. This is bullshit.

Hogan   What?

Veronica   This is one of the biggest mistakes I ever made. Renting this rat-hole, and you skulking around the property like some weird freak—I'm sorry but that's what you are, you are freaking me out! I am done with this.

Hogan   What do you mean?

Veronica   I am done. We are leaving.

Hogan   The kids are sleeping.

Veronica   First thing in the morning. Right now I want you out of here. Go. Park your truck ELSEWHERE. Do you understand me?

Hogan   You're acting like I'm dangerous or something.

Veronica   I will call the police. I swear I will call 911.

Hogan   You think I'm dangerous? You're lucky I was around here today!

Veronica   Yeah, 'cause you were skulking around like the creepy oddball you are.

Hogan   I wasn't —

Veronica   Creepy backwoods oddball freak!

Hogan   You should be *thanking* me!

Veronica   Oh just shut up and get out of here, will you please? We'll be gone in the morning. Then you can move back into this dump, with your hockey sticks and your sleazy magazines —

Hogan   You're the dangerous one.

Veronica   Excuse me?

Hogan   Kids who can barely swim — yeah, I watched them, they're not as good as you think they are — Leaving those kids all by themselves in the water while you're off God knows where.

Veronica   No. Don't you *dare* suggest —

Hogan   And it's pretty convenient, isn't it? This threat to leave. Given that you still owe me a third of the rent.

Veronica   It's not a threat and you ain't never getting that money. Ever! This whole deal is *over*! Will you just get out of here now Hogan? Now?

Hogan   Where did you go anyway?

Veronica   What?

Hogan   While the kids were swimming.

Veronica   Nowhere.

Hogan   You weren't in the house.

Veronica   I got a phone call. It was important. I had to walk down the road to get a decent *signal* — I told them to come up on the beach —

Hogan   You should have just asked me. I would've stopped work, watched the kids.

Veronica   Look, what do you want? You want me to thank you again?

Hogan   You never thanked me the first time. After I jumped in the lake, saved a drowning child.

Veronica   I was right there the second I heard her yell!

Hogan   After you heard her yell maybe the third or fourth time.

Veronica   Third time, first time, who cares?

Hogan   Well I was already there pulling her out and you just seem pissed off about it

Veronica   I'm not.

Hogan   You sure have been acting pissed off about it.

Veronica   Sorry. I — I'm glad you helped me out. I am. But I was just down the road within earshot and three more seconds I would have waded in and grabbed her wrist just like you did only you beat me to it.

Hogan   Little girl drowning and you make a phone call.

Veronica   Oh for God's sake she wasn't *drowning*, she —

(*The phone rings.* **Veronica** *jumps.*) Jesus.

Hogan   Maybe you should get that.

Veronica   Why?

Hogan   She's gonna let it ring until somebody picks up.

Veronica   Who?

Hogan   Debbie. My sister in law? Please, just see what she wants. I can't deal with her.

Veronica   That's your problem.

Hogan   She knows I'm here. She's done this before. That phone's gonna keep ringing.

Veronica   So answer it.

Hogan   Uh-uh. No way.

Veronica   Hogan. Pick up the phone.

Hogan   No.

Veronica   It's gonna wake the kids.

Hogan   Yeah, I know, so you better pick it up.

Veronica   It's your phone. Pick up the goddamn phone.

Hogan   No. (*It keeps ringing.*)

Veronica   Jesus. (*She goes to the phone, furious, and picks up.*)

What. Yes I am the renter. Who is this? Well you can tell me your name too. Uh-huh. Well my name is Veronica Barnes. B-A-R-N-E-S. That's right. Because he rented to me. No we are not "friends." On the internet. Well you're gonna have to talk to him about that.

Hogan *gestures "I'm not here."*

Again, those are issues you will have to take up with your brother-in-law. He's —

Veronica *looks at* **Hogan**, *who makes pleading gestures. Beat.*

No. He's not here right now. Why would he be? It's nine o'clock at night. I don't know where he is. Uh-huh. All right. I don't have a piece of paper. Okay . . .

(*A pause as she listens.*) I see. Okay. I will. Goodbye.

She hangs up.

Hogan   Thanks.

You didn't have to do that.

Beat.

Veronica   She was rude.

Hogan   I told you. What did she want?

Veronica   She said you need to call her. Something about a lawsuit.

Hogan   Yep. Knew it. Remember I told you about that lawsuit over the stupid dock, which wasn't even my fault in the first place! These people on the Homeowner's Association don't care, they just want to see how dry they can squeeze me. You want to know the real bitch of it? I'm a member of the Homeowner's Association! This was my Dad's cabin. I was on the board even for a while in the nineties. So it's like I'm suing myself. It's like if I lose this case I got to go bankrupt trying to pay damages to myself!

Veronica   No, it's not like that at all.

You got a lawyer?

Hogan   Sort of.

Veronica   What do you mean "sort of"?

Hogan   Debbie's a lawyer.

Veronica   Yeah, she sounded like one.

Hogan   What'd she say?

Veronica   Something about, she's worked out a compromise . . . that the homeowner's association is willing to drop the complaint, but you got to vacate the property.

Hogan   What?

Veronica   That's what she said.

Hogan   Oh that is just bullshit! Who said she could even negotiate on my behalf? She never formally agreed to represent me. Vacate the property? What does that even mean?

Veronica   It sounds pretty obvious.

Hogan   It's bullshit! It's a blatant conflict of interest! My brother and I co-own the property. It was left to us jointly. So she comes along and negotiates a "compromise" that just happens to produce the outcome she's wanted all these years, which is to get the place all to herself? It's ridiculous! It'll never stand up in a court of law. I'll appeal. I'll appeal this all the way to the Supreme Court if I have to.

Veronica   What are you talking about? You're not even in court.

Hogan   "Vacate." She is just completely out of control.

Veronica   Maybe if you asked her before you rented she wouldn't be so upset.

Hogan   I don't have to ask her permission.

Veronica   Maybe you do. If you co-own the place. And they pay the utilities — she must have paid the phone bill. And you didn't even ask them before you put it online. You didn't even tell them till a few days ago.

Hogan   She told you that?

Veronica   Yes.

Hogan   Why are you on her side all of a sudden?

Veronica   I'm not on anybody's side. But it seems like maybe she's got a point. Especially if you're keeping all the rental money for yourself.

Hogan   What? She told you that too?

Veronica   No. That I just figured.

Beat.

Hogan   Look, here's the thing. She comes here — they all come here to use the lake in the summer, right? Her and my brother and their kids. I have my own kid I'd like to bring up here! But I can't, right? I can't, and they act like they're the only one with any right to it. They just show up whenever they want. Sometimes they want to have cook-outs with other families. Parties . . . The girls — they got twin girls, my nieces — they both drive now, they show up on their own, bring their boyfriends — I'm living here!

Veronica   So don't live here.

Hogan   WHERE THE HELL AM I SUPPOSED TO GO?

Veronica   How do I know? God, I'm sick of listening to you complain. I got problems of my own!

Hogan   Oh boo-fuckin'-hoo.

Veronica   You don't even know.

Hogan   At least you got your kids with you, you know? Count your fucking blessings. And a fancy job —

Veronica   I lost my job.

Beat.

Hogan   The nursing job?

Veronica   Yes.

Hogan   When?

Veronica   Week before I came up here.

Beat.

Hogan   That why you never paid me the last third of the rent?

Veronica *gives a dismissive gesture.*

You should have just told me. Look, it happens.

Veronica   Not to me.

Hogan   It's happened to me maybe twenty, thirty times.

Veronica   Yeah well you're a loser.

Beat.

Hogan   You didn't have to say that.

Veronica   Sorry.

Hogan   Not just losers who get laid off.

Veronica   I didn't get laid off.

Hogan   You got fired?

She makes a "bingo" gesture.

Still doesn't mean it was your fault.

Veronica   Oh it was, there's no doubt about that.

Hogan   Come on.

Veronica   It was.

Hogan   What'd you do, poison somebody? Give em the wrong injection?

Veronica   No.

Hogan   What?

Veronica   It doesn't matter.

Hogan   Did you —

Veronica (*Near tears*)   I REALLY DON'T WANT TO TALK ABOUT THIS ANYMORE, IF YOU DON'T MIND.

Beat.

Hogan   Look. Finish the week. I'll stay out of the way. I'll go in town during the day and at night I'll park at the far end of the property and be gone again at daybreak, you won't see or hear me. I'll clear up all the stuff with my family, it won't affect you. Those kids are having a good time. You don't want to disappoint them and you don't want a hassle from that girl's dad for bringing her back early. You don't want to waste your car rental. And the weather's supposed to be terrific next few days. I'll even spring for the inner tubes. Okay? Now you're never gonna get a better deal than that.

He puts out his hand. Beat. Then **Veronica** *reluctantly shakes it.*

All right.

He starts to go.

Veronica   Hogan.

He stops.

Thank you. For the girl.

Hogan   Any time.

Beat.

Veronica   Can I ask you something?

Hogan   Sure.

Veronica   Why can't you bring your own daughter up here?

Beat.

Hogan   I sent her an email back in May. Guess what? I'm finally building that diving platform. It'll be ready this summer. You can come up and visit. This is before I even knew she'd be going to school an hour away. You can swim. The cabin's still here. The lake's the same as it ever was. Everything's the same. It bounced back. She changed her email. I called her mother to get the new one. She said, in this voice, this very precise voice, she said she was asked, by our daughter, not to give it to me, and she felt she should respect our daughter's preference.

(*Shrugs.*) Well, that's her preference.

He exits.

FADE.

Scene Four

Night. **Veronica** *bagging surplus groceries. She starts to fold a pile of kids' clothes. She stops for a moment, listening to the night. It's quiet. Beat.*

The sounds of a truck. Headlights in the window. Motor turns off. Truck door opens and closes. Lights stay on.

Veronica   Hogan?

Hogan (*off*)   Yep.

Veronica   Turn those lights off.

Hogan   Oh.

The lights go off. **Hogan** *enters. A bottle of Old Granddad. He looks a little unsteady.*

Hogan   Told you I'd stay away.

Veronica   Uh huh.

Beat.

Hogan   Getting ready to go?

Veronica   Yes.

Hogan   Tomorrow morning.

Veronica   Yep.

Hogan   How were your last days? Was I right about the weather or what?

Veronica   They were real nice.

Beat.

Hogan   Just thought I'd check to see you needed anything else before you go.

Veronica   No, I think we're okay, thanks.

Oh. One of my kids broke a cereal bowl. You tell me how much it cost and I'll pay for it.

Hogan   That's all right.

Veronica   No, take it out of the damage deposit. I don't want to –

Hogan   It's just a bowl. Forget it.

Beat.

Did we end up doing a damage deposit?

Veronica   Yeah, in the first two payments, remember?

Hogan   Right, yes.

Oh – But your third payment never –

Veronica   We said we'd forget about all that.

Hogan   Right, right, right right right.

Veronica   Let's not go through this again, please. I've had a real nice couple days –

Hogan   Of course. No.

Beat.

Veronica   So you still have to return my damage deposit.

Hogan   Yes. Absolutely. I'll do a quick walk-through tomorrow, then send it off first thing.

Beat.

Veronica   Oh, I dropped a coffee mug too. I tried to glue it but it wouldn't glue so I threw it out.

Hogan   Don't worry about it.

Unless it was my 1980 Lake Placid Miracle on Ice mug.

Veronica   I think it was, yeah.

Hogan   Shit.

Veronica   I'll pay for it.

Hogan   That was a collector's item. There's no way you can afford to replace it. If you could even find a replacement.

Veronica   Well you shouldn't have left it here if it was so valuable.

Hogan   I didn't think you'd *use* it.

Veronica   Why wouldn't I use it? It's a coffee mug.

Hogan   It's clearly a collector's item.

Veronica   Then you shouldn't have left it on the shelf with all the other cups and glasses.

If it's so important to you –

Hogan   Never mind, just forget it.

Veronica   I'll pay for it.

Hogan   FORGET IT I SAID.

Veronica   I'm sorry.

Beat.

Hogan   So I brought you something. Little farewell gift.

He gives her a wrapped present.

Just to sort of say no hard feelings kind of thing.

Veronica   Oh. Well, thank you.

Hogan   Open it.

She does. It's a book.

Veronica   "A Child's First Book of Birds."

Hogan   See I saw this and I thought this would be the one for a seven year old. See it's got pop-up pages? And you can pull that flap and make the wings beat, there's a bunch of stuff like that, and check this out:

He presses a button and the book emits a bird-call.

For each one you can hear the actual call. That's pretty incredible, huh? Tiny little speaker in there somehow. So your boy can really learn them now.

Veronica   That's – Thank you very much. That's very . . .

Hogan   Of course you're leaving. But there's birds in the City too, right?

Veronica   Yes.

Hogan   There's an inscription.

She flips to it, reads.

Veronica   "To Veronica, with affection and respect, Terry Hogan."

Hogan   Of course it's really for your son, but I didn't know his name.

Veronica   I'm really . . . thank you, Hogan. I don't know what to say.

Hogan   Okay then.

He starts to go. Stops.

Oh. Uh. Earlier today . . .

Veronica   Yeah?

Hogan   I guess around dinner time I saw – I saw a car pull in here. I wasn't watching the place or anything. I was just parked in the woods off the road in and I happened to notice –

Veronica   It was your brother.

Hogan   Shit. I thought so. Did he give you a hard time?

Veronica   No. He was perfectly nice. Apologized for everything. I said there was nothing to apologize for.

Hogan   Oh well that's good.

Veronica   He was looking for you.

Maybe you oughta talk to him.

Hogan   Where'd you say I'd gone?

Veronica   Nowhere. I didn't know where you went.

Beat.

He knows you're hiding from him.

Hogan   I wasn't hiding from him.

Veronica   Whatever, avoiding him.

Hogan   I just went to get something to drink.

Veronica   Well it looks like you succeeded.

Now maybe you should go now, finish your drink in your truck.

Hogan   You really don't think much of me, do you?

I'm not gonna sit and just guzzle this down alone in the woods in my truck.

I use a glass.

Veronica   Okay.

Hogan   Can I borrow a glass?

Veronica   It's your cabin.

He goes, gets a glass, returns.

Hogan   You want some?

Veronica   No.

Beat.

Hogan   Okay then. I guess that's it. I won't be around here in the morning, so good luck and take care and all that.

He starts to go.

Veronica   Hogan.

You should give that money back.

Hogan   What money?

Veronica   The money your brother said you took from them.

Hogan   What?

Veronica   You heard me.

Hogan   It's bullshit.

Veronica   Uh huh.

Hogan   It's Debbie. She makes up these accusations. She hates me. You know, you've talked to her.

Veronica   He said it was a lot. Like five thousand dollars?

Hogan   (*Dismissive sound*)

Veronica   That sounds serious to me.

Hogan   It isn't true!

Veronica   It's not my problem either way. But it sounds like something you better work out.

Hogan   I will.

Veronica   Okay.

Beat.

Hogan   It's not true, though. My brother, he's basically a good kid. We used to be close before he got married. It's her. She poisons him. It's sad is what it is.

Veronica   You got a record already. Don't be stupid.

Hogan   I don't have a record. Is that what he told you?

She looks at him.

It wasn't anything *bad*. Jeez. Don't look at me like that.

Veronica   What was it?

Beat.

Hogan   Check-kiting.

Veronica   What's that?

Hogan   Writing bad checks, basically.

Veronica   You do it?

Hogan   I guess I did. I mean they proved it in court. It wasn't exactly intentional. I'm not some criminal mastermind. I have trouble keeping track of my net worth sometimes. It was more sloppiness than anything else.

Veronica   How long were you . . .

Hogan   14 months. You know, *that's* probably the thing with my brother. He's like me: bad at keeping track of stuff, a little disorganized, never balances his checkbook . . . Debbie probably noticed some kind of problem with their checking account or something, some little discrepancy, and in her mind, Oh, we're a little short this month, plus Convicted check-kiting brother-in-law I've never liked, *therefore inevitably equals* . . . she jumps to the obvious, or should I say most convenient, conclusion. I bet you anything that's what's going on here. Yeah?

Veronica   Sure, maybe.

Hogan   *Maybe*?

I would never. Not from my own *family*.

Veronica   Okay.

Hogan   You don't believe me.

Beat. She looks away.

Fine. Don't believe me then. I don't give a shit . . .

He grabs his glass and starts to go. The glass slips out of his hand and breaks.

Goddamn it.

He tries to clean it up.

Veronica   It's all right, I got it.

He tries to clean it up.

Hogan   Ow. Shit.

Veronica   What happened? You cut your hand?

Hogan   It's fine.

Veronica   Stop. You're bleeding.

Hogan   I'm okay. Never mind.

Veronica   You got a big piece of glass sticking out of your hand. Let me look at that.

Hogan   Leave me alone. Don't worry about it.

Veronica   Hold still you idiot.

She removes the glass.

Hogan   Ow!

Veronica   Hush. Just stay there.

She exits. He holds his T-shirt against his bloody hand. She returns with her bag.

Sit down. Sit *down* I said.

He sits. She starts to put on gloves.

Hogan   Oh come on, are you kidding me?

Veronica   We can do this right or not at all.

She starts to treat and bandage his hand.

Your hands ain't too clean.

You ain't too clean. When's the last time you did your laundry?

Hogan   Maybe I should just go outside, jump in the water.

Veronica   Nah, you don't want to do that. It's getting chilly.

Just maybe get yourself a shower and change your clothes, you been sleeping in that truck too much. That truck doesn't look too clean either. I'll let you take a shower here if you need to.

Beat.

Hogan   You must really think I'm a piece of shit, huh?

Beat.

Veronica   At least you rented to me.

Hogan   You were the only one responded to the ad.

Veronica   Well this wasn't the only house I looked at. I came up the week before and saw another place nicer. A lot nicer. But the sweet old lady who owned it took a look at me coming up the driveway and said you're too late dear it's just been rented.

Hogan   You gotta expect that kind of thing I guess.

Veronica   I expected it from you. I nearly got right back on the bus when I saw you the first time.

She finishes.

Better?

Hogan   Yeah. You're very good.

Veronica   Well thank you very much.

She cleans up the broken glass.

I sewed a man's finger back on once. Whole tip of his finger. His knife slipped chopping *lettuce*, he said. There were no doctors around, I put it back on for him. Fifteen minutes. He walked out of there, went back to his restaurant where he worked or wherever, I thought, I just put a man's finger back on his hand.

She throws out the glass. She returns.

Hogan   Why'd they fire you?

Beat.

Veronica   I wasn't what I said I was.

Hogan   What are you?

Veronica   I'm a nurse.

Hogan   That's what you said you were.

Veronica   I said I was a nurse practitioner.

Hogan   Oh yeah.

I'm still not that clear on the difference, to be honest.

Veronica   Well there's like a $30,000 a year difference.

Hogan   Okay, that I get.

So you exaggerated a little bit, I don't care.

Veronica   The *hospital* cared.

Beat.

Hogan   Oh. You told *them* –

Veronica   You know, you're like Sherlock Holmes. You're a fuckin genius.

Hogan   Sorry.

Beat.

Veronica   When my husband passed I'd done all the work for that degree except one year. The summer after he died I'd take the kids out sometimes to the beach or someplace? But that's just for the day. And it's a long day, and everybody gets cranky, and you're all exhausted and sandy on the train coming home, and the kids start fighting, and then you're just back in your apartment and somebody's got to make dinner … It's almost worse than when you left that morning. It's like you never went anywhere.

Hogan *nods.*

So when I saw that hospital job opened up … that perfect job I knew I could do as well as anybody … probably *better* …

Hogan   You tweaked your resume a little bit.

Veronica   I submitted a false *transcript*. I *lied* about my *credentials*.

Hogan   Huh.

Beat.

It's actually pretty impressive.

She glares.

I mean to pull that off.

Veronica   I didn't pull it off, that's the point!

Hogan   You did for a while. How'd you get caught?

Veronica   Another nurse in my department wrote a few too many prescriptions for her "friends". After she got arrested they went and did an extra background check on everybody.

Hogan   And they spotted your little creative, whatever.

Veronica   Now I'm probably even gonna lose my regular RN license. I have to go before a review board. I had to beg to get to do *that*. That's why they called. The other day. That's why I had to walk down the road. To beg for a chance to beg the board to keep my license.

Beat.

Hogan   Well I can see why you had to walk down the road to deal with that.

Veronica   I still can't believe I left the kids swimming, I felt so bad afterward I wanted to –

Beat.

So I don't think you're a – what you said. But listen. If you made a mistake, and there's any way to correct it . . . you should really try and correct it.

Hogan   I didn't take their damn money!

Veronica   Hogan.

Hogan   What do I have to say to convince you?

Veronica   I'm just trying to help you is all.

Hogan   Sounds like you're the one who needs help. Just cause you're walking around with a guilty conscience doesn't mean you have to start lecturing me –

Veronica   All right, forget I said anything.

Hogan   I mean it's my *family* for God's sake.

Veronica   All right! I'm sorry. Okay?

Hogan   Okay.

Beat.

Anyway, back to your thing. Here's my opinion:

Veronica   I didn't ask for your –

Hogan   I really don't think you should blame yourself. Okay yes, you screwed up. But it could have been a lot worse.

Veronica   How?

Hogan   Did you say you knew how to do something you didn't know how to do, kill a patient or something?

Veronica   No.

Hogan   All right. So that's a major plus right there. That's huge.

And you probably really needed to, right? Or you wouldn't have done it. You *almost* had the degree, right? The last year of school was probably bullshit anyway, just papers and exams and stuff, you want to move things along, you roll the dice a little bit. That's completely understandable! I mean it wasn't very intelligent but it's understandable.

And you're a good mother, hell you're a *great* mother. You want to take good care of your kids. You want to be able to give them nice vacations, get them swimming in a goddamn lake in the sunshine instead of indoors for once. Don't beat yourself up about it.

Veronica   No?

Hogan   No. You'll be all right. Don't worry. It's all gonna work out, you'll see.

Veronica   Maybe. Maybe I won't.

Hogan   Well, you know what they say. Bad luck runs in streaks. You know, one domino falls and then another one and then another one and another one. Bip, bip, bip, bip, bip. But eventually they have to stop, right?

Beat.

You know, when I got divorced –

Veronica   I really don't want to hear it.

Hogan   Okay.

Beat.

You want to go outside, shoot at some stuff?

She stares at him.

I've got a rifle in the truck. We can set up some bottles and cans on the road, blow off steam. I do it when I'm fed up sometimes. It's surprisingly relaxing.

Beat.

Veronica   You know, I think I would really enjoy that right now.

Hogan   Really?

Veronica   You know what would make it even more fun?

Hogan   What?

Veronica   Blindfolds.

He stares at her.

Hogan   You're messing with me.

She laughs.

Okay.

Beat.

What are you going to do? When you go back.

Veronica   I don't know. I don't know what's going to happen.

Beat. He drinks. He tentatively puts a hand on her thigh.

You're kidding, right?

He removes it.

Hogan   Right.

I'd better go.

He gets up, goes to the door.

Veronica   What are you gonna do? After we leave?

Hogan   No real plans.

I'll manage.

He waves, exits, goes out the truck.

The motor starts. Lights shine into the cabin for a moment, then swing away. It's dark again and quiet.

Beat.

She picks up the bird book. She presses one of the buttons. A bird call. She presses it again.

<u>FADE</u>.

Scene Five

January. The cabin looks uninhabited. Bottles, other rubbish. **Veronica** *appears outside. She knocks. No answer. Tentatively comes in. She has a couple of take-out bags.*

Veronica   Hogan? Hogan?

She looks around. She sets the bags down. While her back is turned, **Hogan** *enters, bleary.*

Hogan   I heard your voice. I thought I was dreaming.

Veronica   I knocked. You didn't answer.

Hogan   I was napping.

Beat.

Veronica   I brought you some coffee.

Hogan   I don't drink coffee. I'm a tea drinker.

Veronica   Oh.

(*Tentative*) Well there's some donuts too. And I got a couple butter rolls, in case you're hungry. And a fruit salad.

Hogan   A fruit salad?

Veronica   Yes. Are you hungry at all?

Hogan   What are you doing here?

Veronica   I have a . . .

(*Resets*) I came to see how you were doing.

Hogan   I'm fine.

Veronica   You want me to put that heater on?

Hogan   It's broken. I've been meaning to replace it.

Veronica   You don't look fine.

Hogan   You woke me up. What do you want?

Veronica   Look, I'm not sure how to . . .

Beat.

I got your envelope.

He says nothing. She digs in her handbag.

I got this envelope sent to my house. Did you send it?

I haven't seen you or talked to you for six months and this comes, no return address, no note, just cash. 4500 dollars cash money. Sent through the mail.

Hogan   So?

Veronica   Did you send it?

Hogan   Yes.

Veronica   Why?

Hogan   I thought you could use it. Given your situation.

Beat.

Veronica   I called here. The phone is, once again, disconnected. I call your brother –

Hogan   Oh Jeez, why?

Veronica   Because I'm looking for you to find out what's going on with this!

Hogan   You didn't tell them –

Veronica   I just asked to speak with you.

Hogan   I don't know why you went to all the trouble. That's what the money was for, to make things a little easier.

Veronica   You really thought I'd keep it?

Hogan   Why not?

Veronica   It's the money you took from your brother.

Hogan   Not all of it. I kept $500 for myself.

Veronica   It's stolen.

Hogan   No, it's missing. The only way they'd know it was stolen was if you showed up on their doorstep like an idiot and tried to give it back to them.

Veronica   I didn't try to give it back. I only talked to them on the phone. We didn't discuss it at all.

Hogan   Good. Keep it.

Veronica   You know I can't.

She sets it down.

Hogan   You find another job?

Veronica   Not yet.

Hogan   So don't you need it? What about your kids?

Veronica   They're – we're getting a little help right now.

Hogan   From who?

Veronica   Hogan. Just listen to me and let me do this. All right? Your brother said they've been trying to reach you but you won't talk to them.

He said he's driven out here and you won't come to the door.

Hogan   I probably wasn't home.

Veronica   He said one time you pulled a gun on him.

Hogan   Oh that is ridiculous.

Veronica   He said you came to the door with your shotgun.

Hogan   I don't have a shotgun. I have a rifle.

Veronica   Whatever.

Hogan   There's a difference. He should know that. It belonged to our Dad. It's a 1940s Remington. It's a collector's item. I might have been holding it when I came out but it's just because he was pounding on the door saying he was gonna kick it in.

Veronica   All right, whatever. I don't care about that. The point is they're worried about you.

Hogan   Right.

Veronica   They are. You think I wanted to get involved with this? I wouldn't be up here if they hadn't begged me to give you a message.

Hogan   Why you?

Veronica   He said there isn't anybody else. Your wife didn't want to get involved, and your daughter just started –

Hogan   All right, never mind.

Veronica   Your daughter just started school, they don't want her upset –

Hogan   I DON'T WANT ANYBODY TALKING TO MY DAUGHTER.

Veronica   They know that! That's why when I called they asked me –

Hogan   Why the hell did they think I'd listen to you?

Veronica   That's what I said. He said you're his friend, aren't you?

Hogan   What'd you say?

Veronica   No, not exactly. But I said I'd try.

Hogan   Try what?

Beat.

Veronica   You can go back there, they said. They – just hear me out now. They asked me to tell you that they'll take you in. At least for a while. Let bygones be bygones. Til you can get things sorted out a little bit. Debbie agrees.

Hogan   You've got to be kidding me.

Veronica   It was her idea, I think. It sounded like she talked your brother into it. She told me. She said, Please try to convince him.

Hogan   Debbie said that.

Veronica   Yes.

Beat.

Hogan   That's why you came all the way up here? To deliver this "message"?

Veronica   Well, like I said, they were very concerned.

Hogan   (*Dismissive sound*)

Veronica   I'll tell you what. I'll drive over there with you if you want. Help you pack up whatever you need here. If there is anything. You shouldn't be staying here now anyway, it's freezing.

Hogan   It's fine once you get the heater on.

Veronica   The heater's *broken*, you said.

I can't be here all night, Hogan. I'd like to get home and put my kids to bed.

Maybe just let me take you over there so you can talk to them yourself?

Hogan   I got nothing to say to them.

Veronica   What would it hurt to stay a couple nights?

Hogan   If you think I'm leaving here you're crazy.

Veronica   Just til you can get yourself together a little bit.

Hogan   I don't need to get myself together!

Veroncia   Look *around.*

Hogan   No. You don't – somehow you have got the wrong idea here. I'm fine, all right? I'm perfectly fine. I know the place could use some straightening up, I've been meaning to get to that but I've been busy, and – You really didn't need to come up here. I don't need any help.

He picks up the cash.

For God's sake I was trying to help *you*!

Veronica   I don't want that kind of help.

Hogan (*Shouts*)   And I don't want your FUCKING SYMPATHY.

He throws the money at her. It flies everywhere.

WE'RE NOT FRIENDS. YOU DON'T KNOW ME. I WANT YOU OFF MY PROPERTY.

Veronica   Oh what, are you gonna pull a gun on me now?

Hogan   TRY ME.

Veronica   GODDAMN IT HOGAN, THEY SAID YOU NEARLY DIED.

Beat.

Debbie said –

Hogan (*scorn*)   *Debbie.*

Veronica   When they pulled you out of the lake –

Hogan   She wasn't there. She doesn't know what she's talking about.

Veronica   "Severe hypothermia." That's no joke. I've seen it.

Hogan   She's making it out a lot worse than it was.

Veronica   You were in the hospital. She said you were unconscious and you didn't wake up for two days.

Hogan   That's an exaggeration.

Veronica   That's a *coma*, Hogan. If whoever it was, that neighbor, hadn't seen you in the ice –

Hogan   There was hardly any ice, the lake never freezes over anymore.

Look, I'm not saying it was a great situation or that I'm not grateful for the help, but you have to understand Debbie's agenda here. Bottom line, she would like to have me declared incompetent. You remember all that shit from last summer. Short of my actual death, that would be the best possible outcome for her. That would get her everything she wants.

Veronica   I only talked to the woman a couple times but she really didn't seem that bad, she –

Hogan   She *hates* me. There is *nothing* she wouldn't say or do. She once ordered me – you are not going to believe this – to "stay the hell away" from her children! What the hell is that? I don't have my own kid around – I'm missing her for Chrissake! – if I offer to take my nieces to the movies or over to Putnam Lanes once in a while – Jesus Christ. This is the woman who accused me of stealing from her –

Veronica   That was true.

Hogan   That was a *fraction* of the money that I would have realized from the sale of this property – from which they were trying to have me vacated, remember? On the way to them taking the whole place for themselves. This is just one more excuse for them to get me out of their way –

Veronica   How the hell did you wind up in the Lake, then?

Beat.

Hogan   Well that –

Veronica   In January.

Hogan   It was an accident.

Veronica   What kind of accident?

Hogan   All right. I admit it sounds a little silly now.

I was trying to fix the dock.

Veronica   In January?

Hogan   I always felt bad about not fully completing that project. And I was out here . . .

I went through kind of I guess you'd call it a rough patch after last summer, you know, after you and your family had gone. I didn't stay here—it didn't seem wise, with all the tensions with my brother and sister-in-law, so there was a period there when I didn't have a firm base of operations, I was sort of floating more or less, you know, sleeping in the truck most nights. But I drove over here one day a couple weeks ago, gorgeous morning, just to check the place out, and it was so clear and sunny I just thought—there had been a little light snowfall the night before so even though the lake only had the thinnest skin of ice on the surface it *looked* thick, with the snow resting on it, it looked like it used to look when we were kids and we could skate after a big freeze.

Veronica   You didn't –

Hogan   What? No. I'm not an idiot. I knew I couldn't walk on it. I took the canoe. But it was such a gorgeous day—I don't know what it was like down in the city but up here it was gorgeous—I guess I just felt like this is the kind of day when you can do *anything*, you know. And maybe I was overambitious before, with the diving platform, but I've still got the lumber I bought, I can at least go out and replace some of the bad planks in the deck. It won't solve the pilings issue but maybe I can get us through another summer or two. I must have just slipped.

Beat.

Veronica   I see.

Hogan   The whole thing is sort of embarrassing in retrospect.

Beat. She's staring at him.

What?

Veronica   They said . . . they found you in the water at night. Not the daytime. At night.

And you were stripped down to your underwear they said.

Beat.

Hogan (*quietly*)   They would say that.

She takes a step toward him.

Veronica   Please. You don't have to –

He backs away, knocking into a chair. Something snaps. He kicks the chair over. Knocks everything off a table. Smashes a lamp. A brief but destructive rampage. He stops, breathing hard.

He puts his face in his hands, weeps. Veronica watches. A long beat.

She goes, gets one of the bags. Takes out some napkins. Hands them to him. He wipes his eyes, collects himself.

Beat.

Veronica   I'm gonna have one of those coffees before it gets too cold.

She takes a coffee. She picks some of the money up off the couch.

You sure you don't want a donut?

Beat.

Hogan   What kind?

Veronica   Glaze or plain.

Hogan   Glaze.

Veronica   Good, I like plain.

They eat. Long beat.

Hogan   Who's with your kids?

Veronica   What?

Hogan   Who's taking care of your children?

Veronica   Oh. Charles. Mia's father. My little girl's friend?

Hogan   The helmet guy?

Veronica   Turns out he's not so bad. I don't see why a 10 year old needs to be a vegetarian, but whatever.

Hogan   He the one helping you?

Veronica   Yes.

Beat.

The board said no. The license board?

Hogan   Oh yeah. Shit.

Veronica   But Charles knows someone who places health care providers with stay-at-home patients. It's not ideal. It's not like hospital work. But I can't be too picky right now. So that might work out, but it hasn't yet.

Hogan   You sleeping with him?

Veronica   What? Shut up.

Hogan   Are you?

Veronica   He's *married*. (*Beat.*) Separated. (*Beat.*) I don't know what we're doing.

Hogan   Well. Congratulations.

Veronica   I guess.

Beat.

Hogan   You want to hear something funny?

Veronica   God yes.

Hogan   I wasn't totally asleep when you drove up. I was kind of dozing. Kind of half asleep I guess. That's why I was so confused to see you, I thought I might be dreaming.

You know what I was thinking about?

Veronica   No.

Hogan   I was thinking about going down to the city sometime.

Veronica   Yeah?

Hogan   Yeah, I had this kind of fantasy I guess you'd call it.

She looks at him.

It doesn't involve you, don't worry.

Veronica   I'm not. That's not what I thought.

Hogan   My daughter's at school there now, right? I was thinking about this the other day. What's to stop me getting in the truck and driving down?

I don't have her contact information but she's in one of the dorms someplace. How many dorms could there be? She's on a soccer scholarship. It shouldn't be that hard to find the playing fields. Anyway, I could track her down and take her to lunch.

(*Smiles*) I've got the cash.

We could go someplace really up-market. White tablecloth kind of thing. Actually, she's 18, she probably wouldn't want that. What do 18 year olds like? I'd hate for it just to be pizza. Whatever, that doesn't matter. I picture just surprising her on the street outside her dorm as she's coming in from practice. Like she turns a corner and I'm standing there and she stops and I just say "Can I buy you lunch?"

And maybe it would be a little awkward at first. I mean of course it would be. Maybe she'd want to bring along a friend.

That would be fine, if it would make her more comfortable. A couple friends. The more the merrier, long as I'm buying.

You could even come. With your kids, I mean we'd have to coordinate a little bit, I'm not sure how that fits in with the rest of it, the spontaneous part, but we could get a big round table someplace like a Chinese restaurant, with the dishes in the middle and one of those spinning disks, what are they called?

Veronica   Lazy Susan.

Hogan   Right. You can just turn it and everybody can help themselves to whatever they want.

Veronica   That sounds good.

Beat.

Hogan   I'm not going over there –

Veronica   Just eat. We don't have to decide that right now.

Hogan   Will you let me finish?

I'm not going over there with anybody thinking it wasn't an accident.

Veronica   So it was an accident. We all have accidents.

Beat.

Okay. I'll tell you something funny too.

Hogan   What?

Veronica   My last night here? Back in August? I was sitting right there packing up the kids stuff, folding their clothes . . .

Hogan   Yeah?

Veronica   We had an okay couple days you know, toward the end, and I was sitting there alone and it was nice and quiet for once, those damn crickets and frogs had shut up . . .

Hogan   They do that when it's going to rain.

Veronica   Really?

Hogan   Yep.

Veronica   How do they know?

Hogan   I don't know. Air pressure maybe?

Veronica   Huh.

Anyway. You know what I remember thinking? Even after everything that happened that week?

That I wish I could just stay here. In this shitty little cabin.

Beat. She laughs. He laughs too.

Hogan   Well, we can't.

Veronica   No.

CURTAIN.

The New York Idea

Adapted from the original (1906) by Langdon Mitchell

The New York Idea opened at the Lucille Lortel Theater, produced by Atlantic Theater Company, on January 26, 2011 with the following cast and director:

Directed by Mark Brokaw.
Mrs. Philimore: Patricia O'Connell
Miss Heneage: Patricia Conolly
Thomas: Tom Patrick Stephens
Sudley: Peter Maloney
Cynthia Karslake: Jaime Ray Newman
Philip Philimore: Michael Countryman
Matthew Philimore: Joey Slotnick
Fiddler: John Keating
John Karslake: Jeremy Shamos
Wilfred Cates-Darby: Rick Holmes
Vida Philimore: Francesca Faridany
Jacqueline: Mikaela Feely-Lehmann

Characters:

Mrs. Philimore, elderly
Miss Heneage, elderly
Sudley, 50s

Cynthia Karslake, 30
Philip Philimore, late 40s
Matthew Philimore, late 30s

Wilfred Cates-Darby, 30s
John Karslake, 30s

Vida Philimore, 30s

Thomas, a butler
Fiddler, a cockney
Jacqueline, a French maid

Act One

Scene One

Parlor of **Philip Philimore***'s house.* **Mrs. Philimore** *and* **Miss Heneage**. *Elaborate tea service.* **Mrs. Philimore** *reads from a card.*

Mrs. Philimore   "Mr. Philip Philimore and Mrs. Cynthia Deane Karslake announce their marriage, May twentieth, Nineteen hundred and six, at three o'clock, Eleven, Washington Square, New York."

What do you think?

Miss Heneage   In my opinion it barely escapes sounding nasty.

Mrs. Philimore   I have spent the afternoon struggling to find the proper form of announcement.

Miss Heneage   That you have failed should not come as a surprise, there being no proper form of wedding announcement between two divorced persons. The only remaining question is to whom the announcement should *not* be sent. The person I shall ask counsel of is Cousin William Sudley. He promised to drop in this afternoon.

Mrs. Philimore   Oh! We shall hear all about Cairo.

Miss Heneage   William is judicious.

Thomas *enters.*

Thomas   Mr. Sudley.

Miss Heneage   Ah!

Sudley *enters. The Women rise.* **Thomas** *exits.*

Heneage & Phillimore   Dear William!

Sudley   Mary. How do you do? Sarah.

Mrs. Philimore   How was your winter? Was it very warm in Egypt?

Sudley   Very. Enough idle chatter. I know I need not say I consider Philip's engagement *excessively* regrettable.

Miss Heneage   Do sit down, William.

Sudley   It's outrageous! He is a judge upon the Supreme Court bench with a divorced wife! And such a divorced wife!

Mrs. Philimore   Would you like some tea?

Sudley   Cream, no sugar.

Miss Heneage   What do you mean, "such a divorced wife?" Have you had news of her?

Sudley   Worse than that. We saw her in Cairo.

Mrs. Philimore   In Cairo!

Sudley   We had not been there a week when who should turn up but Vida Philimore. She went everywhere and did everything no woman should!

Mrs. Philimore   What did she do?

Sudley   She "did" Cleopatra! At the tableaux at Lord Errington's! She "did" Cleopatra, and she did it robed only in some diaphanous material of a nature so transparent that she appeared to be draped in *moonshine*.

That was only the beginning. As soon as she heard of Philip's engagement – and somehow she got the news before I did – she gave a dinner in honor of it.

Miss Heneage (*scandalized*)   What?

Sudley   To which *only divorcées* were asked.

Mrs. Philimore   Are there so many in Egypt?

Sudley   *And* she had a dummy – yes, my dears, a *dummy* – dressed as Philip, seated at the head of the table!

Mrs. Philimore   Oh dear.

Miss Heneage   I disapprove of Vida Philimore.

Sudley   Of course you do. We all do. Let us pray we never have dealings with her again. Now. This . . . *person* Philip is marrying. What is she called again?

Miss Henage   Mrs. Karslake.

Mrs. Philimore   Cynthia. She's just in her room upstairs. She'll be down in a minute.

Sudley   She's not staying here.

Mrs. Philimore   Yes. Mrs. Karslake has no New York house –

Sudley   So the *divorced* woman to whom your *divorced* son – (*to* **Miss Heneage**) *your* divorced *nephew* – is engaged, is *living in your home*?

Miss Heneage   *I* invited her. I disliked the publicity of a hotel in the circumstances.

Sudley   Who is she?

Miss Heneage   She was a Deane.

Sudley (*grudging*)   Her family is an old one. Though the fortune is lost, is it not?

Miss Heneage   Her father was profligate.

Mrs. Philimore   But you cannot blame the girl for that. She was brought up in France and England, in a very gay set. She is what is called a "sporty" woman.

Sudley   Sporty?

Miss Heneage   She is not conventional.

Sudley   And who was her husband?

Miss Heneage   John Karslake.

Mrs. Philimore   He owns Cynthia K.

Sudley   What?

Mrs. Philimore   The famous mare.

Miss Heneage   They were married only seven months.

Mrs. Philimore   Which is a blessing. There are no . . . hostages to fortune . . .

Sudley   And the wedding is to be tomorrow?

Miss Heneage   Tomorrow.

Sudley   Well. A respectable family; sadly we have no strong basis for rejecting her. But I think it will be impossible for me see the young woman. My disapprobation would make itself apparent.

Miss Heneage   I have concealed my own only with a heroic effort of will.

Sudley   The uncouth modern female, the gruesome "Gibson girl," with a cigarette in one hand and motoring goggles in the other – an habitué of the race track and the divorce court –

Cynthia *bursts in, reading a newspaper.*

Cynthia   Listen! Saratoga favorite, six to one, Rockaway, Rosebud and Flying Cloud. At the half, Rockaway forged ahead, when Rosebud under the lash made a bold bid for the lead . . . they were neck and neck for a quarter, then Flying Cloud slipped by the *pair* and won on the post by a nose in one forty nine! Oh I wish I'd been there!

(*Seeing* **Sudley**) Oh hello.

Miss Heneage   Cynthia, this is –

Cynthia   It must be Cousin William. They said you were coming.

Sudley   Yes.

Cynthia   How was Cairo? Are the pyramids as marvelous as they say?

Sudley   You must permit me, Mrs. Karslake . . .

Cynthia   Oh no *please* don't welcome me to the family. All that formal part is over, if you don't mind. I'm one of the tribe now. You're coming to the wedding tomorrow?

Sudley   I had not planned . . . It has never been my practice to –

Cynthia   Oh, but you *must* come! I mean to be a perfect wife to Philip and all his relations. That sounds rather miscellaneous, but you know what I mean.

Sudley   I am very much afraid I cannot.

Cynthia   If you don't come, you'll be a dreadful villain – it'll look like you're not standing by Philip in his hour of need. You'll come, won't you? Of course you will.

Sudley   At what hour did you say the alimony begins?

Miss Heneage *coughs.*

Ceremony.

Mrs. Philimore   Three P.M., William.

Sudley   I will come, Mrs. Karslake. Good afternoon.

(*going*) Good afternoon, Mary. Sarah.

Miss Heneage   Oh, William – I entirely forgot. In regard to the announcements – whom they shall be sent to and whom not. I require your advice –

She follows him out.

Cynthia   So that's cousin William.

Mrs. Philimore   Did you like him?

Cynthia   He couldn't have received me with more warmth.

Thomas *enters.*

Thomas   Mr. Philimore's sherry.

Mrs. Philimore *nods.* **Thomas** *sets glass and decanter on the sideboard.*

Mr. Philimore's *Post.*

He places that too, and arranges a chair, plumps a cushion, etc. **Cynthia** *watches this ritual.*

Mr. Philimore.

Philip *enters. End of a work day. He looks tired.*

Mrs. Philimore   Philip.

Philip   Hello, Mother.

He kisses her. On his way to his chair kisses **Cynthia**.

My dear.

Cynthia   Hello, Philip.

Mrs. Philimore   I'm going to my room to rest awhile.

Philip   What? Yes, good idea. See you at dinner.

Mrs. Philimore *exits.* **Philip** *sits.*

Thomas.

Thomas *pours and hands him a sherry. He drinks.* **Thomas** *opens the paper and presents it to* **Philip**, *who begins to read.*

Cynthia   How was your day, Philip?

Philip (*Noncommittal sound.*)

Beat.

Cynthia   Tell me about your courtroom today, Philip. Were there any shocking crimes?

Philip   No my dear. All rather routine.

Cynthia   Were the lawyers very long-winded?

Philip   To the point of catatonia.

Cynthia   Did you bang your gavel at them?

Philip   What? Oh, no, no . . .

Hmf.

Cynthia   What?

Philip   These damned anarchists. And the suffragettes are at it again, too. Well, let them blow each other up, I say.

Thomas *has been very discreetly and quietly refreshing the tea service, but even the slightest noise seems to annoy* **Philip**.

Cynthia   You seem a little more tired than usual.

Philip   I suppose I am. I hate to tell you that over a case today I actually slumbered.

Cynthia   It must have been a very dull case.

Philip   A hatmaker suing on seven counts.

Thomas *goes to blow out the alcohol lamp on the table. He has to blow twice.*

Confound it, Thomas! Can't we simply have a little peace?

Thomas   I'm sorry, sir.

Philip   Puffing and wheezing and blowing like an automobile in an ecstasy!

Thomas   I beg your pardon, sir.

Cynthia   It's fine, Thomas. You can go now.

Thomas *exits.*

Philip   Sorry Cynthia. It's just because I so value this time with you. This hour of sherry and serenity. It's quite as if we were married already.

Cynthia (*stares at him*)   Yes, it is.

She picks up her racing paper.

Philip   What's that you're reading?

Cynthia   Just running over the sporting news.

What? I fancied Rhododendron would come in an easy winner. He was blown off the track by Nonpareil!

Philip   The market is in a deplorable state of anemia . . .

Cynthia   Oh – he was ridden by Henslow. He's a rotten bad rider. No steel . . .

Philip   Hm – here's a report of my hat-maker's case. Haggerty v. Philimore.

Cynthia   Philimore? I thought you *heard* the case.

Philip   Yes. Oh, I see. Ah, the suit was brought by Haggerty, a hat-maker, against . . . well, Mrs. Philimore. The *former* Mrs. Philimore.

Cynthia   And you didn't remove yourself?

Philip   Why? Do you think me incapable of remaining impartial?

Cynthia   It's your former wife!

Philip   What difference could that possibly make?

Cynthia   How will you decide?

Philip   I expect I shall have to decide in her favor. Haggerty's plea was absurd on its face. Said he hadn't received payment for a *peacock-feather* hat. Preposterous. No such thing exists. How could it? It would be six feet high.

Cynthia   Did you see her?

Philip   No. Last I heard she was in Egypt.

Cynthia   Well that's good. I'm sure you'd find it very painful to see her again.

Philip (*mild*)   No.

Cynthia   No?

Philip   Why should I? Would you find it so impossible to meet Mr. –

Cynthia   Don't speak of him. He's nothing. I don't even wish to hear his name.

Philip   All right. But what if you should happen to run into him some time? At a party, or –

Cynthia   I won't.

Philip   We travel in the same legal circles. He's argued cases before me in the past and may do so again.

Cynthia   That's your business. I don't care. I never think of him and don't wish to. I never want to see his wretched face again.

She turns a page in her paper.

Agh!

Philip   What is it?

Cynthia   Nothing. A photograph. A photograph of . . . *Him.*

Philip   Him who?

Cynthia   Philip, *him*. My . . .

Philip   John Karslake?

Cynthia   I asked you not to say his name!

Philip   In the racing papers? Let me see.

She gives him the paper.

Philip   That looks like a horse.

Cynthia   It *is* a horse. He's standing beside it.

Philip   Oh yes, I see. And there's a woman who looks a little like you, my dear. Perhaps a bit younger.

Cynthia   That *is* me.

Philip   You didn't say you'd seen Karslake.

Cynthia (*taking the paper back*)   It's an *old photograph*, Philip. For goodness sake.

Philip   Well why on earth are they running it?

Cynthia   My God he's selling her!

Philip   Who?

Cynthia   My pet riding mare! The best horse he has. "Cynthia K." The best horse in the *world*. Look at her, she's an angel even in a photograph. He *can't* put her up for sale. Why would he do such a thing?

Philip (*looking in his own paper*)   Well here's your answer. Karslake's bankrupt.

Cynthia   What?

Philip   The financial column has it. Must be. He's put his country house up for sale, stables . . . something called the "morning star necklace" . . .

Cynthia   My necklace!

Philip   Not any more, now it's at Tiffany's. Here you are – and here I am! ". . . jewels of the former Mrs. Karslake, who is once again to enter the arena of matrimony with the well known and highly respected judge . . ." Well, that's good, anyway . . .

Cynthia   At least he hasn't sold my portrait.

Philip   Is it a Sargent portrait?

Cynthia   Yes.

Philip   Yes, he's selling that too. Sorry – "and the celebrated portrait by Sargent. . ."

Cynthia (*throwing down her paper*)   I can't stand it!

Philip   Now my dear –

Thomas *enters.*

Thomas   Reverend Philimore.

Philip   Matthew! How pleasant.

Matthew *enters.*

Hello Matthew.

Matthew   My dear brother. Good afternoon. I hope the tea's not gone.

Philip   I'm on sherry.

Matthew   Splendid, I'll join you. Dear Cynthia, how charming you look. Why weren't you in your pew yesterday?

Cynthia *tries to collect herself but she's still fuming.*

Cynthia   I . . . had a bit of a headache, Matthew, so I –

Matthew   Spent the morning watching the riders in the park?

She blushes.

Don't be embarrassed. To each his own form of worship, and I can't see that one's sense of awe at God's creation is any less profound when the object of contemplation happens to be a thoroughbred. However, you missed a most original sermon. My text was from Paul – "It is better to marry than to burn." It was a strictly logical sermon. I argued that, as the grass withereth, and the flower fadeth, there is nothing final in Nature, not even Death! And if Death is not final, why should marriage be final? And ergo, the necessity of divorce! You see? All New York was there, and all New York went away happy.

Cynthia   You're such an awful pagan. Here's your sherry.

Matthew   Thank you. (*Drinks.*) My dear, you have such a sad expression.

Cynthia   I don't.

Matthew   I feel as if I were of no use in the world when I see sadness on a young face.

Cynthia   If I'm sad it's only because I'm thinking of all the hours and hours I have to wait before your brother makes me the happiest woman in New York.

Matthew   Ah I see. And are you sure you want him? He is a very dull fellow.

Cynthia   He *is*, and that's what I like about him. He's loyal and steady and affectionate – a true friend. We were friends first, weren't we? – in those grim days when we were each learning the brutal truth that a divorcé has no place in society – and we're still friends, even into our engagement. He's become a lovely habit, one I intend to keep.

Philip   I certainly hope so.

She kisses him.

Thomas *enters.*

Thomas   Mr. John Karslake.

Cynthia   *What?*

Thomas (*checks the card again*)   Pardon me. Mr. John Karslake's *trainer,* Mr. Fiddler.

Philip   Really, Thomas. Will you please make a practice of reading the *entire card* before you speak?

Thomas   Sorry sir.

Fiddler *comes in.*

Fiddler   Afternoon, gentlemen. Ma'am.

Cynthia   Fiddler, what are you doing here?

Fiddler   Note for the Judge, ma'am. From Mr. Karslake.

He hands it to **Philip**.

Nice to see you again, ma'am.

Cynthia (*still rattled*)   Yes, it's lovely to –

Philip   He wishes to call.

Cynthia   Why?

Philip   He needs to see me on a matter of business.

Cynthia   He can come to your office!

Fiddler   Mr. K. said it's urgent, sir. Wants to stop by soon as possible.

Cynthia   Philip, *no.*

Philip   It's out of the question.

Fiddler   The guv'nor will be very disappointed sir.

Cynthia   Good.

Philip   I'm sorry, it can't be helped.

Fiddler   Right.

He starts to go.

Cynthia   Fiddler?

Fiddler   Ma'am?

Cynthia   How are the horses?

Fiddler   Not well.

Cynthia   What do you mean?

Fiddler   They're miserable, the lot of them. Golden Rod, Tender Tempest, Lorelei, Fancy Ken, Caligula – the whole stable's like a bloody infirmary, excuse me. Cracked hooves. Sore tongues. Flaccid nostrils. Coats with all the gloss and glow of an army blanket.

Cynthia   That's awful! What about Cynthia K.?

Fiddler   A stranger. Off her feed, dead-eyed, bloody poor concentration. Not the same creature she used to be.

Cynthia   Oh no . . .

Fiddler   Not since you threw us over, mum.

Cynthia   *Fiddler.*

Fiddler   Just like the guv'nor, sorry to say.

Cynthia   That will do, Fiddler.

Fiddler   Yes mum. I'll be off, then.

Fiddler *turns to go.*

Philip   Ah, just a moment.

Fiddler   Sir?

Philip   You, ah, you take care of this mare, this "Cynthia K."?

Fiddler   You don't miss a trick, sir.

Philip   I should like to buy her.

Cynthia   Philip!

Philip   Why not? You're fond of her, aren't you?

Cynthia   Fond of her? I adore her!

Philip   Then what better wedding present? I want the horse. We'll stable her in town, you can ride every day if you like.

Cynthia (*kissing him*)   Oh you dear, dear man!

Fiddler   You'll have to take this up with Mr. K, sir.

Philip   Of course. Have him contact me.

Fiddler   May I point out sir, he is outside circling the block as we speak, having hoped to see you in any case on an unrelated matter?

Cynthia   I don't want to see him.

Philip   You can retire upstairs.

Matthew   The sooner they meet, the sooner we can have you back in the saddle where you belong.

Cynthia   Oh of course you're right. I'm being silly. Go, Fiddler. Tell Mr. Karslake we would be *most* happy to take advantage of his bankruptcy.

Matthew   Oh you are wicked.

Fiddler   Right.

Fiddler *exits.* **Philip** *goes to ring for* **Thomas**.

Cynthia   Cynthia K.! Philip, you are a darling. Now I have to get something marvelous for you.

Philip   My dear, I've already received the greatest gift I can imagine: your hand.

Matthew   This is threatening to become rather wet. Perhaps I should go.

Cynthia   Nonsense. You must bask in our happiness.

Thomas *enters.*

Thomas   Sir?

Philip   Now Thomas. We are expecting a caller, a Mr. Karslake. I wish to have *ample warning* before you show him in. Is that understood?

Thomas   Perfectly sir.

Thomas *goes.*

Philip   That way you'll have time to get upstairs.

Cynthia   I know it's foolish, thank you for indulging me. I just don't have your nonchalance about facing former spouses. Though I wonder if you'd be quite so cool if yours weren't halfway around the globe.

Matthew   Who's halfway around the globe?

Cynthia   The former Mrs. Philimore. She's in Egypt.

Matthew   No she's not. She was in her pew on Sunday.

Cynthia   Are you sure?

Matthew   Sure? She nearly caused a riot. She wore a hat festooned with peacock feathers that set the whole place buzzing.

Philip   Hmf.

Matthew   The view from the pulpit was splendid but she had half the congregation straining their necks to see around her.

Cynthia   She is terrible.

Matthew   Then, reports reached me that she was seen outside on Fifth Avenue, in full view of the church steps and the wider world beyond, smoking *a cigar*.

Cynthia   You're joking.

Matthew   That's what I was told. She's quite the provocateur, is our Vida Philimore.

Cynthia   What do you mean *our*? She's not *our* anything. (*to* **Philip**) Are you listening to this?

Philip (*reading his newspaper*)   Typical Vida.

Matthew   Only she could get away with it. She's so deliciously avant-garde.

Cynthia   She's a show-off.

Thomas *enters.*

Philip   Ah. (*to* **Cynthia**) My dear –

Cynthia *prepares to leave.*

Thomas   Sir Wilfred Cates-Darby.

Cynthia *stops.*

Cynthia   Oh.

Philip   Who on earth is Sir Wilfred Cates-Darby?

Thomas   I don't know sir.

Philip   Sounds English. Perhaps he's a friend of that Fiddler fellow.

Cynthia   I've never heard of him.

Matthew   I have. He was at church on Sunday too. He's come from London for the season. Making quite a sensation, socially. Titled, rich as Croesus, tremendous horseman, everybody's wild about him.

Philip   Well. Show him in, I suppose.

Thomas   And . . . Mr. John Karslake.

Cynthia   *What?*

Matthew   They've come *together*?

Philip   You're sure it is Karslake this time? It's not Karslake's bootmaker or his piano-tuner?

Thomas *gives him the card.*

Thomas   Yes sir I'm sure. It was a confusing situation. You told me to give you ample warning about Mr. Karslake but I didn't know if that applied to Mr. Cates-Darby as well.

Philip (*to* **Cynthia**)   You'd better disappear, my dear. (*to* **Thomas**) Just have them wait for a moment in the hall.

Matthew   I wouldn't do that.

Philip   What? Why not?

Matthew   If it got around – and it *will* get around – that you left *Wilfred Cates-Darby* waiting in your hall you'd be finished socially.

Philip   Oh for heaven's sake Matthew, I don't give a fig about nonsense like that.

Matthew   I know you don't, but think of Cynthia. She's young, she has a life to lead, she's got social handicaps enough –

Cynthia   Matthew!

Philip   Oh all right . . . so show in Cates-Darby but leave Karslake waiting.

Matthew   No, no. He'll think you're afraid to see him because you're marrying his former wife.

Philip   Then show them *both* in.

Cynthia   No, you can't do *that* –

Matthew   He *must*. You shall just have to face him, my dear. It's the only way.

Thomas   Actually, she could have been gone by now if she'd left when I first announced Mr. Karslake.

Matthew   Dammit, we're running out of time!

Philip   Thomas, *show both gentlemen in*.

Thomas *exits*.

Sorry Cynthia, but it can't be helped. I'll keep things short, I promise.

Matthew (*to* **Cynthia***; French pronunciation*)   *Courage*.

She's mad at both of them. She stomps away.

Thomas *enters*.

Thomas   Mr. Karslake and Mr. Cates-Darby.

John Karslake *and* **Wilfred Cates-Darby** *enter*.

Philip   Good evening, gentlemen.

John   Evening, Judge. (*to* **Matthew**) Hello, here's the church. How are you, your Reverence?

Matthew (*eyeing* **Cates-Darby**)   We are *most honored* –

John   Oh, right. Sorry. The Reverend Philimore, his brother Judge Philimore, Sir Wilfred Cates-Darby.

Cates-Darby   Reverend, a pleasure. By George that was a racy sermon of yours yesterday. Enjoyed it awfully.

Matthew   You're too kind, Sir Wilfred.

Cates-Darby   Call me Billy.

Matthew   Oh, I couldn't.

Cates-Darby   Course you could. And Judge, I had the pleasure of meeting Mrs. Philimore at church on Sunday. You're a lucky devil, your wife's a damned handsome woman. Most extraordinary hat. Glad I was seated well to her right. But grand girl. Bit of the leopardess in her, eh? Do you know she gave me a *cigar* on the street afterwards! You could have knocked me over. Lit it for me!

Philip   Ah. Yes, well, you see –

Cynthia *stands, showing herself to* **Cates-Darby** *and* **John**. **John** *starts.*

Cynthia   Excuse me.

Beat.

John   Hello, Cynthia.

Cynthia   Hello.

Philip   And, ah. Sir Wilfred . . . (*He's not sure how to introduce her.*) Mrs., ah, Cynthia Karslake.

Cates-Darby   Mrs. Karslake? (*to* **John**.) Hello, I'd no idea you had a wife, old boy.

Philip   Ah, no, you see –

Cates-Darby   Rascal never told me!

Matthew   No, it's –

Cates-Darby   Here we are all week staying up half the night over cards and brandy and what-not and he never says a word, the devil. And such a charming, lovely, *lovely* thing.

Cynthia   Thank you, Sir Wilfred.

Cates-Darby   Billy, please. All for it, this marvelous American informality. Determined to drag some of it back across the pond with me. Well, Mrs. Karslake, let me tell you, you're deucedly lucky to be married to this fellow, all appearances to the contrary. He's a capitol chap.

Cynthia   I am very glad you think so, *Billy*, but I am not Mr. Karslake's wife.

Cates-Darby   Sorry?

Cynthia   I am to be married to Mr. Philimore.

Cates-Darby   Oh. Eh – what?

Philip   And I am not Mrs. Philimore's husband.

Cates-Darby   Sorry, my brain must be boiled. Reverend, you're a churchman and all that, can you straighten me out?

Matthew   It's a bit awkward . . .

Cynthia   Oh just tell him, Matthew.

Matthew   Well, you'll recall my sermon . . . Mrs. Philimore *was* my brother's wife; he divorced her –

Philip   Incompatibility.

Matthew   – in Rhode Island a year ago. Cynthia *was* Mr. Karslake's wife; she divorced him –

Cynthia   Cruelty.

Matthew   In Sioux Falls, seven months ago. Tomorrow, she is to marry my brother.

Cates-Darby   Extraordinary! Is all New York like this?

Matthew   Increasingly.

Cates-Darby   And here you all are, calling on one another, perfectly civilized, nothing out of the ordinary. That's what I was talking about. America! It's simply delightful.

John   Yes it is.

Cynthia   Would you care for some tea, Sir Wilfred?

Cates-Darby   I would indeed.

She goes to pour it, ignoring **John**.

Philip   Please, sit down, sit down.

Cynthia   Do you like your tea strong?

Cates-Darby   Middling. One sugar.

Cynthia   Lemon?

Cates-Darby   Just torture a lemon over it.

John   I'll have a cup too.

Cates-Darby   So, you're marrying tomorrow, eh?

Cynthia   At three o'clock.

Cates-Darby   Qualified congratulations.

Cynthia   Qualified?

Cates-Darby   I hate to see a pretty woman married.

Cynthia   Oh, but I'm sure you don't admire American women.

Cates-Darby   Some I admire awfully.

Cynthia   And you've no one at home?

Cates-Darby   Funny you should ask. I came over here for the sport, cards and races and so on, but I'm thinking of acquiring a New York girl while I'm at it. They're so *modern*, stimulating – fully electrified, you might say. Damned shame I seem to have caught you between husbands.

She smiles, hands him his tea, begins pouring **John***'s.*

Philip   So. I understand you wanted to see me on business.

John   I understood the same.

Philip   Yours first, then.

John *gives him an envelope.*

John   Just your signature, Judge. Bar association business. Dull stuff.

Philip   Dull and routine. You couldn't have left it at my office?

Cynthia   Yes, couldn't you?

John   Well. I was in the neighborhood, and I . . .

Cynthia *gives* **John** *his tea.*

Cynthia   Your tea, Mr. Karslake.

John   Thanks. And I would have called, but it seems you don't have a telephone.

Philimore   Not in my home, or in my chambers either. I don't see the point. Silly things going off all hours of the day and night, jangling the nerves, upsetting everyone. And what can they do that the post or a wire can't? Tell me that.

John (*he sips*)   I beg your pardon. You must have forgotten, Mrs. Karslake – very naturally, I expect – but I don't take sugar.

Cynthia *glares and takes the cup back. Over the following she adds multiple teaspoons of sugar.*

In any case, Fiddler said you were a man in the market for a horse.

Philip   Not any horse. Your mare "Cynthia K."

John   Ah. He didn't tell me that. You sure you want that one? I've a whole stablefull of fillies wanting good homes.

Philip   I'm sure.

John   You want her for yourself?

Philip   I, ah, I sometimes ride, yes.

John   She's rather lively for you, Judge.

Philip   I'm not without experience in these areas.

John   I warn you, she's especially tricky. She's high-strung, and changeable. Are you sure that's the type of thing you want to take on?

Cynthia (*giving* **John** *the tea*)   He's more than capable, aren't you darling?

Philip   I should think so.

John   Well, I'm glad to hear it. (*He tastes the tea, grimaces, and puts it down.*) But I'm afraid she's already sold.

Cynthia   *What*?

John   Had to take the first offer I got. The wolves are at the door.

Philip   Yes, I heard you were forced to sell your country place. Damned unfortunate.

John   My house here too. I'm selling everything. If I was long of hair I'd sell that.

Cates-Darby   I've been trying to let him win at cards all week. No good.

Cynthia   Can't you cancel the sale? Philip really wants her very badly. I'm sure he could match whatever you're getting.

Philip   Well, yes, I suppose –

John   Impossible. The buyer's very determined. Promised to beat any other offer.

You could have Fancy Ken.

Cynthia (*scorn*)   Fancy Ken.

Cates-Darby   I say, she's taking it rather hard, isn't she?

Philip   What about the ah, the painting. Sargent, wasn't it? Have you a buyer for that?

John   No.

Philip   All right, I'll take your portrait then.

John   It's not my portrait. It's a portrait of Mrs. Karslake. And I've made up my mind to keep it.

Cynthia   You have?

John   Yes. You never know. A Sargent may be valuable one day.

Cynthia   Oh, it's *maddening*. How on earth did you come such a cropper?

John   Streak of blue luck.

Cynthia   I don't see how it's possible –

John   It all started when Galahad ran third in the thousand dollar stakes for two-year olds at Belmont.

Cynthia   Ugh, Galahad. I never had faith in that horse.

John   Well I did, and it cost me eighty thousand.

Cynthia   *Eighty?*

Matthew   Dear Lord.

John   And then when I was down at St. Louis on the fifth I laid seven to three on Fraternity –

Cynthia   Oh no wonder.

John   With her record she ought to have romped to an easy winner.

Cynthia   She doesn't have the stamina! Look at her barrel! Agh, I've told him a hundred times, you've no business at the window without a decent handicapper by your side, it's like a baby with a loaded pistol.

John   Yes, well, anyhow, at Saratoga Geranium finished me off.

Cynthia   You didn't lay odds on *Geranium*! He wasn't acclimated! He was ridden by O'Connell and he's sluggish on a muddy track, everybody knows that! It's sheer imbecility!

Cates-Darby (*to* **Cynthia**)   See here, who do you like at Belmont tomorrow?

Cynthia   Why, are you going?

Cates-Darby   Oh, I thought I'd pop over if the mood struck.

Cynthia   Could I come?

Cates-Darby   I'd be delighted.

Matthew   Cynthia.

She looks blank.

The wedding?

Cynthia   Oh, yes. Sorry.

Anyway, tomorrow I like Felicity.

John *snorts.*

Oh? And who do you –

John   Carmencita, of course.

Cynthia   *Carmencita* is a lazy, badly-trained, foolish little filly – She'd shy at her own shadow! Felicity will come in first and I'll lay you three to one she'll beat Carmencita by five lengths. How's that for fair?

John   Sorry. I'm not flush enough to take you.

Cynthia   Philip, dear, lend John enough for the wager.

Matthew   Cynthia!

Philip   I . . . I don't think . . .

Cynthia   Well why on earth not? It's a sure winner.

John   It's a sporty idea, Mrs. Karslake, but perhaps in the circumstances –

Cynthia   You stay out of it. Stake him, Philip! We can't lose, I guarantee it.

Matthew   It does seem to me that there is a certain . . . impropriety in lending the former spouse of one's fiancé the funds to wager against oneself . . .

Beat.

Cynthia   You're right. I'm sorry Philip . . . Matthew. I forgot myself.

John *prepares to go.*

John   Well. You'll have to excuse me. I shall be late for my creditors' dinner.

Cates-Darby   "Creditor's dinner"?

John   Fifteen of my most sporting creditors have arranged to give me a blow-out at Delmonico's. I can't afford to disappoint them.

Matthew   Literally.

John   I was told to bring friends. They think I don't have any. What do you say, Billy?

Cates-Darby   Is it really the custom here for a bankrupt man –

John   This is New York. Our customs are invented anew on an hourly basis. Come on. I'll show you a gang of creditors worth having.

Cates-Darby   Wonderful! Extraordinary place, this.

John   Matthew, See you in the pulpit . . . Judge. Sorry we couldn't come to an arrangement.

Philip   Yes, well, can't be helped . . .

Cates-Darby   Delightful meeting you, my dear Mrs. . . . do you know I'm not sure what to call you? "No-longer-Mrs.-Karslake-not-quite-Mrs.-Philimore."

Cynthia   Perfect, Sir Wilfred.

Cates-Darby   Billy. Best of luck.

Cates-Darby *and* **John** *start out.*

Cynthia   John?

He stops.

Who bought her?

John   Sorry?

Cynthia   Cynthia K. Who was the buyer?

John   Vida Philimore.

(*Off* **Cynthia**'s *shock.*) I know. I had no idea she was interested in horses.

John *and* **Cates-Darby** *exit. Beat.*

Matthew   Good gracious. I didn't realize the hour was so late. I must get home, begin preparing tomorrow's ceremony. Do you know, I couldn't be more excited? I doubt I shall be able to sleep tonight. I think I know how you both must feel . . .

Matthew *goes.*

Philip *sits and takes up his paper again.*

Philip   Well. That was amiable enough. See? All that fuss for nothing. Shame about the mare. Ah well. We'll find you another, if you like.

Cynthia *paces, agitated.*

Do sit down, Cynthia, you're making me nervous.

Cynthia (*sharp*)   Am I?

Philip   Oh dear. You're upset.

Cynthia   I'm fine.

Philip   No, of course, forgive me – this has all been most disagreeable for you. My advice: forget all about it, have a sherry and compose yourself. Dinner's in half an hour . . .

Mrs. Philimore *and* **Miss Heneage** *enter.* **Cynthia** *goes to the sideboard.*

Miss Heneage   There, my dear Mary, is the list as I have now revised it. I took Cousin William's suggestions. He was strongly of the opinion that the announcement should be sent *only* to those people who are really in society.

Mrs. Philimore   It's just as well to be exclusive.

Miss Heneage   And of course they won't be coming to the house or witnessing the ceremony, so that stain is avoided.

Cynthia *downs a sherry. She pours another one.*

Miss Heneage   And I have excluded the Oppenheims. And the Fitzgeralds . . .

Mrs. Philimore   We should, of course, include those new Girardos . . .

Miss Heneage   No. I dislike Italians and I don't care for common people, any more than I care for common cats.

Cynthia *downs another.*

Mrs. Philimore   Still, I do feel we should include the Girardos – he has a seat on the exchange –

Miss Heneage   Very well, I shall include the Girardos –

Cynthia *finally snaps, lets out a cry and smashes her glass on the ground. The* **women** *start.*

Miss Heneage   Mrs. Karslake! What on earth is the matter? Mrs. Karslake?

Philip   Cynthia?

<u>FADE</u>

Scene Two

The next morning. **Vida Philimore**'s *boudoir.*

Vida *in a dressing gown. It looks like she has only recently gotten up. She picks up her watch and checks it. She lights a cigarillo, squints at the daylight.*

Jacqueline *enters. French ladies' maid. She carries a very large flower arrangement.*

Vida   What time is it?

Jacqueline   Half past eleven, madam.

Vida   My watch has stopped; please wind it. And pull the curtain, won't you? Daylight is so garish.

Jacqueline   These flowers came for you this morning.

Vida   Put them over there.

Jacqueline   Do you wish to know who sent them, madam?

Vida   Jacqueline, I appreciate that you are new here and still learning the rules of the house, but I don't wish to be addressed as "madam." This isn't the court of Louis-the-whichever. Call me Vida.

Jacq   Vida, madam?

Vida   It is my name.

Jacq   It is your first name.

Vida   This is America in the twentieth century and I am an egalitarian to my bones.

Jacq   Yes . . . Vida. (*giggles*) It is exciting.

Vida   I'm glad you agree. Now, who sent the flowers?

Jacq (*reading the card*)   Sir Wilfred Cates-Darby.

Vida   Hm. That rather strikingly well-formed Englishman I met on Sunday. I can't say I'm surprised. He gave me an outrageously penetrating look when I lit his cigar on the church steps. We'll be seeing more of him, I predict. Anything else come?

Jacq   No, Vida.

Vida   You're sure you didn't overlook, say, a wedding invitation?

Jacq   I am sure.

Vida   No surprise there either. A comet would have to strike Manhattan and plunge it into the sea before Philimore *mère* and *fils* would flout the least convention. Not to mention that gargoyle of an Aunt. I shall just have to spend my afternoon riding in the park.

Jacq   I did not know you kept a horse, Vida.

Vida   It's quite new.

(*A bell, off.*) That'll be the fellow bringing the animal now. He's a cockney. Twiddler or Piddler or something. Show him in. And find out where to put it. And what they like to eat.

Jacq   Yes Vida.

Jacqueline *goes.* **Vida** *looks at the card and smiles to herself. She arranges her hair.*

Jacqueline *enters. With her is* **Cynthia**.

Vida   Hello.

(*to* **Jacqueline**) This is not the person I was expecting.

Jacq   She said she came about the horse, Madam. I thought you would want me to –

Vida   Does this look like a little Cockney man to you, Jacqueline?

Jacq   No, Vida.

Vida   Nor to me. She looks like a very pretty, slightly anxious young woman.

Jacq   I am sorry I made this mistake of letting her in.

Vida   Well, nothing to be done about it now. Though in the future please remember I am not at home before noon to either tradesmen or women who are marrying my former husband.

Hello, Mrs. Karslake.

Cynthia   You know me.

Vida   I recognized you from your portrait, my dear.

Cynthia   My portrait?

Vida   Yes.

Cynthia   But it hangs in John's – in my husband's – in my *former* husband's private study –

Vida   And it doesn't begin to do you justice. Mr. Sargent has been after me to sit for him for ages, but now that I've seen you in the flesh I think I shall say no. You're exquisite.

Cynthia   How do you know John?

Vida   It's not a big town, my dear, not really. And we've become quite good friends, in the last – what is it? Seven months or so . . .

Before **Cynthia** *can pursue this:*

Jacqueline, bring coffee. Five sugars and quantities of cream for me. (*to* **Cynthia**) I find single life very thinning. How do you take yours?

Cynthia   I don't drink coffee, thank you.

Vida   Tea then, for Mrs. Philimore. Excuse me, it's not three o'clock yet. Mrs. Karslake.

Jacqueline *goes.*

Won't you sit down?

Cynthia   Mrs. Philimore –

Vida   Vida, please.

Cynthia   Mrs. Philimore. I'm sorry to come unannounced –

Vida   I think it's refreshing. I am violently opposed to this rampant, decadent formality *strangling* our social intercourse –

Cynthia   – But I have to speak to you about Cynthia K.

Vida   Who?

Cynthia   My chestnut mare.

Vida looks blank.

The horse you're buying from Mr. Karslake.

Vida   Ah yes, the horse. But I'm not *buying* it. I've bought it. Oh dear, is his name really *Cynthia K.*? That's unfortunate. Do you think he'd mind if I changed it?

Cynthia   No, she's a *mare*, she – (*starts over*) Mrs. Philimore, I am getting married today –

Vida   Yes, I know. Have I not given my congratulations?

Cynthia   Philip, my fiancé –

Vida   How is dear, steady, dependable Philip?

Cynthia   He's fine, but he –

Vida   I wish you both every happiness. Is he still graying as heavily around the temples? And that balding patch he has in back – I always thought it looked so distinguished and judicial.

Cynthia   He – The *point* is, he intended – he wanted to –

Vida   Won't you give him my very best today? For some reason I wasn't invited to the ceremony –

Cynthia   Mrs. Philimore, please –

Vida   Please, *Vida*.

Jacqueline *enters.*

Jacqueline   Vida! Coffee. And tea for Mrs. –

Vida   Philimore.

Cynthia   Karslake.

Beat while **Jacqueline** *pours.* **Cynthia** *is frustrated with how this is going; Vida pleased.* **Jacqueline** *finishes and goes.*

Cynthia   Now. If you'll *please* let me –

Vida   Do you know, Cynthia – May I call you Cynthia? I've been hoping for a chance to sit and chat with you. We should have become friends long ago, our situations are so similar. Tell me, have you found life as a New York divorcée terribly socially isolating? I had feared it would be, but I've come to think if anything the *opposite* is true –

Cynthia   Will you just be quiet for a moment and *listen*?

You've been trying to throw me off my stride since I came in. I'm not a fool. You like informality, here's informality. Cynthia K. is *mine*. I can't imagine my happiness without her. Philip wants to buy her for me, for the wedding. I want you to let him.

Vida   But my dear, you don't know what you're asking.

Cynthia   I know precisely what I'm asking.

Vida   But I am such a passionate equestrienne –

Cynthia   You don't know a stallion from a gelding. I can't imagine why you'd go to all the trouble –

Vida   Can't you?

Beat.

Cynthia   To . . . annoy Philip? To get under his skin, deny him a pleasure . . .

Vida   Don't be ridiculous. I didn't even know he wanted to buy it until just now.

Cynthia   Then *why*? Is it something to do with John?

Vida   Do you mean Mr. Karslake?

Cynthia   Yes!

Vida   Well why on earth should you care?

Jacqueline *enters.*

Jacqueline   A Mr. Cates-Darby is here.

Cynthia   What?

Vida   What an entirely anticipated pleasure.

Jacqueline   Yes, He's very handsome.

Vida   Isn't he?

Jacqueline   Shall I show him up, Vida?

Vida   Please.

Cynthia   Can't you wait? I don't want to have to talk to him now.

Vida   You'd better go then.

Cynthia   *I'm not leaving without that horse.*

Vida   Aren't you a tenacious little thing.

Cynthia   You've no idea.

Beat.

Vida (*airy*)   Well, you're welcome to wait in the club room upstairs. I keep it for my gentlemen visitors. Though there's no telling how long this interview will last.

Cynthia   I'll wait.

Vida   You'll find whisky, a stock ticker and the racing papers.

Cynthia   Fine.

Cynthia *stomps out.*

Vida   My God. I like her.

Jacqueline *shows* **Cates-Darby** *in.*

Jacqueline   Sir Wilfred Cates-Darby.

Cates-Darby   Mrs. Philimore.

Vida   Sir Wilfred.

Cates-Darby   Won't you call me Billy?

Vida   Oh how disarming. And I'm Vida.

Cates-Darby   I had a feeling you would be.

Vida   Billy, I'm quite overwhelmed! First the flowers and now this unexpected visit . . .

Cates-Darby   Well, I –

Jacqueline *is lingering, ogling* **Cates-Darby**

Vida   That will be all, Jacqueline.

Jacqueline *goes reluctantly.*

I just wish you weren't encountering me in my *dishabille.*

Cates-Darby   A woman like you could wear a potato sack and it'd make no difference.

Vida   Oh surely you exaggerate. I haven't even done my hair –

Cates-Darby   I like a lady just after she's got up in the morning. And just after she's got in bed at night.

Vida (*mock scandalized*)   Billy!

Cates-Darby   Sorry, that was a bit bold, wasn't it?

Vida   Outrageously, scandalously bold. Do sit down.

Cates-Darby   Thanks, I will.

Vida   It's most original of you to come this morning. I don't quite see why you did.

Cates-Darby   Sheer admiration.

Vida   But we barely spoke on Sunday. I had no conception that you even took notice of me.

Cates-Darby   What? Oh, no, sorry, the admiration was for Cynthia Karslake.

Vida   Pardon?

Cates-Darby   Met her yesterday. She's a pip. Just a ravishing girl, and full of spirit. She's engaged to that Judge, Philimore. You know, your former –

Vida   Yes I know who they are.

Cates-Darby   They're marrying today at three.

Vida   You'll have to forgive me, *Billy*, if I don't quite see how it is that your vaulting admiration for Mrs. Karslake brings you to my boudoir today.

Cates-Darby   Right, I'm getting to that. So as I say, I was jolly well knocked over by Mrs. Karslake yesterday. I mean, she's really bowled me a googly. Couldn't say anything then, you understand. Standing between her two husbands. Damned awkward to try to make love to the girl right there. But it started me thinking. I want to marry. Now, she's a sticky wicket, right? Practically speaking. One husband already, and another one on the way . . . What to do? I was turning it over and over in my mind last night, trying to sleep after a rather debauched evening out, and do you know what? I thought of you.

Vida   How very flattering.

Cates-Darby   The way you looked through that cloud of smoke as you were lighting my cigar, eyes cast down, lips slightly parted . . . Well, it gave me an idea.

Vida   I cannot wait to hear it.

Cates-Darby   Easier to show you.

He takes her by the waist and kisses her. She doesn't respond at first. Then does. Then breaks off.

Vida   Sir Wilfred! I never –

Cates-Darby   Look here, Vida. You and I aren't bottle babies. You're a modern woman, and I've knocked about. And we both know there's a lot of nonsense talked about, oh, you know, "the one and only," that a fellow can't awfully well be smashed by two at the same time, and so forth. All rubbish!

Vida   I'm not sure I follow you.

Cates-Darby   May I be brutally frank? Cynthia's my favorite, but you're running her a very close second.

Vida   What a fantastic person you are.

Cates-Darby   I knew you'd take it that way.

Vida   And what's next, pray?

Cates-Darby   Just the usual. The, ah, same old question, don't you know. Will you have me if she won't?

Vida   I don't believe that *is* the same old question.

Cates-Darby   Come on. I sail home in a week. I'd like to take you with me. I'd like to see you at the head of my table.

Vida   And Cynthia at the foot.

Cates-Darby (*taking hold of her again*)   Vida –

Vida   Take your hands off me, sir.

Cates-Darby   Oh come on, don't be like that.

Vida   Do you really expect me to stand in line for you, like some . . . *immigrant* woman at a delicatessen, waiting for her number to be called? And you're the Bologna sausage?

Cates-Darby   Now you've hurt my feelings. I'm not an icicle, you know. I'm offering myself, and my affections. (*Beat.*) And my home in Somerset. And my townhouse in London. And my villa on Lake Como. And my castle and rather extensive grounds in Scotland . . .

Vida *is softening.*

Do you really find me so repulsive?

Vida   Of course not. In fact I rather like looking at you. And you must be a splendid lover.

Cates-Darby   I am.

Vida   I won't be second to Cynthia Karslake.

Cates-Darby   And if the next few moments, spent properly, had the effect of reordering my preferences, what then?

Vida   I . . .

Jacqueline *enters.*

Jacqueline   Mr. John Karslake is here.

Cates-Darby   I say, what the devil is he doing here?

Vida   I haven't the slightest idea.

Cates-Darby   He's a fine chap but I really don't want him to see me in such a state of suspense. It would shatter all his notions of me. Tell him to go away.

Vida   I can't do that.

Cates-Darby   Course you can.

Vida   Look, just make yourself scarce for a moment or two. I'll see what he wants and once he's gone we shall resume precisely where we left off. You can wait upstairs, in the club room.

Cates-Darby   Oh very well.

Cates-Darby *goes.* **Vida** *nods to* **Jacqueline**. **Jacqueline** *goes.*

Vida *tries to compose herself. Then stops, horrified, remembering:*

Vida   Oh God, the club room!

She starts to dash out but **Jacqueline** *comes in.*

Jacqueline   Mr. Karslake. He's not bad either.

Vida   Yes, that will do, Jacqueline.

John *enters, looking haggard.*

John   Hello, Vida.

Vida   John.

John   I was afraid you wouldn't be receiving yet.

Vida   On the contrary, I've had a very busy morning.

John   I just got up. Trying to pull myself together after a brutal night out with my creditors. We must've drunk half of Delmonico's cellar. A fitting end to my career as a sport.

Vida   Can I have Jacqueline bring you something?

John   No. I won't stay long.

John *seems a little distracted and irritable.*

Vida   Why have you come?

John   I brought Cynthia.

Vida *starts.*

Your horse. Cynthia K.

Vida   Oh, of course. I thought your man was going to do it.

John   Fiddler? Yes, he was, but I decided I might as well come myself. One last ride.

Vida   And how was she?

John   Oh, wonderful. Alluring, spirited, a joy.

Vida (*a small smile*)   The horse?

John (*irritable*)   Yes of course the horse. Have a look for yourself, she's just on the street outside.

Vida *glances out the window, very briefly.*

Vida   Hm. Very nice.

Beat.

I'm curious, why did you part?

John   Because you bought her, why do you think?

Vida   John. Not the horse.

John   Oh what on earth do you want to talk about *her* for?

Vida   You've seen her recently, haven't you?

John   Saw her yesterday at Philimore's.

Vida   I thought so.

John   Why?

Vida   You have that dark look on your face.

John   That's just Delmonico's vengeance.

Vida   No it's not. It's the look you'd have whenever you even heard her name spoken. You couldn't stay away, could you?

John   I promise you, the future Mrs. Cynthia Philimore is the farthest thing from my mind.

Vida   I know you too well.

John   Yes, well, that's the other reason I came.

Vida. I've enjoyed . . . knowing you these last few months. But I don't think it should continue.

Vida   I don't either.

John (*a little surprised*)   Oh. Good.

Vida   You've been a lovely refreshing sherbet between dishes but now I think I'm ready for the next course.

John   That's . . . more or less how I felt. I wouldn't have put it quite that way . . . So, do you know what your "next course" is going to be?

Vida   Possibly. If it hasn't been served to another diner already.

And yours?

John   I'm not the least bit hungry.

Vida   Why *did* you and Cynthia part? You never told me.

John   Why does the hawser part from the tug? She couldn't stand the tug.

Vida   I'm afraid maritime metaphors are lost on me.

John   Oh I don't know. Why did you and Philip part?

Vida   Oh, Philip. He was entirely too substantial for me. And I think he regarded me as some sort of uncanny foreign species, like the platypus. But you and Cynthia, you were peas in a pod. What happened?

John   Don't ask me what happened. We met, we married, we parted . . . It was all so senseless. Perhaps it's how she was raised. She was actually *bred* to be contemptuous of reality. It's appalling. She – would you mind if I had drink?

Vida   Not in the least.

John *pours himself some over the following.*

John   I blame her father. Died with a lie on his lips and a lien on his property. Can you believe she used to say I reminded her of him?

Vida   Shocking.

John   Dear old Dad smashes up the family fortune and what lesson does the daughter take? Life's a joke, money's water, marriage is burnt almonds and moonshine and a yacht and three automobiles . . .

Vida   Were you never happy?

John   Happy? We were *blissful*. It was perfect – for half a year we were a world unto ourselves, and then one day . . . I was in my study. I'd just lost a big case, a big fee, and was trying to buckle down for the next one and salvage my tottering legal career – and in sails Cynthia, mad to see "Searchlight" run in Baltimore. And I'm to put my hat on and take her. I gather all my pathetically thin supply of self-control and say No – and bang she goes off like a stick of dynamite – what did I marry her for? And I got mad and she got mad, she called me a dullard and I called her something worse and something worse again, and she said marriage is a failure, or at least it was with me, and I said maybe she'd better try somebody else then, and she said she would. She dropped her ring on my desk . . . knocked over a chair and marched out the room. (*He still can't believe it.*) And that was it.

Vida   She broke your heart.

John   Oh the devil she did. But by God I'm glad you bought that horse. I know the thought of Philip's former wife astride her beloved Cynthia K. is driving her absolutely *insane* right now.

Vida   Yes. So insane she tried to talk me out of it.

John   What? When?

Vida   This morning. She's upstairs now. She's quite desperate I don't take possession of it.

John   My God, that girl. She's unbelievable.

Vida   She's still in love with you, you know.

John   What? Don't be ridiculous.

Vida   It couldn't be more obvious.

John   She's marrying Philimore in three hours!

Vida   Yes, because of all the other men in New York Philip is the one who reminds her least of you.

John   That's absurd. She –

Cynthia *bursts in and rushes to the window.*

Cynthia   Cynthia K.! She's outside! I saw her from the clubroom window! Oh look at her, isn't she a darling? Is Fiddler –

She turns and sees **John**.

Mr. Karslake. Hello.

John   Hello.

Cynthia   I'm here . . . I only came to . . .

John   I couldn't care less why you came. (*to* **Vida**) Mrs. Philimore, the animal is yours. A pleasure doing business with you. You can arrange payment with my office at your leisure.

John *starts to exit.*

Cynthia   Wait. Please. John.

I know you're only selling her to torment me. It's all right – I don't blame you. There's blame enough to go around. Even if we did make a mess of our married life, it's all over now and can't be helped. Can't we be friends? Let's be reasonable and kind to each other.

John   Are you joking?

Cynthia   No. Now is the time to shake hands, and put by anger and pride –

John   Oh very nice. Now that there's something you want from me.

Cynthia   I'm extending my hand! I'm determined to be generous, I'm prepared to forgive you for everything you ever did to me –

John   That I did to you? You murdered my happiness!

Vida   Perhaps I should wait outside.

John   No, stay. I'll make short work of this. (*to* **Cynthia**) You're a wonder. You talk to me of *kindness*. You threw me over! You turned your back on *me* without a second's thought, but for Cynthia K. –

Cynthia *starts to object.*

Oh I know that's what brought you here, don't deny it – For her, you beg, you simper, you debase yourself before a *stranger* – no, she's worse than a stranger, she warmed the same bed you'll be conquering tonight! There's no price too high, no humiliation you wouldn't bear for the sake of your four-legged love –

Cynthia   At lease *she was constant*! At least with her a girl knew what she'd got – dash and nerve, a dear who'd run all day and dare any jump without shying or slowing or running to her study for her law books –

John   *Because she's a damned animal*! Horses can't practice law in the state of New York, check the statues!

Cynthia   She gave me more affection than you ever did! More loyalty and devotion. Of course I want her back. If I can't have you –

Cynthia *stops herself.*

John   Yes, if you can't have me you'll take her husband and my stable, you've made that very clear. Well you can have the Judge, Mrs. Soon-to-be-Philimore, and my blessings, but I'll see you in Hades before you put a foot in Cynthia K's stirrup ever again.

Cynthia   Oh you're horrible! Horrible!

Cates-Darby *enters.*

Cates-Darby   I say, what's all the shouting?

John   Oh God, not you too.

Cates-Darby   That's a nice way to talk. After we set the town on fire last night, eh?

John   What are you doing here?

Cates-Darby   None of your bloody business, old boy. No disrespect intended, of course. (*noticing* **Cynthia**) I say, the girl's crying.

He offers her a handkerchief.

Cynthia   I'm fine.

Cates-Darby   Poor little thing.

Cynthia   I'm sorry. I don't know what's the matter with me.

Cates-Darby   I do. You're marrying the wrong man. Anyone can see that.

Cynthia   Don't be ridiculous. (*starting out*) I have to go . . .

Cates-Darby   It's like I told you upstairs. You've got to have a *whim* for the fellow you marry.

Vida   A what?

Cates-Darby   A whim. A . . . special liking.

Cynthia   I like Philip just fine, thank you.

Cates-Darby   No, no, it's more than that. I'm talking about something else entirely. How to put it? A sort of, ah . . . well, I don't want to bring a blush to any cheeks. Let's just call it a whim. You know. (*indicates* **John** *and* **Vida**) Like he's got for her.

Cynthia   *What*?

John   I haven't!

Cates-Darby   Oh come on old boy. After what you told me at your creditors' dinner? (*to* **Vida** *and* **Cynthia**) We were both a bit bladdered, and the talk became rather frank, I don't mind telling you.

Cynthia (*to* **John***; disbelief and fury*)   You – and she haven't –

John   Thanks very much Billy.

Cates-Darby   What? (*getting it*) Oh dear, I hope this doesn't come as a *surprise* to anyone . . .

Vida   Sir Wilfred, I thought you had a "whim" for me.

Cates-Darby   I do. Nothing's changed. Told you before. If she says no, I'm all yours.

John   Says no to what?

Cates-Darby   I asked her once already, upstairs. Said she didn't know me well enough.

Vida   She doesn't.

Cates-Darby   That's easy enough to fix.

John   You mean, says no to *you*?

Cates-Darby (*to* **Cynthia**)   My motor's on the corner. What do you say? We can be there in an hour. Spend the whole afternoon together if you like.

Cynthia   Where?

Cates-Darby   Belmont Park, of course.

Vida   What?

Cates-Darby   We'll do the races, and dine at Martin's . . . You'll get to know me, see if any feeling develops on your end.

Cynthia   Sir Wilfred, you're awfully nice, but I'm to be married at three –

Cates-Darby   Postpone it. Here.

He rings for **Jacqueline** *and goes to a writing table.*

John   Are you out of your mind? You can't do this.

Cates-Darby   Nonsense. Couldn't be easier. There: "Unavoidably delayed, stop, postpone ceremony til seven-thirty."

Jacqueline *enters.*

Jacqueline   Yes?

Cates-Darby   Yes, we need you to send a wire. (*Holds out the paper to* **Cynthia**.) There you are, sign that and away we go.

Cynthia *hesitates.* **John** *snatches the paper.*

John   She is not going to Belmont with you.

Cates-Darby   Hello.

John   An hour before her wedding? It'll ruin her! It's worse than eloping! Tell her, Vida!

Vida   Since I have an interest in the outcome I'll only say it will be viewed as a wild affront to every social norm, and I therefore envy you.

Cynthia   Good.

Cates-Darby   Shall we then?

John   No! I absolutely forbid it.

Cynthia   *You* forbid it?

Cates-Darby   I say old man, I think the girl can do as she likes.

Cynthia   That's right. Thank you!

John   Cynthia, don't be a fool. Your life, your reputation –

Cynthia   Oh I'm a fool, am I?

John   I'm just watching out for your interests –

Cynthia   Then watch this.

She snatches the paper and signs it. She gives a coin to **Jacqueline**.

Have it sent to the Philimore's, Eleven Washington Square. Quickly before I change my mind.

Jacqueline *takes it and curtseys.*

John   Vida, say something.

Vida   Jacqueline, while you're out, pick up a pineapple and a some Bath-buns at the grocer's. I haven't had breakfast and I'm famished.

Jacqueline   Yes Vida.

Cynthia (*giddy*)   I can't believe this. It's too marvelous! Goodbye, Mr. Karslake. Goodbye, Mrs. Philimore. (*out the window*) Goodbye, darling, *darling* Cynthia K! We're off to the races!

She sweeps out with **Cates-Darby**

Cates-Darby   Cheerio.

Vida *and* **John** *are alone.*

John   My God.

Vida   Yes, that was rather unexpected.

John   It's awful.

Beat.

Vida   Well, you'd better go. I have so much to do to get ready for tonight.

John   Tonight? Where on earth are you going?

Vida   With you, of course. To the Philimore's.

He looks blank.

To the *wedding*. Oh don't be so stupid. Dear, silly John, did you think this was *over*?

END OF ACT ONE

Act Two

Scene One

The same night. **Philimore**'s *parlor, now set up for a wedding ceremony. Flowers, etc.* **Mrs. Philimore**, **Miss Heneage**, *and* **Sudley**. *Tense atmosphere.* **Mrs. Philimore** *checks her wristwatch.*

Mrs. Philimore   Twenty to ten.

Sudley   We've been waiting since *half past two.*

Mrs. Philimore   Those poor choir boys.

Sudley   You sent them away, I hope.

Mrs. Philimore   I told Thomas to give them supper. Should we notify their parents, do you think?

Miss Heneage   It's an abomination.

Mrs. Philimore   Perhaps that's a *bit* strong . . .

Miss Heneage   Not nearly strong enough. I haven't been forced to stay up this late since the night Garfield was shot.

Sudley   I now seriously regret that I went to the expense of a silver ice-pitcher.

Beat.

Mrs. Philimore   I don't wish to be censorious, or to express an actual opinion, but it is an unusual bride who keeps her wedding party waiting for eight hours.

Miss Heneage   I don't believe Mrs. Karslake means to return here or to marry Philip at all.

Mrs. Philimore   Has anyone seen Philip?

Sudley   He said he was going for a walk. Matthew went with him. That was two hours ago.

Miss Heneage   I shouldn't be surprised if he's drowned himself in the East River.

Mrs. Philimore   Sister!

Miss Heneage   It's what I would do. It's the only way to ameliorate a really severe social setback.

Thomas *enters, goes to* **Mrs. Philimore**

Thomas   Telegram for you, ma'am.

Miss Heneage   Who's it from?

Thomas   Mrs. Karslake.

Mrs. Philimore   Oh –

Sudley   Give it to me.

Miss Heneage   To *me*, Thomas.

Miss Heneage *grabs it and starts to open it.*

Mrs. Philimore   Thomas, how are the choir boys?

Thomas   Sleeping in the butler's pantry.

Mrs. Philmore   In the pantry?

Thomas   I told cook to lend them a blanket.

Mrs. Philimore   Oh good.

Sudley   Well? What does it say?

Miss Heneage   It's unintelligible. "Delayed. Automobile threw a rod." – What on earth does that mean? "Home by nine-forty-five, hold the church." Hold the church?

Sudley   It's from Belmont Park!

Miss Heneage   She went to the *races*?

Sudley   Dear God.

Miss Heneage   I knew it! She's run off for good!

Mrs. Philimore   But . . . "hold the church" – surely that means –

Sudley   I consider a young woman who has spent her wedding day wagering on horses to have broken her engagement.

Miss Heneage   Indeed. The maid can pack up her belongings. Send the choir boys home.

Mrs. Philimore   Oh let's not wake the poor dears . . .

Miss Heneage   *Send them home.* And when Mrs. Karslake arrives –

Sound *of a car horn off. They freeze.* **Sudley** *looks at his watch.*

Sudley   Quarter to ten precisely. It's her.

Mrs. Philimore   Well that's a relief of a sort.

Sudley   She is not setting foot in this house. Not while I am here.

Miss Heneage   Nor I.

Thomas *checks the window.*

Thomas   It's Mr. Cates-Darby's car.

Miss Heneage   The Englishman? She went with *him*?

Sudley   Disgraceful!

Mrs. Philimore   Perhaps we should at least listen to what she has to –

Miss Heneage   Never! Thomas! Bar her entry!

Mrs. Philimore   Surely that isn't necessary . . .

A door opening, off.

Miss Heneage   She's coming in. Do something!

Sudley   I'm going to become unwell.

Sudley *swoons.*

Mrs. Philimore   Cousin!

Miss Heneage   Sit down, William. Thomas, fetch water –

Sudley   I don't think I can endure this.

Cynthia *enters, bright. She's in driving-gear: goggles, veil, duster.*

Cynthia   Hello all!

She bumps into a piece of the moved furniture.

Whoops. Sorry.

She takes her goggles off, looks around.

Dear me. It looks like a smart funeral.

I see you got my wire, so you know where I've been.

Miss Heneage   To the *race-course.*

Cynthia   Yes. Oh it was lovely. I never was so surprised in my life as when I strolled in to the paddock and they all gathered round, the old gang – Jimmy Withers, Jack Deal, Monty Spiffles, the Governor and Buckeye . . . They actually *cheered* for me. You should have seen it. I started blubbering like a baby . . .

Sudley   We concluded you desired to break your engagement.

Cynthia   What? Why?

Miss Heneage   You are eight hours late!

Cynthia   The car broke down. I told you in the wire. If not for that I would have been back by six at the latest.

Mrs. Philimore   Oh, well that does sound very (*reasonable*) –

Miss Heneage   Silence, sister, I'll manage this. (*to* **Cynthia**) So you actually still intend to marry Philip?

Cynthia   Why shouldn't I?

Miss Heneage   "Why"? You stroll in here, on this sacred occasion, *in goggles*, stinking of the paddock, speaking of *Buckeye* and *Monty Spiffles*, having practically *eloped*, having created a scandal and disgraced our family –

Cynthia   How on earth does it disgrace you?

Miss Heneage   I am speechless.

Sudley   Madam, you are leading a *fast life*.

Cynthia   Not in this house. For the last six weeks I've laid away in the grave, and I've found it very slow indeed trying to keep pace with the dead. Oh, I refuse to take any of you seriously.

Philip *and* **Matthew** *enter quietly at the back, unseen.*

Miss Heneage   Well you shall take this seriously. *Pack your things*. You are no longer welcome in this house.

Cynthia   What? Oh for heavens sake. Mrs. Philimore –

Mrs. Philimore   I can't . . . It's all very confusing. I don't know what to say . . .

Sudley   I do. I am going, and as I leave I shall do myself the pleasure of calling a hansom for Mrs. Karslake –

Philip   Call a hansom, Sudley, and when it comes get into it.

Sudley   My dear sir –

Philip   You heard me, get out.

Sudley *goes.*

(*to* **Miss Heneage**) Aunt, don't make it necessary for me to say what I think of you.

Miss Heneage *goes in a huff.*

(*to* **Mrs. Philimore**) Mother, I desire to be alone with Cynthia. I expect both you and Aunt Sarah to be ready for the ceremony a half hour from now. Matthew.

Matthew *helps* **Mrs. Philimore** *out.*

Philip *gives his coat to* **Thomas**, *who exits.* **Philip** *and* **Cynthia** *are alone. Beat.*

Philip   I won't be jilted. You understand? I intend to marry you. I won't be made ridiculous.

Cynthia   Philip. I didn't mean to make you –

Philip   Then why did you run off to Belmont Park with that fellow? I've spent the last two hours walking up and down the Avenue trying to work it out. On our wedding day. Why did you do it?

Cynthia (*lamely*)   Because he asked me to.

Philip   Do you love him?

Cynthia   Sir Wilfred? No, don't be ridiculous. I've just been so . . . *bored.*

Philip   Bored? In my company?

Cynthia   Philip. I am afraid that one can't just select a great and good man and say, I will be happy with him.

Philip   Of course not. No one expects that. When you promised to marry me you told me you saw marriage as the rational coming together of two people. You said you were through with juvenile infatuation.

Cynthia   Yes I know I said that.

Philip   And I agreed we'd *earn* our happiness. Build it, by the sweat of our brow . . . slowly, laboriously, brick by brick . . .

Cynthia   Yes, but I think Sir Wilfred may have been right about something. He said a woman should marry only when she has a whim for the man.

Philip   A *whim*? Oh fine. Marry for whim! The New York idea of marriage. Marry for whim and leave the rest to luck and the divorce courts. That was the former Mrs. Philimore's theory too. But it's nonsense, you must see that. A woman of your mental caliber. No. Something else is at work, some obscure, primitive female feeling, corrupting your better judgment. Cynthia, what is it you feel?

Beat.

Cynthia   I feel like a fool.

You never felt a fool did you?

Philip   No, never.

Cynthia   I thought not.

Philip   Well whatever your feelings, which I won't pretend to understand, I conclude you are prepared to marry me.

Cynthia (*resigned*)   I came back. I'm here, aren't I?

Philip   So, you . . .

Cynthia   I'm a woman of my word. I will.

Philip   Very good then. Run to your room. Throw something pretty on. In half an hour I'll see you back down here.

Cynthia *nods and starts to go.*

And Cynthia?

(*She turns.*) I may not be fitted to play the love-bird. I . . . may not coo and cuculate like a wood pigeon, but I . . . I esteem you.

She starts to go again. She sees her telegram on the table, picks it up.

Cynthia   Philip. Did you say you'd been out walking these past two hours?

Philip   Yes.

Cynthia   Then how did you know where I'd gone, and with whom?

Philip   Karslake told me.

Cynthia   *John*?

Philip   He came to my office.

Cynthia   Why would he do that?

Philip   I've no idea.

Beat. Then she goes.

Philip *looks at the telegram, then crumples it with finality and throws it away.*

Thomas *enters.*

Philip   Thomas, set out my morning coat and –

Thomas   Mr. John Karslake.

Philip   What? I can't see him now. Show him the door.

But **John** *has already come in.*

John   I've seen the door. It's a handsome door.

Philip   Your humor is strained. I thought I'd seen the last of you tonight.

John   I'd expected a warmer reception, Judge. After the good turn I did you earlier –

Philip   Look, what do you want? I've finally got things back on track. If Cynthia comes down and finds you here God knows what will ensue.

John   So she came back.

Philip   Yes.

John   Said No to Billy.

Philip   Of course. She's a sensible girl and he's a preening ass.

John   Judge.

Philip   I know he's your great friend but I shan't apologize.

John   Good for you. Well. That's really all I needed to know.

Philip   Karslake? Is that why you came? And why you alerted me earlier?

John   She's just so damned *impulsive*. Goes careening off at the flick of an eyelash. Billy's not a bad fellow but for Cynthia he'd be a disaster. I'd rather see her married to you than him.

Philip   Well. That's . . . damned decent of you.

John   Don't thank me.

Philip   I wasn't *thanking* you exactly . . .

John   God knows who she'll ricochet onto after you.

Philip   What do you mean, after me?

John   Wake up, Judge. The modern American marriage is a wire fence. The woman's the wire, the posts are the husbands. One, two, three, and onward, post after post, up hill, over the horizon, all the way to the Dakotas.

Philip   Well I'm not so cynical. I still believe in constancy, monogamy –

John   Monogamy's as extinct as knee-britches. You're living in the dark ages. You want to call up Central. "Hello, Central! Give me the present, New York City, 1906." Oh I forgot. You don't have a phone.

Philip   You'll forgive me but I have to get dressed for the ceremony.

John   You're forgiven.

Oh, Judge. One more thing. The Sargent? It's yours if you still want it. Call it a wedding gift.

Philip   But . . . you said it would be terribly valuable in the future.

John   Yes. But it's worthless to me now.

Philip   Thank you.

John   I'll have it sent over tomorrow.

Mathew *enters, agitated.*

Matthew   My dear brother. Aunt Sarah Henage refuses to let herself or mother take part in the ceremony, she –

Sees **John**.

Oh hello. I'm sorry. My Aunt has made me very warm. Everyone's nerves are a bit frayed, given the hour, and . . . Mr. Karslake, you know I am very fond of you but forgive me if I suggest that your presence here now might not be entirely –

John   Don't worry, Reverend. I was about to make myself scarce.

Matthew   Oh thank God.

Thomas *enters.*

Oh Thomas. I seem to have misplaced a small handbag or satchel containing my surplice. I shall need it. And can you see what's become of the choir boys? I'd have thought they'd be practicing by now –

Thomas   Yes sir. (*Announces.*) Mrs. Vida Philimore.

Matthew   What?

John   Of course.

Philip   Vida? You must be joking!

Vida *enters. She looks alarming – walking unsteadily, wearing a mud-splattered formal dress and the giant peacock feather hat, which is however completely smashed on one side, the feathers sticking out at right angles.*

Matthew   Dear Lord!

Philip   Vida!

Vida   She *threw* me.

John   What?

Vida   That revolting animal *reared* in the middle of Washington Square and pitched me headlong into space. I landed on the pavement before an oyster vender, three women of very doubtful virtue, and a hurdy-gurdy man. It's a wonder my spine wasn't shattered. The vicious creature.

John   Do you mean Cynthia K.?

Vida   If you're referring to the loathsome little nag you delivered to my doorstep this morning, yes.

Philip   Vida, you don't ride.

Vida   Well how hard should it be? And I did *nothing* to it, apart from giving it a little jab on the back of the head with my parasol tip when it refused to make the turn onto the block. And now look at me. Of course I shall be suing.

Philip   Suing whom?

Vida   I do hope you'll be hearing the case, Philip. After your *brilliant* adjudication of my last one.

Philip   Vida, why have you come?

Vida   For one of two mutually exclusive purposes, depending. If Mrs. Karslake has thrown you over and run off with Sir Wilfred Cates-Darby, I am here to offer what consolation I can. If on the other hand you are still to be married, I am here for the ceremony, and to claim Sir Wilfred myself.

Philip   You weren't invited.

Vida   Nevertheless.

Philip   And what on earth do you want to marry him for?

Vida   To unite my soul with his, of course. Also I have never felt entirely happy about accepting the alimony the courts compelled you to grant me: it is woefully inadequate to the style of life I require. Come now, don't leave me in suspense.

Philip   Oh for God's sake. Of course I'm marrying Cynthia.

Vida   How fortunate for me! Won't you accept my wedding gift of a charming and spirited chestnut mare. She's out on the curb, unless she's galloped off somewhere.

John *indicates for* **Thomas** *to see to it.* **Thomas** *exits.*

Now. Where is Sir Wilfred?

Philip   He's not here.

Matthew   Brother –

Vida   Do you know where he's gone? I should like to telephone before the ceremony . . .

Philip   No! You will just have to –

Matthew   Brother, remember, Aunt Sarah, and mother –

Philip   Yes, yes. I'll deal with mother, have Thomas wrangle Aunt when he's done with the horse. Now if you'll excuse me the hour is late and I must get dressed.

(*to* **Vida**) And it's out of the question your staying.

I thank you both for your concern but the greatest gift you could give me now is your immediate absence from my house!

Philip *and* **Matthew** *exit.* **Vida** *and* **John** *are alone.* **John** *prepares to go.*

Vida   You're not leaving.

John   Course I am. And you are too.

Vida   But I have a very important reason for staying.

John   Oh for God's sake Vida. Stop stirring up trouble. You've a clear shot at Sir Wilfred now, there's nothing to gain by tormenting Philip.

Vida   I'm not staying for that. Don't be insulting. I'm staying for you.

John   What?

Vida   To help you. You want Cynthia, don't you? That's why you couldn't stay away.

John   Don't be ridiculous.

Vida   Then why did you come?

John   I *came* to . . . to –

Vida   To what?

John   To give the happy couple my *gift*, and . . .

Vida *starts to laugh.*

Vida   Oh John. You're so guileless and transparent. It's why we could never succeed. You love her. As she loves you.

John   I *hate* her. And as for her loving me, you were witness to that tender scene this afternoon –

Vida   And it couldn't have been clearer that you're aching for one another.

John   You're out of your mind. That fall off the horse scrambled your brains.

Vida   Now listen. I've worked it all out. Getting her back will be quite simple. All you have to do is make love to me tonight.

John   What?

Vida   At the ceremony. Make her think you're mad for me – that we're engaged, even. Jealousy and her competitive instinct will take care of the rest.

John   If you think this . . . *scheme* out of a shoddy French farce will accomplish *anything* –

Vida   Of course it will, if you play your part properly, and don't shy from the vigorous physicality of which I know you to be capable.

John   Goodbye Vida.

He starts to go.

A BLAST of organ from off, playing the wedding march. **John** *stops, startled. The organ abruptly cuts off.* **John** *and* **Vida** *look at each other, confused.*

What's –

Matthew *comes in, harried.*

Vida   Are the nuptials begun and aborted already?

Matthew   What? Oh, the organ, no – that was my attempt to revive the choir boys. It seems they discovered in the pantry a supply of rum kept by the cook. They're in no condition to perform, I'm afraid . . . I didn't think the two of you would be here still.

John   Tell her. I've been trying to leave for the past quarter hour.

Matthew   Well really, you must –

Cynthia *hurries in, breathless.*

Cynthia   Am I late? I heard the organ. Ridiculous to make it a conventional thing, you know, come in on the swell of the music and all that, as if I'd never . . .

She sees them and stops. **John** *stares at her. She looks beautiful.*

Mr. Karslake and Mrs. Philimore. Why am I not surprised?

Vida (*whispers to* **John**)   *You should begin <u>now</u>.*

John (*mouth dry*)   I beg your pardon, Mrs. . . . Cynthia . . .

Vida (*to* **John**)   *Commence "the Scheme." Go on. Embrace me.*

John   Stop it. (*to* **Cynthia**) We were just, ah . . . that is, *I* was about to . . .

Vida (*to* **John**)   *Take my hand at least.*

She takes **John**'*s hand. He pulls it away. She takes his arm, drawing close.*

Vida   Mrs. Karslake, you're glowing. Doesn't she look simply irresistible to you, John?

John   No she does not.

Vida   Mrs. Karslake, we wanted to offer our congratulations –

John   No *we* did not.

Cynthia   Well, thank you very much.

John   No, that's not what I –

Cynthia   I won't be distracted by this. Matthew can we please get on with things?

Matthew   I am trying . . .

Thomas *comes in.*

Cynthia   Thomas, where is Philip?

Thomas   Mr. Philimore will be down in a few moments, ma'am. He's very sorry, but there's a button off his waistcoat.

Cynthia (*exasperation*)   A button?

Thomas   I would have been quicker in repairing it ma'am, but I had to first chase on foot, and then capture, curry, feed and water the horse.

Cynthia *freezes.*

Cynthia   What horse?

Vida   Your namesake, my dear. A gift from us both on your wedding day. I say "both" – I was terribly reluctant to part from the magnificent creature, but John at length persuaded me. Your happiness is everything to him, you know.

Beat. She looks at him.

Cynthia   John?

John   Yes, that's right.

Vida   He really is the kindest and most tender-hearted fellow. Aren't you, you darling, darling man?

She kisses **John**. *He breaks away quickly. Then looks at* **Cynthia**. *She looks shaken. Maybe* **Vida**'*s plan is working. He turns to* **Vida**. *With some effort:*

John   More your idea than mine, sweetheart.

Vida   Oh nonsense.

John   Nonsense yourself, you . . . you grand old pip of a girl.

John *takes her hand and kisses it.*

Vida   Really, John, not here . . .

She grabs his face and kisses him. **Cynthia** *seethes.* **Matthew** *looks very uncomfortable.*

Cynthia (*fierce*)   Thomas. Tell Mr. Philimore he is to come downstairs *at once.*

Matthew   But we're not prepared –

Cynthia   I don't care about the waistcoat, I don't care about his relations or your choir boys, I just want this done with. Go, Thomas.

Thomas goes.

(*to* **Vida** *and* **John**) Thank you for the gift of my rightful property. Now goodbye, and I look forward to our never *ever* meeting again.

Matthew, put on your surplice.

Matthew *starts to go.*

Vida   Oh Matthew. That reminds me. When you're finished here, won't you come over to Mr. Karslake's house?

Matthew   Whatever for?

Vida   Just a small party.

John *looks at her.*

We're having champagne and lobster and a few dear friends at midnight. And we would like – nay *need* – you to be there, too.

Matthew   Very well, I suppose . . .

Matthew *goes.*

Vida (*to* **Cynthia**)   Enjoy your evening. Wedding nights are so magical and rare, aren't they my dear?

(*sweeping out*) Come, love.

Vida *exits.* **John** *and* **Cynthia** *are alone for a moment.* **John** *starts to go.*

Cynthia   My *God*, Jack. I knew you were in awful straits, but *that*?

John   Good night, Mrs. Philimore.

Cynthia   You cannot seriously intend – It's self destruction. You're throwing yourself away!

John   There's nothing to get exercised about. It's just a small party.

Cynthia   With *champagne and lobster*? Don't play the fool with me. And *Matthew* . . . Have you an ounce of sense? *Vida Philimore*?

John   What about her?

Cynthia   Don't you know what she's like? Do you have *any idea* the things she did to Philip? He told me – wore him half to death – kept him up til all hours every night and then without his knowing put brandy in his coffee to make him lively at breakfast.

John   I hope you were taking notes.

Cynthia   I wouldn't mind you marrying again in the abstract, but *her*? A woman like that, all languor and loose frocks –

John   She's a modern girl. I happen to admire it.

Cynthia   You won't do it. I don't care what you say. I liked your father, and for his sake if for nothing else I'll see his son doesn't make a donkey of himself a second time.

John   Forgive me, I thought I'd been divorced. I begin to feel as if I had you round my neck still.

Cynthia   You have! You shall have if you attempt to marry her. I'll follow you, and I'll tell Vida – I will! – I'll tell her what sort of a dance you led me on –

John   Do, and while you're at it tell me, please, because I still have no idea!

Cynthia   You don't know how to make a woman happy! Not for long. Oh you're quick out of the gate and splendid round the turns but you fade in the home stretch because you've no idea what's in our hearts or heads, or who we really are, because you don't know who *you* are.

John   I've never heard such –

Cynthia   I never knew which John I'd wake up next to, the daredevil or the drudge, the lover or the *lawyer*. *You* decided when we'd live for the moment and when the moment was done. And it was always done too soon. God knows who Vida thinks she's getting but either way she'll soon be disappointed. I'll tell her that. I'll tell her everything –

John   Will you?

Cynthia   To save you from yourself, I will.

John   And why do you care what happens to me?

Cynthia   I don't.

John   Then how dare you pretend –

Cynthia   I don't pretend!

John   How dare you look me in the face with the eyes that I once kissed and pretend the least regard for me? Oh, I begin to finally understand you now. There is no *you*, just a collection of caprices, of "whims" – a firefly, flitting about. And the fire you gleam with is so cold a midge couldn't warm his heart at it, let alone a man. You care for nothing. You married me for nothing, divorced me for nothing, because you *are* nothing.

Beat. She's really wounded.

Cynthia   Jack. What are you saying?

John   The worst things I can think of.

The organ begins again, the wedding march.

I believe that's your cue, Mrs. Philimore. Go. Prance up to the alter and claim your happiness. If you can.

He goes.

Cynthia *sinks into an armchair.*

Matthew *enters with* **Philip**. *Finds the room empty.*

Matthew   Oh thank God.

Bustling about.

Well. It was impossible to find my surplice, Philip, but it is an age of informality, I suppose. You look splendid, that's the important thing.

Philip   I thought you said Cynthia had come down.

Matthew   Yes, when I left she –

Cynthia *rises.*

Cynthia   I am here.

Philip   My dear.

Matthew   Ah, good. Cynthia. In lieu of the choral fiasco let me tell you the words of the hymn I have chosen to sing myself:

(*sings, badly*) "Enduring love, sweet end of strife/O bless this happy man and wife."

Cynthia   I think I need a scotch.

She goes to the sideboard and pours herself one.

Matthew   My dear. In the pomp and ceremony of this occasion, there should be sufficient exhilaration . . .

She downs it and pours another.

Mrs. Philimore *enters.*

Philip   Ah, mother.

Mrs. Philimore   After all, it shouldn't matter too much *who* the girl is. The important thing is we will all still live together . . .

Cynthia *watches* **Philip** *maneuver her into place. She drinks.*

Matthew   Wonderful . . . And where is Aunt Sarah?

Thomas *escorts* **Miss Heneage** *in. Scowling, she starts to go again, but* **Philip** *takes her arm and steers her into place.*

Cynthia *pours another drink.*

My child, I really don't think that my Bishop would approve, of, ah –

Miss Heneage   Get on with it, then!

Matthew   Yes, of course. Philip stands here. Mother. . . All is in readiness. And the music should trail away now . . .

It doesn't.

Thomas (*shouts*)   SHUT IT!

It cuts off.

Matthew   And we may begin.

Matthew *begins to sing the hymn again; it sounds awful.*

Cynthia *is still at the sideboard, clutching her glass, staring at them.*

Cynthia?

She doesn't answer.

Philip   Cynthia, dear?

She's still frozen.

Miss Heneage (*shouts*)   Mrs. Karslake!

Cynthia *sets down the glass.*

Then slowly walks to her place next to **Philip**.

FADE

Scene Two

An hour later. **John Karslake**'*s study. Law books, clutter. The Sargent portrait of* **Cynthia**. *Scattered in various places around the room are a sewing basket; a lady's gloves; a lady's hat. One chair is conspicuously turned over.*

Cates-Darby *enters.*

Cates-Darby   Hello?

No one here. He's about to go when he looks again at the room. Steps in, noting the portrait, the ladies' things, the chair.

Fiddler *enters.*

Fiddler   Oi, how'd you get in?

Cates-Darby   I beg your pardon. Are you speaking to me?

Fiddler   I ain't speaking to Nellie Bly, am I? How'd you get in?

Cates-Darby   The door was unlocked. And there's no one attending.

Fiddler   Whole staff's been sacked. Lack of funds. I'm the only one left on the payroll, and it's not clear how long I'll last. Mr. K's moving out of here day after tomorrow.

Cates-Darby   Where is John?

Fiddler   Dunno, do I? Now what are you doing here?

Cates-Darby   I say, you're not very deferential, are you?

Fiddler   This is America, guv. It ain't like back home.

Cates-Darby   Couldn't you at least make a gesture in the direction of class distinction?

Fiddler   What sort of gesture?

Cates-Darby   I don't know, tug of the forelock, bit of perfunctory groveling, something like that? I think we'd both be much more comfortable.

Fiddler   Nothing doing. (*Offering from a box on John's desk.*) Cigar?

Cates-Darby   Don't mind if I do.

Fiddler *takes one too. They smoke.*

Fiddler   I take it Mr. K. didn't know you were coming.

Cates-Darby   *I* didn't know I was coming. After Mrs. Karslake rejected my offer of marriage in my automobile on our way back into the city I of course made straightaway to Vida Philimore's – only to learn, after an extended bit of banter with her rather saucy ladies' maid, that Vida'd gone to Cynthia and Philip's wedding! Well, I foresaw my *persona*'d be *non grata* there, so went to look for John at his club, hoping for a round or three of cards, in vain as it turned out. So here I am now at his home.

Fiddler   Well I've got no more idea where anybody is than you do.

Cates-Darby   Why is that chair upside down?

Fiddler   Mr. K.'s orders.

Cates-Darby   How odd.

John *enters. Glum, distracted air.*

Fiddler   Here's the man now.

John   Fiddler. Listen, see if you can find a crate in the cellar to pack up that painting, all right?

Fiddler   The portrait? Are you sure, sir?

John   Quite sure. And when you're done hire a wagon right away, I want it out of here tonight.

Fiddler   Right.

Fiddler *goes.*

Cates-Darby   Hello, John.

John   What are you doing here?

Cates-Darby   Well, after Mrs. Karslake rejected my offer of marriage in my automobile on our way back into the city, I of course made straightaway to –

John   Never mind. I don't care, really. I see you found the cigars.

Cates-Darby   If you don't mind my saying so old boy, you look like a rugger pitch after a nasty scrum.

John   I'm just tired is all.

Cates-Darby   You didn't go to Philimore's I hope.

John   Briefly. I chose not to stay for the festivities.

He checks his watch.

Which I presume are now concluded . . .

Cates-Darby   Yes, must be.

You wouldn't know where I could find Vida, would you?

John   Actually, I thought she'd be here by now. She said she was coming over.

Cates-Darby   How fortunate! Why?

John   All part of an elaborate and rather stupid charade.

Cates-Darby   Oh good, I adore charades!

John   No, not like that. It's –

Fiddler *enters.*

Fiddler   Fishmonger's here, guv.

John   Fishmonger?

Fiddler   Says he's brought the lobster.

John   The lob – Oh for God's sake. She didn't have to actually go and *order* it.

Fiddler   There's a case of champagne too, guv. Want me to ice it?

John   No.

Cates-Darby   I wouldn't mind a glass of the bubbly stuff.

John   Go to the Haymarket then. I'm not entertaining tonight.

Cates-Darby   You certainly aren't. You're bloody depressing, in fact.

John   Send it all away, Fiddler.

Vida *sweeps in.*

Vida   Don't you *dare* send it away.

Billy, Hello.

Cates-Darby   Vida!

Vida   Let me guess. You've been looking everywhere for me.

Cates-Darby   I have.

Vida   I'm so sorry to be late. I had to go home and change after my incident with Cynthia-the-horse, as opposed to Cynthia-the-wife-of-my-former-husband.

Cates-Darby   You look ravishing.

Vida   That was the intention. Now what on earth have you been up to all evening?

Cates-Darby   Well you see, after Mrs. Karslake – now, I gather, Mrs. Philimore – rejected my offer of marriage in my automobile on our way back into the city –

Vida   Stop there. The rest is immaterial.

Twiddler, go at once and boil eight or ten of the lobsters, remove the claws and tails and set them out with quantities of lemon halves and melted butter.

Fiddler   I ain't your cook.

Vida   No, but you're John's, and it's his party.

John   It's not my party, because I'm not having a damned party.

Fiddler   And I ain't his cook neither. And anyway I don't know anything about them lobsters. The large hoofed land mammals is more my line.

Vida   We are not expecting miracles. Simply do your best. My girl Jacqueline can help you; she's waiting in the kitchen.

Fiddler (*to* **Cates-Darby**)   The saucy Frenchy one?

Cates-Darby   And no mistaking.

Fiddler   Right, see you all at supper then.

Fiddler *goes.*

Vida   He will wash his hands, won't he?

John   Vida, since you appear to be inhabiting a fantasy world of your own creation, let me remind you that the notion of a wedding party here tonight was a *ruse* – one that *you* concocted; one, moreover, that *didn't work* . . .

Vida   Fantasy? What fantasy? We *are* having a wedding here tonight.

John   For God's sake, we are not getting married.

Vida   *John.* Of *course* we're not.

She turns to **Cates-Darby**

Sir Wilfred Cates-Darby. (*demure*) If I'm not mistaken, my delicatessen number has been called.

Cates-Darby   I believe it has.

They embrace. Then **Vida** *breaks away and turns to* **John**.

Vida   We have champagne; we have lobster; when the Reverend Matthew finishes his duties at the Philimores we will have clergy. May we not have your house for the evening?

John   Of course you can.

Vida   Dear man. Even in the face of his own crushed hopes he is generous to others.

She kisses him on the cheek. **Cates-Darby** *shakes his hand.*

Cates-Darby   Thanks old boy. Good heavens. I'm going to have a wife! Won't they be surprised back home. Now how about some of that champers while we're waiting for the church, eh?

Vida   Good idea. I'm desperately thirsty. It happens whenever I get married.

Cates-Darby *exits.* **Vida** *follows. Then stops, looks at* **John**.

Vida   John?

John   I'm fine. I just want to be alone for a moment.

Vida *goes.* **John** *looks around the room. Then at the portrait. He stares at it a moment, then takes it down from the wall. He goes to the overturned chair. He hesitates, then reaches down to right it. But before he can –*

Matthew *enters.*

Matthew   Hello? There was no one at the door.

John   Reverend. You're late.

Matthew   Yes, well I ah, I've been . . .

John   You've been a busy man tonight.

Matthew   Yes. It has been somewhat . . . hectic.

John   Well. Vida'll be very glad to see you. She's upstairs.

Matthew *looks around the disordered room, at the portrait of* **Cynthia**.

Matthew   How are the, ah, preparations going here?

John   Everything seems to be in hand. Go on, go up to the parlor, have a glass of champagne and get to work. They're only waiting for you, really.

Matthew   Aren't you coming?

John   What for?

Matthew   It is traditional that the groom be present at the ceremony.

John   Oh. (*A short laugh.*) Yes well there's been a slight change of plans since we last saw you. Vida's getting married but not to me. To Cates-Darby.

Matthew   Sensible. I approve.

John   So do I. The British Empire will never be the same.

Matthew   John –

John   Matthew, if you don't mind I'm not much for conversation at the moment.

Matthew   Yes, but I really think you should hear about –

John   Please? I enjoy the latest gossip as much as any of your parishioners, but not tonight. Not now.

Matthew   Very well.

Starts to go.

Shall I take up her hat and gloves?

John   What? Oh, those aren't Vida's.

Matthew   Oh. (*mortified*) I'm *sorry* . . . of course I should not judge . . . you are a bachelor . . .

A small smile from **John**. *Then he gets up, making a visible effort to shake himself out of it.*

John   Do you know, I'm a fool? I'm bankrupt and bereft but there's food and drink upstairs, and coal in the fire, and friends celebrating . . . Why wallow?

Matthew   Yes, why?

John   Be a sport, Karslake, you blithering ass.

Matthew   I think that's a most commendable attitude.

John   Come on, Reverend, I'll take you up to the party.

John *leads* **Matthew** *out.*

Beat.

Jacqueline *comes into the room backward, dragging in the large crate for the painting. It's heavy and she struggles with it.*

Jacqueline   Monsieur Karslake? Your strange little man Fiddler took charge of *les homards* and sent me to the basement for this box you wanted. It's very heavy . . .

She lets it fall and sees no one is here.

Monsieur?

She shrugs and turns to go.

Cynthia *is at the door.*

Allo.

Cynthia   Oh. Jacqueline. Hello.

She looks at the painting and crate.

So. He's shipping me off, I see. Well why shouldn't he?

Jacqueline   Madam?

She looks at the portrait.

Oh, that's you! It's very good. Yes, maybe this is what the box is for.

Cynthia   Is . . . Mr. Karslake at home?

Jacqueline   Oh yes madam. I believe he is upstairs, for the wedding.

Cynthia   The wedding.

Jacqueline   Yes madam.

Cynthia   I see. So it's actually going on now, is it?

Jacqueline   Yes, they are very likely being wed this instant.

Cynthia   Oh. Right.

Jacuqeline   Is very joyful.

Cynthia   No doubt.

Jaqueline   Shall I tell them you are here, Madam?

Cynthia   What? Oh, no. I'd rather go without, ah . . . I'll just go.

She starts to leave. One last look around.

My God this room is in an awful state. Well, I suppose it's your mistress' problem now. Or more likely yours.

Jacqueline   Sorry? I do not understand.

Cynthia   Look, she left her hat, her gloves . . .

Jacqueline   That is not her hat.

Cynthia *examines it.*

Cynthia   It's mine.

Jacqueline   Yours madam?

Cynthia   And my gloves . . . is that my sewing box? And . . .

She goes to **John**'s *desk. Picks up something and looks at it. It's her wedding ring.*

And the chair . . .

Jacqueline   Why is that chair turned over?

Cynthia   Because I threw it over. On the day I threw *him* over. He left it all. Just as it was on the day that I . . .

Jacqueline   On the day that you left him?

Cynthia   That's right. Typical John. Preserves it all in amber. Not just the room but the fury he felt. He's keeping it all fresh, nursing his wrath, feeding his hatred for me like a bonfire burning in his breast . . .

Jacqueline   Oh no Madam.

Cynthia   No?

Jacqueline   This is the wrong interpretation.

Cynthia   How on earth would you know?

Jacqueline   I realize this is not the moment for a lengthy account of my life prior to present events, but suffice to say I have much experience of men, and this is clearly a man who is burning, yes, but burning still with love for you.

Cynthia   Ridiculous.

Jacqueline   Nevertheless.

Cynthia   Oh what does it matter? He's married now . . .

Jacqueline   That's true. Oh well. C'est la vie.

Jacqueline *exits. Beat.*

John *enters. He sees* **Cynthia***, stops, shocked.*

Cynthia   Mr. Karslake.

John   Mrs. Philimore.

Beat.

Cynthia   Congratulations.

He looks blank.

Jacqueline told me that you've just –

John   Oh, yes.

I should say congratulations to you.

Cynthia   Yes, you should.

John   Congratulations.

Cynthia   Thank you.

Beat.

John   Do you know, for a moment I thought . . .

Cynthia   What?

John   You'd come to make good on your threat.

Cynthia   Threat?

John   To warn Vida of all my miserable failings.

Cynthia   Oh! No, no. Don't be ridiculous . . .

Beat.

John   Anyway. The one you ought to congratulate is the bride. She's upstairs. I'm sure she'd be happy to receive you.

Cynthia   You've left her all alone?

John   No. Billy's with her. She's in good hands.

Cynthia   Ah. That's all right then. But I think I'd better not.

Beat.

John   It's good you're here, actually.

Cynthia   Is it?

John   My gift to you and Philip is there. You can take it with you when you go.

Cynthia   You're very kind.

John   Kind may be putting it too strongly. I apologize for my . . . unpleasantness at your home earlier.

Cynthia   Unpleasantness may not be putting it strongly enough.

John   In any case, you were right before. We should be civilized to one another.

Cynthia   We'll probably see each other quite often.

John   Probably.

Cynthia   At the theater, or –

John   Here and there, on the street . . . Yes, it's very likely.

Beat.

Well. I suppose the really civilized thing to do would be to offer you a drink and toast your happiness.

Cynthia   Our mutual happiness, you mean?

John   Yes, precisely.

Cynthia   It would be pleasant to say yes. But I really can't stay.

John   Of course not. Forgive me. It's your wedding night.

Cynthia   And yours.

Beat.

John   Why did you come here, then?

Cynthia   Sorry?

John   To my house. Now. Why did you come?

Cynthia   I came . . . (*scrambling*) Really, Mr. Karslake. I *came* to get my hat. And my gloves. And my sewing kit.

John   You're planning on doing some mending tonight?

Cynthia   It seemed wrong to leave my personal things in another man's house. Indecent even.

John   Of course. I admire your sense of propriety.

Cynthia   Thank you. So if you don't mind . . .

John   Take anything you like.

She gathers her things.

Right the chair even.

Cynthia   Oh, the chair. How embarrassing.

John   Nothing embarrassing about it.

Cynthia   Shameful reminder of what a temper I had.

John   You did have a bit of a temper.

Cynthia   When provoked.

John   Like the day you threw my slippers out the window?

Cynthia   Yes, because you tried to take my fan from me by force.

John   Because you were about to strike my face with it.

Cynthia   I wasn't! I was gesticulating in exasperation –

John   *Dangerously* near my face –

Cynthia   Because you'd said we couldn't put five thousand on Searchlight in the Preakness –

John   I had a trial to prepare! And it was a bad bet besides –

Cynthia   According to whom? Those pathetic broken down amateur touts at your club, who don't know the track or do their research – agh, they're so glib and smug and always wrong, and I was right –

John   Yes, you were. (*truthful*) You always were.

Cynthia   Not always.

John   Near enough.

Cynthia   I should have let you prepare your trial.

John   I lost my trial. You won your race.

Cynthia   Well that's all done now, anyway.

John   Yes. My sporting days are behind me and good riddance.

Cynthia   Mine too, I suppose.

John   Well. I'll let you get back to your husband

Cynthia   And you your wife.

A look. Then she starts to go.

John   Cynthia.

She stops.

You didn't know I'd kept your things.

Cynthia   And you're not dressed for any wedding. Not even your own.

John   I don't have a wife. That was all a lie. She's married to Cates-Darby.

Cynthia   I ran out before the ceremony. I won't be going back.

Beat.

John –

They are in each others' arms. They kiss.

John   Cynthia, darling. It's still too late. I'm ruined, remember? We could never again live as we did before.

Cynthia   I don't want to live as we did before. I don't care that we haven't a dime between us.

John   We haven't a *penny*.

She frowns. Beat. Then looks at the Sargent.

Cynthia   How much do you think I'd fetch?

John   At auction or on the open market?

Cynthia   Doesn't matter. As long as we have cash in hand by noon.

John   Noon?

Cynthia   For the fourth at Saratoga, tomorrow, *Ticonderoga* – it's 25 to 1 but she's a *gem*, it's going to be sunny and Fanshaw's riding her!

John   My God.

If we hurry we can catch the midnight train.

They kiss. Then grab the painting and run from the room.

CURTAIN.

Summer, 1976

Summer, 1976 opened on Broadway at Manhattan Theatre Club's Samuel J. Friedman Theatre on April 25, 2023 with the following cast and director:

Director: Daniel Sullivan
Diana: Laura Linney
Alice: Jessica Hecht

Characters:

Alice
Diana

1.

Diana   We became friends, as you often do, through our children.

I didn't like her child, actually. A little girl, Holly – I hate the name Holly – her nose was always running, her mother constantly calling her over and wiping it for her whenever she came over to play with my daughter, Gretchen.

The girls would ask to use my studio for art projects. My art studio was *strictly off limits,* which Gretchen knew, so that meant Holly put her up to it: She'd certainly calculated that I wouldn't want to look unkind and controlling in front of my friend, her mother – small children are devious that way – that I'd be forced to say Of course, kids! Run amuck in my studio. And while you're at it never mind your own colored pencils and Big Chief pads, use the rapidographs that I bought in art school with the proceeds from my grandmother's savings bond! And the Strathmore Bristol Board too!

But I showed them – NO, I'd say very firmly, you may *not* use my studio, that is where I *work*, it's not a place for play, Gretchen you *know* that and Holly you'll find a box of tissues in the bathroom, why don't you carry it *with* you?

And now leave the Mommys alone, we're talking. Go outside.

And they'd slink off appropriately cowed. And Alice and I would be alone to talk and sometimes share a joint she'd brought.

Parents who can't or won't control their kids aren't upset when you do it for them. They're grateful and ashamed.

Alice   The pot came from Merle, a student who was painting our house at the time.

My husband Doug taught at Ohio State and we had a nice little house. Merle was one of his students who needed money so we hired him that summer. Despite being pretty stoned most of the time he did a good job, but he was slow.

We'd been in Columbus for three years and there were a bunch of young faculty parents with small children on tight budgets so we started this thing, it was a babysitting co-op.

Really Doug started it. He's an economist – he worked it all out, he had a rubber stamp made and he stamped out these coupons – although he called them "shares" – and distributed them to all the parents in the group.

The idea was you could trade these "shares" for babysitting, an hour or two hours or whatever at a time. That way no one had to pay cash for child care, you could just exchange these papers back and forth and around, like if you went out Wednesday night you'd spend two or three shares but you'd get them back when you sat for somebody else on Friday, and it would all work out in perpetuity somehow; Doug had proved it mathematically.

Sure, whatever.

We didn't go out that much. I was bored that summer. Doug was working and I mostly just hung around the house supervising Merle, tanning, reading paperback novels and watching Holly splash around in her little inflatable pool.

One afternoon another woman in the co-op called me up. A professor in the Art Department. She had a project to finish and she needed sitting for her daughter, Gretchen. I told her sure, bring Gretchen over.

Both girls were about five and they played all afternoon. When she came to pick Gretchen up she tried to give me three shares for the three hours but I was like come on, this wasn't *sitting*, the kids were *playing*, they were entertaining each other. I benefitted too, I got to read *Shogun*.

She was kind of thrown by that and annoyed, like, "But isn't there a system?" She seemed kind of uptight.

I was like, if you want to give me the shares, OK, but I really don't care, it's all sort of bullshit anyway, right? I mean, Doug just *made* these with his rubber stamp, they don't actually have *value*.

She said of course they have value because we *assign* them value, like any currency or monetary instrument.

She said "monetary instrument."

I really didn't want to get into a whole philosophical debate about it and also I sort of immediately hated her so I took the shares and she took her kid home.

The problem was Holly and Gretchen had hit it off, and soon they wanted to spend every afternoon together.

Diana   Of course I could tell she didn't like me, this sleepy-eyed little hippie with her shorts and her coconut oil and her sun-bleached paperback copy of James Clavell's depressingly middlebrow novel *Shogun*, which she was toting around proudly like it was *The Brothers Karamazov*.

There is no one more condescending and judgmental than a self-imagined "free spirit" smugly encountering a "square," but let me tell you I knew exactly what she was up to on I'd say it was about the third afternoon she brought her daughter over, and I had politely offered her an iced tea – it was a very hot afternoon – as we sat on my screened-in porch watching the girls in the yard, and she said No thanks and opened up her little macramé handbag and lit up a joint instead!

When she offered it to me I knew she was expecting a shocked stammering and fluttering of hands and an opportunity to feel superior so I showed her: I took the biggest deepest hit I could and held it for an age and blew it out and didn't hand the joint back but took another *massive*, really industrial-vacuum suck before demurely relinquishing it.

The look on her face!

Alice   Yeah, she fucking bogarted it for like five minutes, and I was like, come on lady, I only took it out because it was the only way I could imagine getting through the next ten minutes before I could make an excuse and leave. I'd already had to look at her art since four or five of her, like, pieces were scattered around on the porch – she said she worked out there sometimes – and get a mini-lecture about each one, except strike the "mini" part.

They *were* good.

I pointed out one I particularly liked.

Diana   It's not finished.

Alice   I still like it.

Diana   None of them are.

Alice   Why not?

Diana   That's just how it is.

Alice   Okay.

They weren't just one thing, one medium: they were paintings with ink drawing and things scratched away or glued on, you know, a variety of techniques in each one, sort of like Paul Klee, who I'd always liked, but by an American and a woman.

Diana   She muttered something about Paul Klee as we talked about my work and the pot clicked in, and I was surprised.

Sorry – I was, first, briefly but keenly *chagrined*: I was no longer influenced by Klee *at all*, it was something I had worked very hard to get *away* from, actually, I'd sweat *blood* to expunge the embarrassingly jejune infatuation I'd had with his work as an art student.

But I was surprised that she knew him.

Alice   We got hungry of course and were digging through her fridge when the kids came in for popsicles. She gave them some neon-colored store-bought ones from the freezer which Holly was *ecstatic* about since I only made the homemade orange juice kind which admittedly *were* kind of gross but you know, they were cheap; and the kids went back outside, and we tucked into her leftovers which were *incredible*: it turned out she was a *serious* cook, we ate cassoulet out of a Tupperware, cold (*microwaves were still rare then*) – God, I can still remember how fucking delicious it was, sitting on her kitchen floor stoned on a summer afternoon.

After that, yeah, we were friends.

2.

Diana   Who was Gretchen's father? A boy I had met in art school, and gotten pregnant by on our second date – he took me to see *Beneath the Planet of the Apes*, which disheartened me, but not enough to overcome the sheer and as it turned out fleeting animal lust I felt for that lush-lipped, golden-haired, deeply not-bright glass-blower.

Smells are powerful and the erotic for me remains deeply bound up with the chemical tang of the art supplies that were always close at hand during those intense, formative sexual experiences. Oil paint; the photographic developer in the darkrooms where so many humid couplings took place; varnishes and patinas; blown-glass pigments . . .

But back to the boy. Two dates was enough; after that – and a third afternoon's farewell fuck when I went by his place to retrieve the case containing the diaphragm I had neglected, in a moment of madness, to use during date number two – I avoided him on campus and ignored his phone calls and eventually he got the message – he was just too dull, the poor thing.

He dropped out of school the next semester. I've no idea where he wound up.

Sometimes when I stumble onto one of those touring craft fairs they erect next to farmers markets in the summertime – you know, the ones with the candles and the leather notebook covers and the table lamps made of old typewriter parts or God knows what aesthetic atrocity – if I spot a hand-blown glass display tended by a man the right age (beard, greying ponytail, thick middle) I'll think: This could, in theory, be the father of my daughter.

Not that I care all that much.

Alice   A couple times I wondered about Gretchen's father but never asked, figuring bad divorce, but who knows, maybe death? Since she never brought it up? At all? 'Til one day – this was after we'd been hanging out for a couple weeks maybe – she told me her art school story.

And I was kind of surprised. It was hard to square. I should describe her house so you understand. It was incredibly orderly, and incredibly nice, with all this very carefully chosen midcentury modern furniture that she knew the history of and would describe for you in *great detail* – don't get me wrong: it was really interesting, everything she said was interesting, she really knew a lot, like, *everything* about 20th century art and design. You could see how she must have been a really good teacher.

And I mentioned her food – her kitchen was the same as the rest of the house: *immaculate*, and *thought-out*: spice jars alphabetized, copper pots hanging just so in order of size, that kind of thing.

So I couldn't quite square it. This meticulous, very controlled person. And just having a baby like that, like, kind of accidentally and randomly and what-the-hell.

And then, all the fancy gourmet food, but junky store-bought popsicles. Or seeming so uptight, but *really* enthusiastic about my grass.

So it made me think – I mean, this is obvious now but it seemed like a big revelation at the time, I was young – that people aren't just one thing.

And it made me kind of question myself.

Diana   She thought of herself as a "free spirit" but she was in the most conventional of marriages: she wasn't working, she was essentially living like a 1950s housewife.

She just *thought* she was unconventional because her house was messy. I mean that's all it was really.

When I went over there – we alternated afternoons – I was horrified. It wasn't just the clutter, or the makeshift college-apartment furniture, the brick-and-plank bookshelves, the art exhibition posters *in no frames – just tacked up directly to the wall!* It was the whole bullshit bead-curtain-in-the-doorway gestalt of the place. The house *badly* needed a paint job and rather than hiring professionals it was being done by a graduate student, *by himself*: one shambolic goon with a roller on a rickety ladder. It was taking all summer! A job that could have been done in 4 days by professionals!

Alice   We couldn't *afford* professionals!

And yeah we had shitty furniture but we'd put all our money into the house and Doug was always working – he was up for tenure the next spring and this summer was make-or-break, he was finishing 3 different articles and figured he had to get at least 2 published before the tenure committee met if he was going to have a shot; we didn't have time to, like, *decorate*.

She said, don't *decorate*. Just buy *one good piece*.

I said I don't know what that means!

Diana   I will show you what it means.

Alice   So we drove to Cleveland. To a place she knew, a *gigantic* dusty auction house crammed with furniture from estate sales, defunct Great Lakes resorts, bankrupt corporations, that kind of thing.

Diana   I knew the owners, a pair of brothers, Arthur and George.

Alice   And not just furniture. Chandeliers, carpets, mantelpieces, strips of moulding, and those wood panel wall things . . .

Diana   *Wainscotting.*

Alice   . . . Whole *ceilings* that had been removed from fancy houses somehow. I'd never seen anything like it! She bargained for me when I saw what I wanted: a desk.

Diana   I said You don't want a desk, Alice, you want something to pull a room together. Your living room sofa is a hide-a-bed, for God's sake, replace that!

Alice   But I liked this desk.

Diana   It *was* interesting. A 1930s tubular steel Bauhaus design, a bit banged up but the real thing; not cheap.

Alice   No way could I afford it.

Diana   I bought it for her.

Alice   No WAY am I gonna let you do that, are you kidding me?

Diana   She objected but I could see how badly she wanted it.

Alice   I didn't even know what I'd do with it!

I just felt sure if it was in my house and I was sitting at it I'd do . . . *something*.

But still, she was *not* going to just buy it for me, that is just crazy! I don't even know why you'd *want* to -

Diana   Pipe down and let me bargain.

I haggled with Arthur and George and got them down to a reasonable number.

We put the desk in the back of her station wagon; the hatch wouldn't close all the way but we secured it with twine and drove the 2 hours back to Columbus like that.

Alice   This desk cost *three hundred dollars*. In 1976 that seemed like a fortune. By comparison we were paying Merle 175 dollars to paint the house and that was a stretch for us. It was bananas. I told her I'd pay her back. I *insisted* on it. She sort of shrugged, waved it off.

Diana *does this.*

I didn't know what that meant. Was it "Shut up about it, it's done"? Or was it I *could* pay her back – even though I didn't know how I'd possibly do that. I was kind of too embarrassed to pursue it. I figured – I rationalized it really – that she must have family money.

Diana   I did have family money.

Alice   But still, Jesus! A three hundred dollar antique desk! Doug worked on two filing cabinets and a *door.*

Diana   We set up the desk in a corner of her living room.

The room looked much worse with the desk in it. Everything else was so outclassed.

Oh well. I'd tried.

Then it was time to fetch our respective daughters. We'd spent the whole day together.

3.

Alice   Now it's I think a couple weeks later.

Doug wanted to go to this lecture on campus by some visiting big-wig economist. Apparently he'd told me about it months earlier but I'd forgotten because why wouldn't I?

But it turned out there would be a private dinner party after and wives were "expected," for whatever reason; everybody was supposed to get dressed up and go and kiss this guy's ass, sure, fine. I didn't mind these events. I liked going out, even if the lecture itself would be a snore.

But we didn't have any shares left, you know, the sitting coupons. I'd spent *seven* on the trip to Cleveland, yikes, and I hadn't been taking any from Diana, or her from me – we'd sort of forgotten about using them.

All right, so we're just gonna have to pay a sitter, I said.

And Doug was like, *cash*?

Yeah, cash.

But that would negate the whole point of the *system*. He went to a lot of trouble to set up that system. It's a *cashless, self-sustaining system*!

I was like, well, but it's not. I mean it's not sustaining itself, is it?

It *would*, if we weren't spending more than we were taking in.

Sorry, that was Doug. This is getting confusing. She'll do Doug from here on, OK?

Diana (*as DOUG*)   It *would*, if we weren't spending more than we were taking in.

Alice   All right, Doug, so what do people do in the real world when they're spending more than they take in? They borrow, right? Can't we just get some more shares somehow?

Diana (*as DOUG*)   Alice, they go *bankrupt*.

Diana (*as DOUG*)   And this *is* the real world! Look, the whole, the *fundamental problem* is you're thinking of the co-op as an *abstraction,* one that was only *modeling* real-world behavior, instead of a *functioning monetary system* designed to *constrain* and *optimize* that behavior!

Alice   Oh blah blah fucking blah – this is all happening when we're trying to get dressed for the party and it annoys the *shit* out of me the way he tries to turn everything into a fucking seminar, I'm not one of his goddamn students.

While he was in the bathroom I went to his study and got his rubber stamp and just *made* three new shares, bam bam bam.

Doug! Honey! Good news, whew! I was wrong, I've got a couple shares left after all, we're good for tonight!

So we went to the thing, and actually apart from the lecture we had a decent time.

Diana   Her husband seemed unbearably drab, honestly, but I'd only met him once – the afternoon we brought in the desk and he stared at it with a baffled, resigned look on his face before retreating back into his study. – but she seemed content with him and no outsider can understand what makes another person's marriage tick.

The month of July I recall as a sort of idyll. Me, and Alice, and Holly, and Gretchen, together most days, finding things to do in Columbus. A museum, a movie, the *excellent* zoo, a dairy outside of town that made their own ice cream.

There were endless commemorations with band concerts and fireworks that bicentennial summer and Alice and I went to several with the girls. Doug, who I was told hated fireworks, usually stayed home. I *adore* fireworks.

I began to like Holly much more. Her nose stopped running. I'd suggested to Alice she might have allergies and Alice got her checked out and I was right, and she put her on allergy shots and the transformation was wonderful to behold. A bright and ebullient child had been hiding behind all that snot.

And I liked Holly's mother. She knew how to stand up for herself. She knew how to stand up to *me*. One day were lying out by the public pool with our books while the girls splashed around and I guess I'd made one too many snide remarks about her choice of reading material – it was *Coma* by Robin Cook now that she was done with *Shogun*, a step down if that was possible, and she rounded right on me:

Alice   You're a snob, Diana.

Diana   I am not!

Alice   It's OK, I don't mind and you can't help it anyway, but if I want to read crap during the summertime I'm going to do it. All the stuff I know you think I should be reading, the stuff I see on your bookshelves, Henry James and Virginia Woof and Thomas Hardy and *Middlemarch*, I've read them too, you know. I read all that shit in college and grad school. I'm aware *Middlemarch* is "better" than *Coma*. You don't have to educate me on that score. It's a controversial stance you're taking but yeah, when it comes to narrative fiction George Eliot *does* have a slight edge over Robin Cook. OK? Now can you please shut the fuck up and let me finish reading *Coma* in peace because there's a James Michener book about Hawaii I'm dying to get to next.

Diana   I didn't know she'd gone to graduate school.

Alice   I did a year at the University of Iowa. Then I dropped out.

Diana   Why?

Alice   I married Doug. Got pregnant with Holly. And Doug got the job in Columbus.

Diana   Why didn't you continue on at Ohio State? I wanted to ask, but sensed I shouldn't, so I left it there.

Our growing intimacy was cemented one afternoon the night after a fireworks display – it might have been the big one on the fourth of July, actually – when I thought I was going to die.

I'm not trying to be melodramatic. I'm trying to be accurate to my sense of things at the time.

I'd always suffered from migraines. "Suffered" is both the conventional term and *le mot juste*; the best description I can give you of the experience is, it's as if someone were trying very hard but failing to extract your eyeballs through a hole in the back of your skull.

The only thing worse than a migraine is a migraine when you have a small child to look after.

You cannot function.

In the past if I was lucky and it hit after dinnertime I could put Gretchen in front of the television – PBS only darling, you know the rules, promise me – and crawl into bed with an icepack on my face and a vomit bucket on the floor – sleep would be impossible but with luck *please, please Christ please* by dawn the demonic surgeon will have set down his tools and I could stagger out, find Gretchen drowsy and stirring on the couch, and pretend Mommy just had a little cold, it's much better now, should we make blueberry pancakes? Even as the thought of them made me retch and gag.

But this time it came a little after noon. You know when it's coming. There's no pain at first. Colors have a nervous vibrancy and you feel this strangely giddy dread. Nothing to be done. Here it comes. Batten down the hatches.

I called Alice. Please come over, *now*. I'm going to need you.

Alice   Doug was working, as usual. I left Holly at home with him. The way Diana's voice sounded scared me. I hadn't known her long but I'd never heard her voice sound like that.

I found her dry-heaving in her bathroom, and pressing her face against the tile for the coolness, and crying.

Somehow I got her into her bedroom. She wanted the place sealed up, no light, and the air on full blast even though she was shivering. I just did what she said. I was kind of freaked out. I didn't know anything about migraines and thought I should probably take her to a hospital but she begged me to just do what she asked, so I did.

I stayed the rest of the afternoon, and all night, and the next morning. I kept Gretchen calm, let her watch all the crap TV her mother usually forbid (I think *Charlie's Angels* was on), made her supper. Emptied her Mom's puke bucket and brought her wet washcloths I chilled in the freezer. She finally came out of it around 2 PM the next afternoon.

Diana   As much as the giddiness that precedes them, there's a species of joy *following* the migraine that's equally strange.

Because it's not simple joy at the release from pain – the joy you'd expect.

It's a different feeling.

An awareness of how much pleasure there is to be taken in the world. That you only possess in such intensity *because* you've endured the hateful thing. And somehow, *gratitude* to the hateful thing for making the awareness possible.

The cup of coffee she made for me when it was finally over and I came out into my kitchen was the most delicious thing I'd ever tasted.

Alice   Doug was pissed he lost a day of work. Well, tough.

4.

Alice   The next thing to tell you about is when I started to get the distinct impression that Merle was into me.

Look, I'm not super-vain, I never have been, I wasn't going around always thinking guys were trying to get into my pants, but I was reasonably cute back then and it was summer and I was laying out in a bikini a lot or at least a bikini top, and Doug was up in his office all the time and Merle took frequent breaks.

Mustache; jean shorts; sun visor; John Lennon glasses, Jimmy Connors bowl haircut, Jesus sandals, Muppets T-shirt. Not bad. Not great by today's standards, but an OK look then.

I couldn't have been more than 3 or 4 years older than him. Actually we might have been the same age. But he still spoke to me weirdly formally, calling me by my last name – actually my *married* name which I didn't even use – asking if it was OK if he could go inside and use the bathroom or get a drink of water or whatever.

Keep in mind there was a power dynamic between us because not only were we employing him but my husband was his master's thesis advisor, but it was still ridiculous. I said, Merle, you don't have to ask me every time you want to go inside. Just do whatever you need, OK? And call me Alice.

After that he relaxed a little, and we became kind of friendly, and chatted sometimes, and this was when I'd sometimes buy a joint or two off him, and things were cool.

But then one day he seemed to be going up and down his ladder *a lot*, and finally on about the fourth trip inside in like an hour I said, Jeez, Merle, you're pissing like a racehorse today.

He *froze*, turned *really* red, and his chin trembled, and it looked like he was going to cry!

I was like, *What the hell?*

Oh my God, Merle, I'm *so sorry*. I didn't mean anything. I don't know why I said that. That's just a stupid phrase my granddad used to use. I don't care how much you piss, I mean pee, I really don't. Or whatever you're doing in there.

He just stammered, like, No, no, no, it's nothing, and *shot* back up his ladder like a squirrel and didn't come down the rest of the day.

Diana   Well *obviously* the frequent trips inside were so that he could walk by and ogle your tits in your bikini top.

Alice   What? Come on, you're out of your mind.

Diana   Of course! That's why he was so embarrassed when you called him on it! Don't play *faux naif*, Alice. You've probably been all flirty, playing the hip hausfrau, sharing his drugs and giving him the eye, don't deny it.

Alice   I –

Diana   And don't make me spell out what he was *doing* in there on each of those trips after ogling you in your bikini top either.

Alice   Now *that* is ridiculous. Not four times in one hour.

Diana   Maybe not four, no. But unless he has a medical condition I can think of no other solution to the Case of the Peripatetic House Painter.

Alice   Well now I was worried he really *did* have a medical condition that made him have to pee all the time and I seemed like a huge bitch for making fun of him about it.

I mean, look at it from his point of view – he's working his ass off in the hot sun all summer *seriously ill* –

Diana   Oh come on, he doesn't have a *medical condition.*

Alice   -- and there's this little spoiled nitwit lounging on a towel *mocking* his condition while he desperately tries to complete the job *her husband*, who holds his career in his hands, is paying him *a pittance* for – God, I felt like Marie Antoinette or something.

Diana   If you feel so guilty why don't you just fuck him?

Alice   Diana!

Diana   Well why not? I've seen him. He's all right in a goonish sort of way. I've seen the way he paints your house. He's patient and meticulous. That bodes well for sexual competence.

Alice   Ugh.

Diana   Why not give it a try?

Alice   I'm married!

Diana   Yes?

Alice   That *means* something to me. Jesus! I don't just go around sleeping with other guys just because I want to.

Diana   So you do want to. With – what's his name?

Alice   Merle. No, I don't!

Diana   You said you did.

Alice   Not with Merle.

Diana   But generally?

Alice   No!

Diana   Are you sure about that?

Alice   Will you cut it out? Why are you doing this?

Diana   I want you to be happy, Alice, that's all, and you're clearly not.

Alice   Of course I'm happy!

Diana   Are you?

Alice   I – Are *you*?

Diana   No. I'm not. Thank you for asking.

The difference between us is I don't try to fake it.

Alice *gets up and leaves.*

She stormed out of my house.

Alice   God, she really pissed me off.

Diana   I was surprised. What had I said?

Alice   I didn't talk to her for a few days.

Diana   I called. She didn't answer.

Alice   I just let the phone ring.

Diana   What had I said?

Alice   That thing of telling me how I "really" felt, what I "really" wanted, only I was too stupid or naive or whatever to realize it? That especially got to me. Like she was the adult and I was the child. She wasn't older than me. Maybe by a couple years. Like *she* had all the life experience. Why? Because she was alone? She obviously thought she could "improve" me. That stuff with the desk and everything – the desk was immediately buried under mail and magazines and other crap, by the way; I never used it, not even to pay bills, I just sat at the kitchen table. Maybe I'd made a mistake getting so close to her so fast.

Diana   Eventually she did pick up.

Alice   Yeah?

Diana   Look, I have tickets to the Emerson String Quartet at Weigel Hall on Thursday night, they're young but they're supposed to be very good.

Alice   Great.

Diana   Do you want to go?

Alice   I can't. Doug and I have got a thing.

Diana   Clearly a lie.

Are you lying?

Alice   You tell me, Diana, you're so perceptive and wise about everything, right?

Diana   It was like talking to a teenager.

Well, that's too bad. I would have liked to go with you.

Alice   Yeah, well.

Maybe I was overdoing it. But I still didn't want to see her.

Really awkward pause. She still hadn't hung up.

What?

Diana   The thing is . . .

Alice   What?

Diana   I still need babysitting.

For the concert. I'm still going to go. I'm not about to waste the tickets.

Alice   Yeah, uh, sorry, I'm not going to *sit* for you, Diana, I told you, Doug and I –

Diana   We both know that's not true but nevermind. No, the point is I'm out of shares, I wondered if you could loan me some?

Alice   No. I'm out too.

Diana   Why do we both always seem to be out?

Alice   Cause Doug's system is stupid.

Diana   Well, you and I haven't been making use of the shares, that probably warped things a bit, you can't blame poor Doug for that.

Alice   Uh huh.

Look, I guess I can maybe get you some more shares.

Diana   No, you don't have to do that, I'll find a local high school girl and pay cash.

Alice   No, it's OK. I can get you some, it's no problem.

Diana   Don't do anything "illegal."

Alice   It's fine. I'll leave them in an envelope on our front porch, you can pick them up whenever.

Diana   Well, thank you.

Alice   Sure. Okay then.

Diana   Okay.

Alice   It was definitely uncomfortable. I don't know. I don't think it was my fault.

Diana   Something had happened. Some corner turned in the friendship. Some ground lost. How much?

Alice   Still, I'd promised her the shares so after I hung up I went to Doug's study and got his stamp and made a bunch for Diana. I made a bunch of extra ones for myself too in case I needed some sometime.

When Doug suddenly *burst* into his office, scaring the *shit* out of me, I barely had time to jam the stamp into the back pocket of my shorts.

Hi! Just getting an envelope!

He looked really upset. He said he needed to talk to me.

We begin to hear Shostakovich's String Quartet #8.

Diana   In the end I couldn't find a sitter so I took Gretchen to the concert.

That night the very charismatic young string quartet was playing Shostakovich Eight, that most harrowing, gutting cry of bitterness and pain.

Shostakovich wrote the piece, in case you've forgotten, in a spasm of agonized self-loathing for his capitulation to Stalinism, and in physical agony from his encroaching degenerative nerve disease besides.

I tried to explain all this to Gretchen before the performance but somehow it didn't seem to pique her interest much. She'd hadn't wanted to come in the first place. She'd wanted to stay home and watch "Charlie's Angels," her "new favorite show."

How did the music affect me?

To my surprise I found myself unmoved, and experienced old Shosty's exquisite and well-earned despair as merely lugubrious, and tiresome, and too easy to succumb to.

I wanted my friend with me, to roll her eyes and make rude comments, and make me giggle behind my program at the solemnity of everyone around us.

I *miss* you –

Alice   Doug said.

And there were tears in his eyes!

Diana (*as DOUG*)   I feel like I never see you.

Alice   Well, you're working so much.

Diana (*as DOUG*)   I know! I know, I know, I'm not blaming you. It's not your fault. It's me. These fucking papers –

Alice   The journal articles he was trying to finish so he could get tenure hopefully.

Diana (*as DOUG*)   – I'm trying to finish them but they just won't *stay finished*, they keep getting away from me, half the time I don't even know what the hell I'm saying with them anymore . . .

Alice   It was very unlike Doug to ever express any doubt about his work, that was one area where he was totally confident, arrogant really, he thought he was really a hot shit young academic and his sort of nerdy swagger was something I actually found quite sexy about him when we first met.

Hey, hey, hey, you're gonna get them done. They're gonna be great. You're gonna blow the tenure committee *away* –

Diana (*as DOUG*)   Anyway, that's not the point. I don't want to talk about work. It's *me*.

Alice   You?

Diana (*as DOUG*)   I mean us. I mean . . .

Alice   An eternity here while Doug paused for breath, then made a visible effort to reset and start again:

Diana (*as DOUG*)   I know you've been alone. I know you're stuck with all the child care. You don't complain, but I know you must be lonely and bored, you must be really frustrated with me, and –

Alice   I haven't been lonely.

Diana (*as DOUG*)   Yeah, I know, your friend, the art adjunct woman, that's great but what I'm saying is, I'm *sorry* the summer's been such a drag. Let's just go *away*, OK? Let's go away as a family for a couple days

Alice   Wait, *adjunct*? I thought she was a professor.

Diana (*as DOUG*)   Who?

Alice   Diana. My friend.

Diana (*as DOUG*)   Are we talking about the same person? The one who gave you that weird desk?

Alice   Yes.

Diana (*as DOUG*)   No, no, I don't think so. I think she's just part-time.

Alice   No, she's in Fine Arts.

Diana (*as DOUG*)   No. She teaches continuing ed or something like that, she's not in the Department.

Alice   Oh.

Diana (*as DOUG*)   Anyway, look, let's leave tomorrow.

We'll drive up to Sandusky and find an inexpensive motel on the Lake and swim and . . . Alice?

Alice   What?

Diana (*as DOUG*)   Are you listening? What do you say?

Alice   Sorry. I – yes. Of course. Of course, Doug. Yes.

He kissed me.

I was really touched.

Except my shorts were ruined – the ink on the rubber stamp bled through the pocket and wouldn't come out.

Doug went to tell Holly about the trip.

Diana   Let's surprise Holly! I said, and bundled Gretchen into the car the next morning around 10 AM and drove over to their house.

The envelope with the co-op shares was on the porch where she said it would be, but the house was empty and their car was gone.

Lanky Merle was mixing paint in the driveway. He told me Alice, Doug and Holly had gone on a little vacation, he wasn't sure how long they'd be away.

Alice hadn't said anything about a vacation to me.

Gretchen burst into tears on hearing her friend was gone. I think she misunderstood the circumstances. "It's only for a few days, darling," I told her, although I didn't know that for sure.

It was already a fiercely hot morning and she'd been looking forward to sharing Holly's inflatable wading pool. Not wanting to disappoint her further, or risk a squall, I asked the laconic Merle if I could let Gretchen use it for a bit. He shrugged, seemingly confused as to why I'd bothered to ask his permission for anything, which to be honest I was too, and soon Gretchen was splashing away contentedly while I sat sweaty and torpid in a lawn chair, watching the loose-limbed and meticulous Merle dipping and stroking with his paint brush – he was on to the fine work on the trimmings now – atop the ladder.

I must have dozed off.

When I awoke my throat was on fire with thirst so I went inside to get something to drink. There was no sign of Merle – he must have been on one of his famous breaks

I was standing at the kitchen sink waiting for the water to run cold when I felt calloused hands on my shoulders and smelled the cool astringent tang of latex all-weather house paint.

I knew immediately what was happening; there was no surprise, no shock as one of the hands moved to a breast, the other to my waist, first, then lower to lift the hem of the thin sun-dress I'd worn that day, by which time I was already ankling out of my underwear. All this without turning around, mind you. I gripped the edge of the sink, and – Oh Christ, what was I *doing*? Had I actually left a six-year-old child alone in a swimming pool while I was inside getting fucked in Alice's kitchen by Merle the fucking house painter? But it was just a splash pool, you couldn't drown in six inches of water, could you? *Of course you could*! This is not good parenting, I told myself, even as I succumbed to a crashing tsunami of lust.

It was then that I heard Gretchen begin to scream.

Alice   We had a nice couple days up in Sandusky. I don't know what else to say about it, really, it was just nice. Good weather, cheap motel but clean, Mom & Pop. Holly and Doug built sandcastles on the beach for hours, we ate take-out hamburgers in the room at night and watched TV all together. Doug and I even made love once, very quietly, under the covers late at night in the motel room, after Holly was fast asleep on the fold-out cot the motel provided. It was just nice.

Diana   She'd been stung by a wasp.

I lurched out of the lawn chair, instantly awake, my child's cries dissolving the sex-dream like smoke.

In the kitchen, an ice cube on the back of her knee where the sting was and an orange-juice popsicle from the recesses of Alice's freezer eventually stilled the sobs.

Merle, who'd emerged stoned from somewhere, looked on stupidly, shuffling in his sandals, a confused, paint-splattered, unhelpful presence. I noticed his toenails. They were long and yellowish. Here was the object of my erotic reverie. Ludicrous. Pathetic. I felt a crunch of self-loathing and self-pity in my guts.

Alice (*as GRETCHEN*)   Why are you crying?

Diana   I'm not, Gretchen Don't be silly.

Alice   When we got back, the house was finished. Trim, everything. Merle had done a *great* job. It looked like a million bucks! I was really impressed.

Doug said we should have a little party, like an end-of-the-summer thing to celebrate and show off the "new" house before the fall quarter got underway. Doug was like a different person after that little vacation. I guess he really needed it.

We decided on a Friday night for the party. I started to make some calls to invite people.

Diana   She called me. It was the first time we'd spoken since she went away. I said I'd be very glad to come, thank you.

Is there anything I can bring?

Alice   No, no, just bring yourself.

Diana   OK. Gretchen can't wait to see Holly, she's missed her.

Alice   Oh, no, uh, it's not a kid's thing. Doug wants to have like a proper grown-up dinner party thing.

Diana   Oh. I see.

Alice   But we can figure out another time to get the kids together, yeah?

Diana   Good, yes.

Alice   Holly's missed Gretchen too.

Diana   You're sure it's all right? If it's all couples the last thing I want is to be in the way.

Alice   You won't be "in the way," don't be ridiculous. We'd love to have you.

Beat

Diana   Where did you go? We happened to stop by the house, we were driving by, you weren't there . . .

Alice   Oh, we just had a chance to get away for a few days, so we grabbed it. Family time, you know.

Diana   That's lovely.

Alice   Yeah, it was really nice.

Diana   A pause here, while I waited for her to say something like What's going on with you? Or What have you been up to?

Alice   So – see you Friday, yeah? Around seven.

Diana   Seven o'clock. See you Friday.

Alice   Was she glad I had called? I couldn't tell.

Diana   Our rift was not healed exactly, but it was a gesture, one I appreciated.

Alice   Did she even want to come at all? I figured, whatever, I'd see her at the party Friday and we'd figure it out probably.

Diana   And I did see her Friday.

But there was no party.

5.

Alice   I started worrying about what to make to eat. I'd been given a Joy of Cooking and a Julia Child by my mother when I got married but as I might have mentioned I was not a great cook so I needed to pick something simple but still impressive hopefully. I was working on that when Doug came into the kitchen. He had a kind of strange look on his face.

Diana (*as DOUG*)   I just talked to Nathan Robinoff.

Alice   Oh great. Are they coming?

Diana (*as DOUG*)   He and Maria are having a little trouble getting sitting.

Alice   The Robinoffs were in the co-op Doug set up, a lot of his departmental colleagues were.

Oh, well, hopefully they can find something.

Diana (*as DOUG*)   I'm sure they will. But it was the *reason* they were having trouble.

Alice   What?

Diana (*as DOUG*)   They asked a couple of other people in the co-op . . .

Alice   Yeah?

Diana (*as DOUG*)   None of them wanted to sit.

Alice   Must be a busy night. Maybe there's other parties.

Diana (*as DOUG*)   No, they *could* sit, but nobody *wanted* to. Because they all have plenty of shares. They have too many already.

Alice   Oh, well, maybe they can just pay somebody.

Diana (*as DOUG*)   I'm sure they can. But it's just . . .

Alice   He went away looking really troubled.

I started to have a sick feeling in my stomach but I tried to focus on the menu issue. I decided I'd make a lasagna, I figured I could handle that, and make a big salad and have lots of bread in case it turned out crap. I was heading out to the grocery when Doug came in again.

Diana (*as DOUG*)   I don't get it. I called a bunch of other co-op members and *everyone's* in surplus. There's some kind of glut in shares. Nobody wants more. Some people are having to spend three or four shares to get an hour's sitting instead of one.

Alice   Oh that's too bad. I'm sure it'll sort itself out.

Diana (*as DOUG*)   No, it won't. Do you understand what this is?

Alice   No.

Diana (*as DOUG*)   It's *inflation*.

Alice   Gosh.

Diana (*as DOUG*)   I don't understand how this is possible. I worked it out very carefully. I can see how the system could go into recession but not how it could be *inflationary*, the number of shares is *fixed*, there's no central bank minting new currency, it's theoretically *impossible* –

Alice   All right, whatever, so people will pay cash. Or – hey! They can bring their kids! We can do a kiddie table in the kitchen, how's that? More fun anyway. Now, how much wine should we get? Do you think people will want red or white?

Diana (*as DOUG*)   Do you know how embarrassing this is? These are my colleagues! This is a model *I designed* and now it's crashing! This is like kindergarten stuff, this is Econ 101 and I look like a total idiot! There's no way the tenure committee doesn't hear about this!

Alice   Should I have told him?

I mean, I wasn't even 100 percent sure it was my fault. Could I have really made enough bogus shares to screw up his whole system? I'd made maybe ten or fifteen for Diana, and a bunch for myself, and yeah I guess there had been a few times I didn't tell you about when I stamped out a few here and there as favors for other people who might have mentioned they were short, or . . . OK, yes, it was definitely all my fault, and he was bound to figure it out eventually.

So I just confessed. I mean, I'm not a sociopath.

Look, it was me, OK? I used your stamp and made the extra shares, I'm really sorry. So, what should we do for dessert, should I just make a pan of brownies, or . . .

I'm not sure how to describe what happened next.

Diana   She'd come to my house immediately afterward in, I suppose, a sort of state of shock. She was quiet. She'd brought Holly and we sent the girls to play. She told me about the co-op business, then descended into incoherence.

Alice   I should have *known*. It was so *obvious*, God! I'm an idiot. Diana. What should I do? I don't know what to –

Diana   What *is* it, Alice? You're not making sense.

Alice   I was babbling, I could barely get the words out.

Diana   She was so pale and shaken at first I feared the worst.

Did he . . . *strike* you?

Alice   What? No. God, no. Doug?

I mean yeah he was super upset, I guess you could say he was kind of panicking about his career and everything, he was convinced that this would sink him with his colleagues, that he'd become a laughingstock, but that just seemed ridiculous to me –

(*To* **Diana** *as DOUG*) I mean, come on, Doug, they're not going to pass you over for tenure because you fucked up a babysitting co-op!

Diana (*as DOUG*)   *You* fucked up the babysitting co-op!

Alice   Whatever, fine, Doug. – Or, yes! *I* fucked it up, so they *can't* blame you, right?

Diana (*as DOUG*)   You don't understand, Alice. I can't *do* this anymore.

Alice   This, what? Teaching? I don't care about that. I'd be *glad*. I hate academia.

Diana (*as DOUG*)   No, this. Us.

Alice   Us?

The *marriage*?

Diana (*as DOUG*)   Yes.

Alice   And he started to tear up again, like he had before, but it was worse this time, much worse, all of a sudden he was *sobbing*, and choking when he tried to get the words out . . .

Diana   So that I don't have to enact the histrionics, which I would no doubt do badly, I'll just summarize for you what Alice told me her husband told her.

The major issue was not the counterfeited shares, or Doug's work troubles real or imagined. No. This was merely the trigger for an anguished outpouring over the state of the marriage generally.

You see, the little vacation – the family getaway which for Alice had been so restorative – had been *determinative* for Doug, he said, and not in a good way. It confirmed for him that he could not go on living the quote "absurd farce" their marriage had become.

By now Alice, in relating this to me, was weeping steadily herself: admitting that there *had* been something off about the little vacation, the Sandusky trip, and not just in retrospect: she knew it at the time. That though they did talk and laugh and "relax" together that weekend, whatever ease they'd managed to contrive was through, and ultimately for, Holly. That a hand grasped during a sunset walk on the beach was inevitably too quickly released; that, finally, there was no giggly, furtive delight, only haste and a sense of obligation, in the silent motel room lovemaking while the child slept.

And it wasn't that Doug was in *love* with the student he'd hired to paint their house that summer. Or *knew* that *he* – or "that" – was what he "really" wanted – in fact he was sure that it wasn't about Merle at all, he actually couldn't wait for him to be *done* and *gone,* for it to all be *over,* Christ, it made him sick to think about it now: the tension, the insanity, the – he used the word again – *farce* of the student's frantic visits upstairs to him in his study while Alice sunbathed in the yard below, the guilt and the fear of it all – not that most of these visits were about sex or anything physical, of course not, they weren't *that* dumb or reckless, most were just anguished cut-short discussions about *what the hell were they doing*? Or sudden declarations of devotion, or quickly withdrawn threats of exposure, or just ugly stupid little quarrels of the kind all lovers have.

Alice   How could I not have seen it?

Diana   I didn't see it either.

6.

Alice   That night she fed us. The four of us sat on her back porch and ate a salad she just threw together out of whatever was in her fridge, only because it was Diana it was *excellent*. And we drank a good bottle of wine she had.

The girls played until it got dark. This is late August, so maybe nine or nine-thirty. And then Diana found them some old jars and punched holes in the tin tops and the girls ran around collecting fireflies in the grass. They asked when they had to go to bed.

Diana   No bedtime! You're on your own recognizance.

Alice   They asked what that meant.

Diana   It's Liberty Hall, girls! You can stay up all night if you want! Run riot! Cry Havoc, and let slip the dogs of war! RAGE AGAINST THE DYING OF THE LIGHT AND LET THE WILD RUMPUS START! You can even . . . *use my art supplies*.

Alice   They looked a little freaked out then, and retreated away from us into the yard with their jars.

Diana   Look at them out there.

Alice   Yes.

Diana   God they are beautiful.

Alice   Yep.

Beat.

Diana   There's something I need to ask you. I don't want you to be upset.

Alice   Okay.

Diana   Do you have any more of Merle's weed?

Alice *digs in her bag. Finds a battered joint. Gives it to* **Diana**. **Diana** *lights it, drags.*

Alice   Better enjoy it. No more where that came from.

Diana *hands it to* **Alice**, *who waves it off.*

Diana   You're not going to?

Alice   I don't feel like it.

Diana *smokes alone.*

Can I ask *you* something?

Diana   Yes.

Alice   Is it true you're an adjunct?

Diana   What do you mean?

Alice   I mean, I thought you were an art professor. I mean, you are an art professor, right?

Diana   At present I teach part time at the University. Continuing ed. Retirees, mostly. I have no degree.

Alice   God, I always thought . . .

Diana   Yes, I know.

I could never quite finish it. The Magnum Opus. The – literal – "masterpiece." My art school friends would say to me, "For Chrissake, just give them something, what is the matter with you?" They were right. "It's an MFA thesis project! They'll take anything! Stick a dildo in a fondue pot and sign it and you're *done*."

Does it matter to you?

Alice   What?

Diana   That I'm a failure.

Alice   Come on. You're not.

Diana   Of course I am. Do you think I wanted to be a part-time art instructor in Columbus, Ohio? Great things were promised me, Alice. I promised them to myself. How could anyone so *uncompromising* not be bound for the New York galleries? Maybe an international career. London or Berlin.

I can simply never finish the work. To my own satisfaction, let alone anyone else's. It's a pity, isn't it?

I've even thought quite seriously of quitting.

Alice   Why?

Diana   I've left enough incomplete. Why add to the pile?

Alice   Stop it. You can't quit. You're *good*.

Diana   Thank you. But you don't, and I mean this with the greatest respect, really know what you're talking about.

Alice   You're not a fucking failure, all right?

I mean if you are, God, what does that make me? I don't even know where we're supposed to sleep tonight!

Diana   Here. You'll stay here as long as you like.

Alice   But what am I going to *do*?

Diana   I don't understand. Do you mean, in *life*?

Alice   Yes, in my life! I don't know *anything*. I don't know who I am. I don't want to lose my family but maybe it's already gone. I don't know what I'm going to do next week, next month, *tomorrow morning – Tell me what I'm supposed to do.*

Diana   Are you sure you want me to?

Alice   Yes.

Diana   When I've done that before you haven't liked it.

Alice   This isn't like before.

Diana   All right.

You should take the opportunity that's been given to you, Alice. That very few of us are ever given. *Start fresh.* Leave behind everything that's caused you to mute yourself. To negate and squander yourself. Become something completely *new*.

Alice   I can't just . . . *do* that.

Diana   You absolutely can.

Alice   What about my marriage?

Diana   You are not your marriage. You don't need it.

Alice   That's easy for you to say. You don't need *anyone*.

Beat.

Diana   Is that what you think?

Alice   Yes.

Beat.

Diana   Then you really don't know me at all.

Alice   Sorry.

Diana   No. I'm not entirely myself.

Alice   Me either. I think I need to go to sleep.

Diana   I'll make up the sofa for you. The girls can sleep in Gretchen's room.

Alice   Is it okay if I just stay out here? I'm too tired to move.

Diana   All right.

Alice   Diana?

Diana   Yes?

Alice   Make sure Holly brushes her teeth?

I woke up very early. The rising sun woke me. I'd slept very hard. I was disoriented for a minute. Then I remembered everything.

I pulled the blanket that Diana must have put on me over my head against the sun and just *cowered* for, I don't know, ten minutes maybe, until it got too hot and I *had* to get up.

Diana   She was gone when I awoke. She and Holly. She'd done the dishes from the night before, folded the blanket.

I assumed she'd gone home. I called her that night but there was no answer.

I called the next day and she *did* pick up.

Alice? It's me, it's Diana.

Alice   Hey, I can't really talk right now.

Diana   I'm concerned. Are you all right?

Alice   Yeah.

Diana   Her voice sounded strained – possibly Doug was in the room – but brisk too.

Alice   Look, thanks for the other night.

Diana   Of course. Is there anything else I can –

Alice   No. Thanks Diana. I'll call you in a couple days, OK?

Diana   Alice, if you need somewhere to go –

But she'd hung up.

I went into my studio. The canvases stacked three deep against the walls.

I looked around the rest of my house.

My God how I hated it. Every stick of furniture. The cabinets of crockery. Every book on every shelf: every title, every spine. The objects I'd selected to *intersperse* with the books: how *unusual,* what an *eye* you have! What a pathetically over-embroidered shroud I'd weaved to drape over my lifeless life.

I knew at once what I must do.

What *Alice* and I must do.

Gretchen and Holly and Alice and I.

Alice   She comes to the house. Gretchen in the back seat. Her car is packed. A U-haul trailer hitched to the back.

Diana   We're leaving.

Alice   What? I don't understand.

Diana   I'm leaving Columbus. I've sold my house and most of my possessions. Everything I own is now in that U-haul. Do you want to come with me or not?

Alice   Where would we go?

Diana   Wherever we want. To be determined.

Alice   Now?

Diana   Yes. Right now.

Alice   I can't just go away with you!

Diana   You absolutely can.

Alice   I pack two suitcases, one for me, one for Holly. Oh, and bring one other thing.

Doug protests, hysterically, but we're already out the door, and into Diana's car.

Diana   We drive.

Alice   We drive all night. Mostly I drive. I'm a better driver.

Diana   And six *more* nights.

Alice   We're driving across the Country!

Diana   Chicago. Cedar Rapids.

Alice   Des Moines. Omaha.

Diana   The Great Plains! We're seeing America!

Alice   America! In the summer of 1976!

Diana   Across Nebraska. Cheyenne, Wyoming.

Alice   Salt Lake City.

Diana   Reno! Carson City.

Alice   Sacramento.

Diana   There's no need to mention Sacramento.

Alice   Part of the journey.

Diana   And finally . . . San Francisco.

Alice   San Francisco!

Diana   Where we found a coldwater flat in a hard-done-by but vibrant and striving district of this then most bohemian and exhilarating of American cities.

And began to shape a life: these two mothers with their two daughters.

Mine is built of course around my art, which, spurred by Alice's encouragement and the freshness of our changed circumstances I attack with a renewed, confident vigor and sense of purpose, soon endorsed, to my delight and astonishment, by the offer of a local gallery show.

Several pieces sell, which leads in less time than I could have imagined to my being taken up by a dealer with a gallery in New York City. Commissions followed, and acquisitions by some smaller contemporary art museums. I am, in a limited but real sense, "known." My bank account now held money I'd earned myself.

Gretchen grows alongside her close friend and quasi-sister Holly. Two beautiful young women, growing up, growing wise, making their mothers almost insanely proud.

Alice in time discovers her own vocation. The inveterate paperback reader discovers she's a writer! Sitting up late at night after the girls have gone to sleep at "the" desk – the one I'd picked out for her, the *one item* she'd salvaged from her former life in Columbus – she begins scratching out sketches and stories – blunt, funny, disarming – like her – which, after some friendly but *firm* editorial input from me, she stitches into a novel-length narrative which becomes a bestselling book in the waning months of the 1970s, later made into a memorable, if minor, film.

And so we live on, two friends, two mothers, two artists, entwined in each others' lives and the lives of our children, our successes and sorrows inextricable too, and owing to a friendship which sustains and challenges us in equal measure as the years, and then the decades, march on.

It's marvelous, isn't it?

Alice   It is. It really is.

Diana   Of course none of that happened.

Beat.

Alice, it's Diana.

Alice   Hey, I can't really talk right now.

Diana   I'm concerned. Are you all right?

Alice   Yeah. Hey, thanks for the other night.

Diana   Of course. Is there anything else I can –

Alice   No. Thanks Diana. I'll call you in a couple days, OK?

Diana   Alice, if you need somewhere to go –

Alice   I had to hang up.

Diana   Alice, if you need *anything* –

She hung up.

Alice   Doug was sitting right there, and honestly I was worried about him at the moment: ever since I'd gotten home after the night at Diana's he was sick, like, literally sick with regret and agony and he couldn't eat, could barely talk, all he could do was hold my hand and beg me to forgive him.

I mean, "forgive?" It wasn't even so much about that as it was more, like, Well, what the fuck are we going to do now? I mean, what does he want, does he know? Does he even want me anymore? Do I want him? And what's best for Holly, and, I mean, everything, Jesus! I mean "forgiveness" is sort of the least of our problems, right?

He agreed with that. He agreed we had a lot to figure out. We had *everything* to figure out and he said we should go into therapy and that seemed like, Yeah, we need to do that. And man, this was going to be a long haul, this was going to be hard no matter what. Plus he still had to finish his work and get tenure (*which he did, incidentally*), plus the school year was starting up and Holly and I had to deal with all that, new clothes and a new backpack and all the stuff that's life-or-death to a kid.

So it was a while before I got back to Diana.

After I finally did we had dinner together once a week or so for a while. It wasn't quite the same as before. She seemed, I don't know, a little preoccupied. God knows I was. She talked a couple times about maybe moving. I think she mentioned San Francisco, which seemed sort of random; she also mentioned New York I think? Finding a cheap place, doing the whole sort of bohemian thing. She even said I should go with her once. Kind of as a joke. At least I think it was a joke. But she never brought it up again.

Through the winter and into 1977 we didn't see each other so much. Doug and I were deep, *deep* into the whole saving-the-marriage thing. Only I'd realized, duh, it *wasn't* a saving-the-marriage thing, it was an Am I happy? thing. Diana was right about that. Jesus, had she been right.

The divorce went through in '78.

That same fall Diana got a new job, at Kenyon College.

We visited a few times, me and Holly. Diana had an even more gorgeous house there, and now she was full-time: a move up, not teaching anymore, some kind of administrative thing. I *think* she was pleased about that, though of course she wouldn't let on. I did get the impression she was lonely. I don't think she had a lot of friends there. She didn't have many friends at Ohio State and it must have been hard coming into a much much smaller place.

Kenyon isn't that far away from Columbus, less than two hours, but you know how it is. The visits got less frequent, and as the girls got older inevitably they didn't have as much in common. They were pen-pals for a while but of course that dropped off.

I got a teaching certificate. Middle-school English. Other teachers will tell you middle school kids are the worst, but I don't know, I like them, they're so crazy and fucked up at that age, it's interesting to try to figure them out, and they're fun, teaching them and reading books with them is fun.

There were men too of course. Some shorter term, some longer. Some nice, some not so much. We don't have to get into all that.

Diana   Years went by.

Alice   Diana sent out cards at the holidays and she always sent me one. She designed the cards herself, they were really beautiful, really meticulous and austere. Not great *holiday* cards actually, but little works of art all the same. I don't send anything, I'm not a card person.

After a decade or so the cards stopped. Maybe I fell off her list.

I wasn't offended or anything. It's not like I had made an effort to be in touch. Sure, I felt guilty about that. I thought about writing or emailing – I even found her email online at the Kenyon Art Department – but so much time had passed it seemed weirder, I don't know, embarrassing somehow to try. You know how it is. You just feel sort of passive and resentful of the thing you know you should have done but didn't, you forget about it for long stretches, until finally on the rare occasions when you do think of it you're just like, well, unfortunately *that's* not ever going to happen.

Then, one day – today – holy shit. I saw her in New York.

7.

Diana   Alice.

Alice   Oh my God.

What are you doing here? I mean, the show, duh, but –

Oh my God.

They embrace.

Diana   How are you?

Alice   I'm good. Do you . . . live here now, or –

Diana   Oh no, no. I just flew in for this.

Alice   Oh! Sure.

Diana   How did you happen to hear about it?

Alice   I didn't. I was just walking by the museum and I saw the banner and I was like, Wow, I've got to –

Diana   Yes.

Alice   It's really something.

Diana   Yes. They did a nice job.

Alice   It's so crowded!

Diana   Well, it's been hyped quite a bit. Overhyped, I should say. "The first complete retrospective." It's not quite true of course. In North America, yes.

Alice   Right.

Diana   Do you live in New York?

Alice   No, no, I'm just visiting Holly.

Diana   What is she doing here?

Alice   Med school.

Diana   Really. That's wonderful.

Alice   She's doing her residency. She took a few years off to have a baby but now she's nearly done.

Diana   You're a grandmother.

Alice   Ugh, God. Yes. I mean it's great, I love it. I love him. I just have a *lot* of trouble thinking of myself that way. It's been almost two years and I'm still not used to it: "Grandma . . ."

Diana   Of course. Of course.

Alice   How is Gretchen?

Diana   She's . . .

Alice   Wait. This is stupid. Just standing here. Do you want to go to the cafe and get a cup of coffee or something? I've seen the show, basically. I mean, I don't want to interrupt your experience or anything –

Diana   Not at all. Let's get a cup of coffee.

Alice   It really was just luck I'd gone in. I had an hour to kill before I had to pick up Nicholas from his morning daycare – you don't have to *send* him to daycare this morning, I'm in town for God's sake, let me have him! I'd practically *screamed* at my daughter, but Holly didn't want to interrupt his "routine," she's very into "routine," I guess it's a thing now – Anyway. I saw the banner with the title of the show. I don't even know if I clocked the teeny connection to Diana, maybe I did subconsciously, because I went in.

Diana   I'd made a point to be in New York for the first week of the 2003 MoMA Paul Klee retrospective. I'd made my peace with Klee and the influence he'd had on my unfathomably distant younger self. I'd even written a short monograph on him for the small online journal published by the Kenyon College Art Department. Very few people read it, but I was pleased with it.

Alice   It was one of those stupid, huge, really crowded shows where you can barely see the art cause of all the people, so I just sort of made a quick circuit of the rooms and was on my way out when I heard someone say my name.

Diana   Alice.

Alice   I knew it was her before I turned around.

At a table:

Alice   I'm so sorry but I only have a few minutes. I have to pick up my grandson at one o'clock.

Diana   It's all right.

Alice   I'd call but they're so strict about pick-up times, it's crazy.

Diana   I completely understand. It's just good to see you.

Alice   It's good to see you too.

Beat.

But hey! I'm not going home until the day after tomorrow, maybe we could meet for breakfast, or –

Diana   I have a four o'clock flight this afternoon I'm afraid.

Alice   Oh.

Diana   I'm taking a cab straight to the airport from here.

Alice   Oh, that's too bad.

Diana   Yes.

Beat.

Alice   I'm just embarrassed I haven't been in touch.

Diana   Don't be. I wasn't much better.

Alice   I loved those cards.

Diana   Thank you.

Alice   People must have been crazy for them. Why did you stop sending them out?

Diana   I suppose I just got tired of making them.

Alice   They were really beautiful. I hope you're making something else.

Diana   I put most of my energy into the Department these days, committee work, there's no end to it.

Alice   I bet.

Beat.

You look great by the way.

Diana   I was going to say the same to you.

Alice   Aw.

Diana   But then I remembered how much I hate when people say that.

Alice   I hate it too! "You look great. . . ."

Diana   *"Considering . . ."*

Alice   Considering the *mileage* . . .

Diana   Exactly. Yes.

Beat.

Alice   Diana.

Diana   Yes.

Alice   You haven't said. How is Gretchen?

Diana   She's . . . had a bit of a rough patch.

Alice   Oh.

Diana   But things are much better now.

Alice   That's great.

You'll tell her we say Hi? Me and Holly both.

Diana   Of course I will. Thank you.

Beat.

Alice   Oh, shit. I hate to say it but –

Diana   You have to go.

Alice   Yes. I'm really sorry –

Diana   No, please. I should go too. I always like to get to the airport early. It's a bit neurotic.

Alice   No, it makes total sense.

Diana   We paid for the coffees.

Alice   I promised this time I would stay in touch. We exchanged contact information like you do, tapped it into our phones, tic tic tic.

Diana   When we said goodbye outside the museum something happened.

Alice   I suddenly found myself with tears in my eyes, hugging her quite hard and saying how much I missed her.

Alice *suddenly embraces* **Diana**, *hugging her tightly. It lasts a moment, then they move apart.*

I swear I hadn't meant to do it. But it's how I felt.

Diana   The hug, yes.

I was surprised. And I suppose still disconcerted by her mention of "cards." I had not sent out "cards," I had sent out *a* card, annually, to her. In fairness, there was no way she could have known this.

And by her asking about Gretchen, inevitable as it was. And by the failure of my usual euphemism of choice, "She's had a bit of a rough patch," to appear as dependably as accustomed. I nearly submitted a blunter accounting: Gretchen's move back in with me; the countless failed relationships; the substance abuse; what I strongly suspect was a suicide attempt two years ago.

I said none of this. What would it accomplish?

I saw Alice make the decision not to press. Did I catch a flicker of pity? I didn't begrudge her her happiness, I didn't want pity in return.

Alice   I told her I'd wait with her while she got a taxi.

Oof, mistake. It took a few minutes and *that* was awkward. Has that ever happened to you? The big emotional goodbye, embrace, so wonderful to see you!, all that stuff, but then something happens and you can't actually *go*, you have to stand there together for a few minutes: it's this weird moment of limbo and there's nothing left to say?

Beat. Sounds of traffic.

Alice   There's a cab.

Diana   Finally . . .

Alice   I watched her get in and pull away. I thought about her waiting for my bus on Sixth Avenue, and on the long ride uptown to the daycare to pick up Nicholas.

I was so glad to see him.

Diana   Do I miss Alice?

I'm not sure. I'm not sure if I miss the person or the memory of those few months in 1976.

It was such a short period of time. We hardly knew each other, really. And we were so different. We were really only brought together by the children.

It's not at all a surprise that we didn't stay close.

CURTAIN